UNBELIEVABLY
ZANY!

RIPLEY

PUBLISHING

a Jim Pattison Company

PUBLISHING

Publisher Anne Marshall
Editorial Director Rebecca Miles
Assistant Editor Charlotte Howell
Text Geoff Tibballs
Proofreader Judy Barratt
Researchers James Proud, Charlotte Howell
Indexer Hilary Bird
Art Director Sam South
Project Designer Rocket Design (East Anglia) Ltd
Cover Design Michelle Foster
Reprographics Juice Creative

Executive Vice President Norm Deska
Vice President, Archives and Exhibits Edward Meyer

PUBLISHER'S NOTE
While every effort has been made to verify the accuracy of the entries in this book, the Publishers cannot be held responsible for any errors contained in the work. They would be glad to receive any information from readers.

WARNING
Some of the stunts and activities in this book are undertaken by experts and should not be attempted by anyone without adequate training and supervision.

Cover image: Tim Cockerill, aka The Great Inferno, performs incredible stunts, such as fire breathing, holding a blowtorch on his tongue and gargling hot molten lead.

Published by Ripley Publishing 2013
Ripley Publishing, Suite 188, 7576 Kingspointe Parkway, Orlando, Florida 32819, USA

2 4 6 8 10 9 7 5 3 1

Copyright © 2013 by Ripley Entertainment Inc.
All rights reserved. Ripley's, Believe It or Not!, and Ripley's Believe It or Not! are registered trademarks of Ripley Entertainment Inc.

ISBN 978-1-60991-070-9

Some of this material first appeared in *Ripley's Believe It or Not! Enter if you Dare!*

Library of Congress Cataloging-in-Publication Data is available

Manufactured in China in November/2012 by Leo Paper
1st printing

First published in Great Britain in 2013 by Random House Books, Random House, 20 Vauxhall Bridge Road, London SW1V 2SA

www.randomhouse.co.uk

Addresses for companies within The Random House Group Limited can be found at
www.randomhouse.co.uk/offices/htm

The Random House Group Limited Reg. No. 954009

A CIP catalogue record for this book is available from the British Library

ISBN 9781847947093 (UK)

Contents

Ripley's World   6

Wacky World   12

Animal Stories   56

Beyond Belief   100

Extraordinary Feats   144

Amazing People   188

Unbelievable Art   232

Extreme Endeavors   276

Eccentric Tales   320

Index   364

Acknowledgments   382

Ripley's World

In December 1918, while working as a sports columnist for the *New York Globe*, Robert Ripley created his first collection of odd facts and feats.

The cartoons, based on unusual athletic achievements, were submitted under the heading "Champs and Chumps," but his editor wanted a title that would describe the incredible nature of the content.

So, after much deliberation, the title was changed to "Believe it or Not!" The cartoon was an instant success and the phrase "believe it or not" soon entered everyday speech.

Ripley's passion was travel and by 1940 he had visited no fewer than 201 countries. Wherever he went, he searched out the bizarre for inclusion as his syndicated newspaper cartoons, which had blossomed to reach worldwide distribution, being translated into 17 different languages and boasting a readership of over 80 million people. During one trip he crossed two continents and covered over 24,000 mi (39,000 km) "from New York to Cairo and back" to satisfy his appetite for the weird.

Robert Ripley with his first cartoon "Champs & Chumps," produced in 1918.

Believe It or Not!

Ripley was always traveling, even though he never really liked flying! Here he is on his return from a three-month trip to Southeast Asia.

He achieved many radio firsts, including broadcasting from Australia, from a falling parachute and even underwater!

Ripley received thousands of entries from fans for his Believe It or Not! contest in 1932.

Ripley's Legacy Lives On

Although Ripley died in 1949 (after collapsing on the set of his weekly television show) his "Believe it or Not!" cartoons are still produced on a daily basis—just as they have been everyday since 1918—making Ripley's the longest running syndicated cartoon in the world.

Intrepid researchers follow in Robert Ripley's footsteps, continually scouring the world and enabling Ripley's to remain the undisputed king of the strange and unbelievable. With a huge computer database of incredible facts, people, and events, a massive photographic archive, and a warehouse stuffed with unique exhibits, Ripley's is able to present a celebration of the amazing diversity of our world, without ever passing judgment. From the outset, Robert Ripley encouraged his dedicated readers to submit material and photographs—a tradition that exists to this day. His weekly mailbag sometimes exceeded 170,000 letters! Ripley, the one man who started it all, was once commemorated in his hometown church of Santa Rosa, California. The entire church was made from a single giant redwood tree.

Believe It or Not!
by Ripley

The ONLY MAN WITH A REVOLVING HEAD!

Laurello

WALKS FORWARD AND LOOKS BACKWARD

SCIENCE DECLARES SUCH A FEAT IMPOSSIBLE

NOW APPEARING IN THE ODDITORIUM

Ripley's Believe It or Not!

BUZZARDS ARE PURE WHITE UNTIL THEY ARE HALF GROWN

Joseph SURRINGTON WHO DIED IN NORWAY AT THE AGE OF 160 LEFT ONE CHILD AGED 109 AND ANOTHER CHILD AGED 9!

MOLLA BJURSTEDT WON THE WOMEN'S NATIONAL TENNIS TITLE 8 TIMES

BILL HAJEK Seattle, Washington PLAYED the PIANO CONTINUOUSLY 14 DAYS and 14 NIGHTS The ODDITORIUM, N.Y. 1939

Daily cartoons are still produced and printed to this day, and appear online and in a number of newspapers around the world.

Ripley's had a very big job on their hands, when they had to exchange one amazing Ripley's car for another at the Believe It or Not! London museum. The only way to get the Swarovski crystal-covered Mini Cooper out of the museum in Piccadilly Circus was to lift it through the roof using a massive crane. A knitted Ferrari sports car was then placed back in through the roof in its place. The Mini is now at home in Ripley's newest museum in Baltimore, Maryland.

The crystal-covered Mini Cooper was transported from the London, England, museum to the brand new Ripley's museum in Baltimore, Maryland.

A giant crane lifted the cars in and out of the museum's roof in the early hours of the morning, forcing some of London's busiest streets to shut.

This knitted Ferrari sports car is now at home in the London Ripley's Believe It or Not! museum.

Ripley's Star Attractions

The Ripley's team is always acquiring new exhibits for the Ripley's Believe It or Not! museums around the world. Ripley's brand new attraction in Baltimore, Maryland, houses some of its most recent acquisitions. The museum has nearly 700 exhibits, and features three genuine shrunken heads and a city made of toothpicks, among many other incredible pieces.

Ripley's Hollywood museum has also been given a magnificent makeover after 20 years in business, and features nearly 600 new exhibits. It is now home to the world's smallest car, a full-size motorcycle made from candy and a vast collection of celebrity memorabilia including over $1.5 million worth of Marilyn Monroe's personal items. Ripley's now have 32 museums worldwide, all filled with unbelievable exhibits.

The new Ripley's Baltimore museum includes a Swarovski crystal-covered Mini Cooper and one of the world's smallest cars.

The brand new interior at Ripley's Hollywood museum was re-opened in 2012.

Located in Baltimore's Inner Harbor, the Ripley museum's façade has a gigantic sea serpent wrapped around it.

Wacky

WORLD

Acid Adventure

Storm chaser George Kourounis from Canada was crazy enough to take a ride in a rubber dinghy in the world's largest acid lake, next to the 8,660-ft (2,640-m) Kawah Ijen volcano in Indonesia.

When the volcano erupts, it can shower the surrounding areas with acid up to 2,000 ft (610 m) away, and this has created a hot lake that contains a deadly mixture of sulfuric acid and hydrogen chloride.

The powerful mixture of volcanic gases and rainwater in the lake creates the vast acid concoction that can reach temperatures of up to 93 °F (34 °C).

GLACIER PRAYERS

For more than 300 years, inhabitants of the Swiss Alpine villages of Fieschertal and Fiesch gave prayers to stop the growth of the Aletsch glacier, Europe's longest, which had caused their homes to flood. However, in 2009, they sought the blessing of Pope Benedict to change their prayers to stop the glacier shrinking. Climate change has seen Switzerland's glaciers, which are a key source of water for hydroelectric plants, melt by 12 percent over the past decade.

LOCKED IN

In an attempt to combat vandalism, the council of Klaipeda, Lithuania, announced that all public toilets in the town would automatically lock in customers if they took longer than five minutes inside.

RAT FREE

In 2003, New Zealand's Campbell Island became the world's largest island to be freed of a rat infestation after a massive poisoning campaign killed off the entire population of 200,000 rats.

ROMANTIC NUTS

At the San Juan Fiesta, held in Ciudadela, Menorca, each June, large crowds of people gather to hurl hazelnuts at each other. Every time a nut hits another person, it is said to represent a kiss.

Stone Home

This stunning and mysterious home is made of limestone rocks and is in Fafe, northern Portugal. Made by an unknown artist, the highly unusual house has been the source of speculation, with many people doubting its very existence. It is extraordinary in appearance and few pictures have been taken of it, but it is indeed real and has become a local icon over the years.

Room with a View

Artists Tiago Primo and his brother Gabriel hung out in an alternative home built on the exterior wall of a building in Rio de Janeiro, Brazil, in the summer of 2009, attracting thousands of visitors. The pair had attached items of furniture, including a bed, a couch and a dresser, 30 ft (9 m) above the street, where they spent up to 14 hours a day.

A THOUSAND WINDOWS

A new, nine-story office block in Jinhua, China, has around 1,000 windows—with one room alone boasting 21 windows. All of the rooms in the building, designed by Japanese architect Sako Keiichiro, have irregular shapes and each floor features its own miniature garden.

TRENCH ART

Ružica Church, located within the Kalemegdan Fortress in Belgrade, Serbia, has chandeliers made from bullets, swords and cannons. Soldiers made them during World War I.

DECIMAL TIME

Following the French Revolution, for two years from 1793 to 1795, France used "decimal time," which had a ten-hour day and 100-minute hours. Clocks and watches were produced with faces showing both standard time with numbers 1 to 24 and decimal time with numbers 1 to 10.

SEPARATE TOILETS

Russian cosmonauts on the International Space Station revealed in 2009 that they have been told by their officials to use only the Russian-built toilet and not the U.S. one.

JOKE KINGDOM

The kingdom of Wallachia, located in the Czech Republic, was founded in 1997 as a practical joke by photographer Tomás Harabis in a bid to attract tourists. King Boleslav the Gracious (aka Czech comedian Bolek Polivka) became ceremonial head of state and Harabis served as foreign minister. Wallachia adopted its own currency, passport, flag, university, navy and state limousine.

ROOFTOP BATH

Silvia Mertens and Pieter Peerlings, architects from Antwerp, Belgium, built a four-story home/office building with a transparent front wall in a space less than 8 ft (2.4 m) wide—and with the bathtub on the roof.

BUTTER BRIDGE

Government officials ordered the surfaces of a 1,000-ft-long (305-m) steel bridge in Guangzhou, China, to be smeared with butter to make it hard for people to climb up and commit suicide by jumping from it. In just one month, eight people killed themselves on the bridge and several others climbed up it with the intention of jumping before changing their minds.

LEGEND COMES TRUE

In a case of life imitating art, on November 18, 2008, officials in Hamelin, Germany—home to the Pied Piper legend—announced that the town was overrun with rats.

MUSICAL CHIEF

A rock formation near Medicine Hat, Alberta, Canada, known as the "Badlands Guardian" resembles the face of a Native American Indian listening to an MP3 player. The contours of the face are formed by natural soil erosion while the "earphones" are actually a man-made road and an oil well.

DOMINANT SUN

The Sun makes up 99.8 percent of all the mass in our Solar System. Everything else—including planets, asteroids, dust and moons—is just 0.2 percent.

FAMILY STREET

No fewer than 69 members of one family live in the same street in Gateshead, Tyne and Wear, England. The Hall family have monopolized Cotswold Gardens since Catherine Hall settled there in 1958. Six of her eight children and their families currently live in the street, along with three uncles and a mother-in-law, and together they occupy 15 houses and have more than 50 pets.

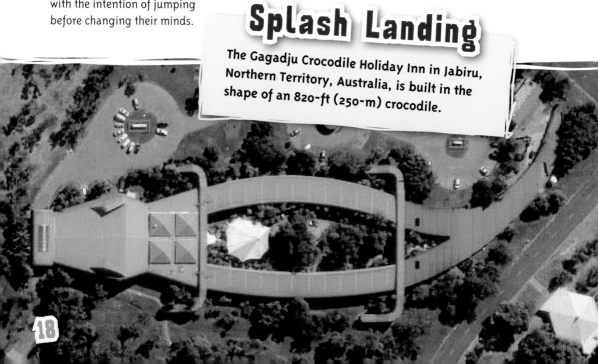

Splash Landing

The Gagadju Crocodile Holiday Inn in Jabiru, Northern Territory, Australia, is built in the shape of an 820-ft (250-m) crocodile.

Famous Face

Ciudad Evita, a city of 70,000 inhabitants located in Greater Buenos Aires in Argentina, was founded in 1947 on the orders of Argentinian president Juan Peron. It was shaped to resemble a profile of his wife, Eva Peron, popularly known as Evita.

NARROW HOUSE

New York City's narrowest house went on sale for a fat $2.7 million in 2009. The 9½ x 42 ft (2.9 x 13 m), three-story home was built in Greenwich Village in 1873, sandwiched between two larger buildings.

WATERS PARTED

When the black waters of the Rio Negro join the brown waters of the Rio Solimões at Manaus, Brazil, to form the Amazon River, they run side by side for several miles without actually mixing.

HOT JUMP

An adventure company in Pucón, Chile, allows people to bungee jump from a helicopter over an active volcano. They are flown into the heart of the smoking volcano and plunge around 450 ft (140 m) toward the molten lava.

SENSELESS LAW

A local law in Skamania County, Washington, details penalties for harming a sasquatch—a mythical beast whose existence has never been confirmed!

FLYING LESSONS

Children at Kingsland Primary School in Stoke-on-Trent, Staffordshire, England, have some of their lessons in a disused airplane. The decommissioned S-360, which used to fly to Ireland and Spain, has been fitted out with desks and laptops.

TYPHOON GUST

Winds from a 2009 Chinese typhoon were so powerful that they blew a bathtub onto 40-ft-high (12-m) power cables. The 75-mph (120-km/h) winds from Typhoon Morakot swept the bathtub up from the balcony of a nearby hotel and deposited it on the overhead cables in Wenzhou, Zhejiang Province.

Rough Weather

Ken Prior, a member of the U.K.-based Cloud Appreciation Society, photographed a brand new type of cloud in 2009. The formation is not officially recognized as yet, but the Cloud Society have named the cloud "Asperatus," from the Latin for "rough" because of the bumpy nature of the formation. Weather data is being gathered to help distinguish the strange-looking cloud. If the relevant authorities accept Asperatus, it will be the first time in over 50 years that a new type of cloud has been found.

DEBT PAID

When the Skylab space station fell to Earth over Western Australia in 1979, the community of Esperance fined the U.S.A. $400 for littering. The fine was paid 30 years later when radio-show host Scott Barley of Highway Radio, based in Barstow, California, raised the funds from his morning-show listeners. He sent Esperance a check for the outstanding amount on behalf of NASA.

GREEN SAND

Papakolea Beach, near South Point, Hawaii, has green sand as a result of olivine crystals found in the surrounding lava cone. Over the years, the sea has eroded the headland, depositing olivine on the beach. The waves have then washed away the lighter grains of sand leaving the darker olivine crystals to form the beach.

ABANDONED CITY

In 2008, a long-abandoned 1,000-year-old city carved into the side of a mountain by the Cloud People tribe was discovered in Peru's Utcubamba province—untouched by looters.

CANYON MOUTH

From the air, the sides of a 130-ft-high (40-m), 3,000-ft-wide (1-km) rocky canyon in the West Darfur region of Sudan appear to form the shape of pouting female lips.

DUST STORM

A huge dust storm covered the Australian city of Sydney in a blanket of red dust in September 2009. The storm originated in the Australian outback before sweeping 725 mi (1,167 km) east to shroud Sydney with dust, forcing people to stay indoors and air-traffic control to divert international flights.

HIGH SCHOOL

A school in Gulu village, Sichuan Province, China, stands halfway up a mountain. Climbing up from the base takes five hours and children walking to school must negotiate a narrow, zigzagging path that is just 16 in (40 cm) wide in places and has a sheer drop on one side. The school has a basketball hoop, but children are allowed only to pat the balls, because if the balls are thrown and go over the edge of the cliff, it would take half a day to retrieve them.

MOZART'S STONE

The Austrian town of Raschala has a plaque on a stone where the composer Wolfgang Amadeus Mozart once stopped to urinate by the side of the road. Each year, so many visitors flock to see the Mozart Pinkelstein ("Mozart pee-stone") that the town has now arranged a festival of music and drinking in memory of the composer's unscheduled visit.

WALKING HOUSE

Danish artists have teamed up with engineers from Massachusetts to design a house that walks. The 10-ft-high (3-m) solar- and wind-powered home has a living room, kitchen, toilet and bed, plus a computer that controls the six hydraulic legs on which the house stands. These legs enable the house to stroll across all terrains and to walk away from flooded areas if necessary.

LIGHTNING STORM

A lightning storm in Saturn's atmosphere lasted for more than eight months in 2009, and emitted radio waves about 10,000 times more powerful than lightning discharges on Earth. They originate from huge thunderstorms with diameters of around 1,900 mi (3,000 km).

Roof Attack

An ordinary small terraced house in Oxfordshire, England, became an international tourist attraction after a 25-ft (7.6-m) fiberglass shark was stuck headfirst into the roof. Known as the "Headington Shark," the sculpture was erected in 1986 by the home's owner, Bill Heine, as a protest against man's inhumanity to man. The building started a six-year battle with Oxford City Council who wanted it removed, but they relented in 1992 deciding to allow it to stay on creative grounds.

Island of the Dolls

Teshuilo Lake lies among the canals of Xochimilco near Mexico City, and on the lake there is a tiny island known as Isla de las Muñecas ("Island of the Dolls").

Many years ago, a young girl drowned there, and the island became a haunted area that people were afraid to enter. A homeless man, Julián Santana, lived on the island for over 50 years, and began to collect and display children's dolls to remember the dead girl and keep her spirit happy. Santana would trade fresh vegetables, which he grew on the island, with local people for their discarded dolls. Although Santana died in 2001, there are still thousands of dolls scattered around the area, mostly hung in the trees.

One of the world's creepiest tourist attractions, the island is filled with old, mutilated dolls.

CANYON CHURCH

Las Lajas Cathedral, near Ipiales, Colombia, was built inside the canyon of the Guaitara River. It was constructed on a bridge spanning the river in such a way that the canyon cliff forms the back wall of the church.

LIMITED TRANSPORT

The principality of Andorra, located in the mountains between Spain and France, has no airports, trains or ports.

LONG TUNNEL

The 10-mi-long (17-km) St. Gotthard road tunnel under the Swiss Alps is almost twice as long as Mount Everest is high.

Before

FIRE WHIRLS

Wind currents and temperature changes can turn a wildfire into a tornado-like column several hundred feet high.

SECRET TREES

The location of Australia's Wollemi pine trees, once thought to be extinct, is secret. Anyone studying them arrives at the site blindfolded.

NO PETROL PRODUCTS ARE IN THIS SQUARE

No OIL

After

Patchwork Pumps

Jennifer Marsh, an artist from Syracuse, New York, wanted to make a statement about oil consumption, so she decided to give the abandoned gas station she walked past each day a much-needed splash of color. Jennifer entirely covered the building and the gas pumps with 5,000 sq ft (464 sq m) of patchwork material. The project received hundreds of colorful panels from all over the world, and Jennifer enlisted a team of volunteers to help her sew them into fabric panels to cover the derelict building, which stands 35 ft (10.6 m) tall and 40 ft (12 m) wide.

Living the High Life

In Torajaland on the island of Sulawesi, Indonesia, when a person dies, an effigy, or doll, is made in their likeness. These dolls are called Tau Tau, and are put in graves, or in the homes of the living, as a blessing. In some places, life-size Tau Tau are placed in cliff faces where they peer down at travelers as they pass. Dug into the same cliffs are the graves of the dead, which are also hung on platforms high up on the cliffs, to prevent possessions being stolen.

WET LANDS

Canada has an estimated two million lakes, covering approximately 7.6 percent of the country's landmass.

ONLY VOTER

The Banej polling station in Gujarat, India, has only one voter—Guru Bharatdas Darshandas, the sole caretaker of a temple in the middle of a forest.

SHED THEATER

Eighty-one-year-old Don Parr from Birmingham, England, spent $15,000 on turning his garden shed into a 1940s movie theater. In tribute to the picture house where he worked as a projectionist back in 1943, he fitted his shed, which measures 18 × 9 ft (4.8 × 2.4 m), with 14 seats from a real cinema. Now fans travel miles to watch old movies on his shed's 6 ft 6 in × 3 ft 3 in (2 × 1 m) screen, which is complemented with hi-tech surround sound.

METEORITE COLLECTOR

Rob Elliott from Fife, Scotland, has collected 1,000 meteorites from around the world, including one that is 110 million years old. He has spent more than 16 years building up his collection, using an old golf club with a magnet on the end as a homemade metal detector. Some of his rarest meteorites are valued at more than $130,000 and his entire collection is worth millions.

CROWDED BENCH

A wooden bench in Masuhogaura, Japan, is more than 1,510 ft (460 m) long—that's over a quarter of a mile—and can seat up to 1,350 people.

DEBRIS COLLECTION

Nearly 400,000 volunteers from around the world picked up a total of 7 million lb (3.2 million kg) of debris from 17,000 mi (27,360 km) of coastline and waterways across the world on a single day—September 20, 2008.

SUBURBAN TEMPLE

Travelers from around the world—as far away as Canada and Nepal—line up in their hundreds to visit Dhirajlal and Sushila Karia's suburban home in the seaside town of Clacton-on-Sea, England, to see a Hindu temple built inside their spare bedroom.

SOLE TENANT

In 2009, a luxury new 32-story apartment block in Fort Myers, Florida, had just five people living in it. Victor Vangelakos, his wife and three children had the large swimming pool, games room and gym to themselves, as most of the other prospective residents backed out because of the global financial crisis.

FREE LAND

In 2009, the village of Rappottenstein, Austria, began offering free land to anyone willing to move there and start a family.

PINK HOSPITAL

To ease the stress of childbirth, the 30-bed Huasheng maternity hospital in Yuanlin, Taiwan, is decorated entirely in pink "Hello Kitty" décor. The hospital's nurses wear pink uniforms with cat-themed aprons and the cartoon cat's likeness even appears on birth-certificate covers.

WHERE'S WALDO?

As part of her Media Arts degree, student Melanie Coles created a 54-ft-high (16.5-m) painting of children's book character Waldo on a rooftop in Vancouver, British Columbia, Canada, so that everyone looking on Google Earth could play *Where's Waldo?*

GOLDEN SEWAGE

The burned waste at a sewage refinery in Nagano prefecture, Japan, is a more concentrated source of gold than the country's largest gold mine! Tens of thousands of dollars worth of gold were found at the Suwa treatment facility in 2008—because a number of precision equipment manufacturers in Nagano use gold in their work and lots of tiny particles of it end up in the sewer system.

VAMPIRES

SHOULD YOU DARE TO TURN
THESE PAGES, YOU HAD
BEST DO IT IN DAYTIME, FOR
VAMPIRES LURK BETWEEN
SUNSET AND SUNRISE...

Vampires, unnaturally pale and apparently frail, are actually freakishly strong, agile and fast. Said to sleep during the daytime, they reveal their true nature at night, seeking victims to quench their thirst for blood. Their fanglike teeth sink into the necks of unsuspecting human prey and drink their fill, topping up their superhuman strength and sucking the life from the body. Occasionally, they will leave a person alive, but the infection they spread transforms any such victim into the next of this undead creed. It's said that death is preferable to an eternity of immortality of the most tortuous kind...

Tales of vampires can be traced back thousands of years to ancient Mesopotamia, but most modern vampire stories have their basis in the folk tales of Eastern Europe. In the 18th and 19th centuries, Gothic horror stories became increasingly popular. Preying on the doubts and fears of a fascinated readership, vampires were a credible explanation for the spread of disease, plague and death. As travelers ventured forth into the far reaches of Europe, they armed themselves with the items thought to safeguard anyone against a vampire encounter. Garlic, crosses, holy water and special bullets were said to target a vampire's weaknesses, and specially made vampire killing kits were also available.

The aristocratic cloaked vampire as we know him today was made famous by Bram Stoker's 1897 novel Dracula. *Movies such as* Dracula *(1931) and* Nosferatu *(1922)—seen above with Max Schreck in the leading role of Count Orlok—helped whip up enthusiasm and a passion for vampires. Bela Lugosi, who starred in the 1931 film, actually fainted at the sight of blood!*

Dracula Did Exist!

Vlad Draculea III was Prince of Wallachia, in southern Romania, in the late 15th century. Also known as "Vlad the Impaler," thanks to his habit of capturing enemies and impaling their heads on stakes, he was a fierce warrior and tyrannical leader who killed many thousands of men in battle. The name "Dracula" comes from the old Romanian for devil or dragon, and is thought to have given the author Bram Stoker his inspiration for the title of his most famous fictional character.

Vlad Draculea's many victims were impaled on poles. According to a German pamphlet published in 1488, a few years after Vlad's death, a nobleman visitor found Vlad among a "mighty forest" of impaled bodies. When the nobleman complained of the smell, Vlad "had him impaled high up so that the smell of the others would not bother him."

Blood Bath-ory

Countess Elizabeth Bathory was no fictional character, but a real-life noble woman who was known as "The Blood Countess." Driven by the desire for eternal youth, she is said to have captured and killed as many as 600 Hungarian girls so that she could drink and bathe in their blood. She was walled up in her own castle as a punishment until her death.

Blood Relatives

Doctors in the 1920s could find no reason for a nine-year-old Haitian girl's poor health and suggested she had a wasting disease. A native doctor was not convinced, and upon searching the girl's body found a tiny pin-prick incision on her big toe. The girl's aunt, Anastasie Dieudonne, confessed to drugging her niece and sucking her blood over a period of nine months.

Time To Kill

Even in the 21st century, vampire tales abound. In 2004, in Wallachia, Romania (home of Vlad Draculea), a corpse was exhumed and destroyed to prevent it from emerging and drinking the blood of living people. The body had a stake driven through the heart, which was then cut from the chest and burned.

Vampire kits first appeared toward the end of the 19th century. Many of them stated their express purpose on the label inside the lid: "This box contains the items considered necessary for the protection of persons who travel into certain little known countries of Eastern Europe where the populace are plagued with a peculiar manifestation of evil, known as vampires." Many of the kits were said to be made by a Belgian gunmaker called Nicolas Plomdeur, and were sold by Professor Ernst Blomberg (1821–1903) of Lubeck, Germany.

This kit is one of over 30 such kits owned by the Ripley collection. Collectors around the world compete to own such kits, and have paid as much as $24,000 for one. This particular kit contains several must-have items:

1 WAX-SEALED VIALS

(containing powdered flowers of garlic, holy water, brimstone, and potassium nitrate)

Each vial is labeled with its contents and says "Specially prepared by Prof. Blomberg." Brimstone and potassium nitrate are components of gunpowder, which could be sprinkled around the grave of a possible vampire or, if a hunter was feeling brave, placed inside the nose, ears and eyes of the body, and then ignited. Garlic has an ancient tradition of having healing qualities, and a reputation of purity much like silver. In ancient times, anyone who didn't like the stuff was condemned as a vampire. It has also been hung outside doorways to protect the home, and handed around in churches to check that the congregation was entirely human. Holy water (ordinary water blessed by a religious figure) will burn the skin of a vampire and cause extreme pain, though is unlikely to kill the creature.

2 GLASS SYRINGE

Most probably used in conjunction with Professor Blomberg's serum.

3 PROFESSOR BLOMBERG'S SERUM

These vials state that a patent was applied for in London, but the exact contents of the serum are unknown. It is speculated that it contains holy water, garlic extract, honey and salt.

4 CRUCIFIX

A ready-made cross can be held up to protect an individual from an oncoming vampire. Other items in the kit are embellished with additional crosses for protection. It may help also to wear a crucifix on a chain around your neck. A strong religious faith can also serve to help the bearer of the crucifix in battle with a demonic force. The form of a cross was believed to drain a vampire of its strength, drive it away, and if touched, burn the vampire's undead flesh. A crucifix—a cross bearing the figure of Christ on it—is considered to be a stronger tool than any other ordinary cross.

5 SILVER BULLETS (not visible)

A hidden pocket in the box contains silver bullets. Silver is renowned for its purity, hence the belief that it can finish off evil creatures such as vampires and werewolves. There is much debate about the validity of this claim, as vampire folklore predates guns with bullets. Many vampire experts accept that modern writers have introduced this aspect of vampire hunting, but also add that silver crosses, daggers, and silver nails in a coffin are effective against candidates for vampirism.

6 PERCUSSION CAPS

This tin stores 100 medium waterproof percussion caps, which enabled muzzle-loading firearms to fire in any weather.

7 PISTOL

The lower part of the case contains several pieces needed to maintain and fire a pistol, such as a powder stick, a bullet mold and a powder flask.

8 POWDER STICK

This was used to pack the gunpowder in the barrel of the pistol.

9 IVORY INCENSOR

Decorated with a silver cross, the incensor was used to burn incense during worship and ward off evil vampires with its divine powers.

10 WOODEN STAKE

Traditionally, a stake through the heart is the best way to finish off a vampire. This stake has a built-in dagger for good measure. Typical woods used are ash and aspen, believed to have powerful anti-vampire qualities. Many medieval bodies were staked through the heart before burial if the corpse was believed to be at a high risk of becoming a vampire—having died through disease or wicked deeds, for example.

11 BRASS AND COPPER POWDER FLASK

Used to hold the gunpowder needed for the pistol.

Other vampire kits also contained a mallet to help drive a stake through the vampire's heart, rosary beads, and icons from various cultures or religions around the world. Shorter-barreled pistols were common, and some were formed in the shape of a crucifix.

This French kit from the 1890s features an ornately carved pistol and powder flask.

This kit includes a "dentol" set of pliers, used to remove the fangs of vampires.

This well-stocked kit includes rosary beads and a Holy Bible.

Cunningly disguised as a book, this kit afforded the owner an element of surprise.

A well-preserved kit, such as this one, recently sold for over $20,000.

Tips for Vampire Hunters

+ It's worth noting a vampire's dislike of daylight. In extreme cases, it can destroy the monster, which disintegrates into dust. Sometimes daylight simply strips the vampire of its strength or power.

+ A vampire prefers to live and feed in darkness. Bear this in mind: If you can maneuver into sunlight, you may be safe.

+ A vampire cannot be killed, as it is undead (technically dead but still moving). But it can be sent back to its grave and kept there.

+ Burning is a good technique for dealing with a vampire—be sure that the entire body and organs are burned, though.

+ A vampire has an amazing capacity to self-heal and restore strength and bodily form. It may take a long time—but the creature has centuries of immortality to play with.

+ Slicing a vampire in two might finish it off—especially if the head is severed from the body.

+ Historically, suspected vampires were staked, their heart removed and burned, and their head chopped off. They were then buried again.

The Düsseldorf Vampire

In the early 1900s, newspapers named a German serial killer "the Vampire of Düsseldorf." Peter Kürten had a violent upbringing and committed many crimes, culminating in several murders. The newspapers reported that he drank the blood of his victims, leading to his grisly nickname. After his trial and execution, his head was dissected to allow a scientific examination of his brain. It was suggested that he suffered from the rare condition known as Renfield's Syndrome, or clinical vampirism, a mental disorder that involves an obsession with drinking blood. Kürten's mummified head is on display in the *Ripley's Believe It or Not!* museum in Wisconsin.

Bricked Up

This 16th-century woman's skull was found in an archeological dig near Venice, northern Italy, in 2006. The object in her mouth is a brick, placed there after death to prevent her rising from the grave and drinking blood.

AUGUST 1970

FEBRUARY 1970

Man Hunts Vampire

Witnesses have told police that they have been frightened by mysterious ghostly figures in the vicinity of Highgate Cemetery, North London. Sean Manchester, vampire hunter, has stated that demonic disturbances are present and should be exorcised. He believes that it is a possessed corpse of a nobleman brought in a coffin to Highgate in the 18th century.

The Dracula Business

As reported by this paper in February of this year, vampire hunter Sean Manchester performed an exorcism on the tomb suspected of containing the Highgate Vampire, after sightings of dark figures and bodies removed from graves in the area created a panic around the cemetery. Manchester stopped short of staking the creature, and the hauntings continued. The vampire hunter now reports that his colleagues have further pursued the cause of the contagion to a mansion in nearby Crouch End, and carried out a full and proper exorcism, resulting in the burning of the vampire, which Manchester believed to be a European nobleman transported to London in a coffin.

Mercy Me

The Brown family of Exeter, Rhode Island, caught tuberculosis in 1892. The mother and then the sister, Mercy, died. When Mercy's brother Edwin was also taken ill, villagers were sure a vampire was to blame. Mercy's body was dug up and looked flush, as if her heart was still alive: a sign she was a vampire. Her heart was burned and the ashes given as medicine to her brother—who was not cured.

Volcano Bath

The thermal baths near Lake Rotomahana, New Zealand, were a rare natural phenomenon, known to some as the eighth wonder of the world. In the 1880s, these men were photographed there, in the shadow of an active volcano, taking a dip in one of the large natural mineral basins filled with warm spring water. These were formed from the mineral silica as water from boiling hot geysers cooled. The "Pink and White Terraces," as they were known, were popular tourist attractions until 1886, when nearby Mount Tarawera erupted, killing more than a hundred local people and destroying the terraces.

STRANGE BONE

Hikers walking in a forest near Landshut, Germany, found a mysterious-looking bone. The police were summoned and discovered a hipbone with artificial joints. They could see no other remains, until they spotted a skeleton in a fir tree 36 ft (11 m) above them. Investigations concluded that a 69-year-old man had committed suicide when he climbed up the tree almost 30 years previously and roped himself to a branch. He managed this despite having hip replacements, as the tree was short enough to climb. But as the tree grew taller, his bones fell to the ground.

IRON PILLAR

The 22-ft-tall (6.7-m) Iron Pillar of Delhi, India, has stood outside in the rain and sun for 1,600 years and yet exhibits little sign of corrosion.

CLIFF BASE

A church in Brittany, northern France, is built into the base of a cliff. The Chapel of St.Gildas nestles under a huge granite outcrop on the bank of the Canal du Blavet.

SMILEY FACE

Although the magnificent Palace of Versailles, near Paris, France, covering 2,000 acres (800 ha) of land, was built in the 17th century, it was not until it was viewed by aerial photography on the Internet that a smiley face was found hidden in the grounds, created by the landscape of the gardens.

CORAL ROADS

Roads on the Pacific island of Guam are made with coral. Guam has little genuine sand on its beaches, just ground coral. Instead of importing real sand from other countries, the coral is mixed with asphalt to build the island's roads.

GHOST TERRITORY

The landmass of the Canadian territory of Nunavut is a million times larger than the European principality of Monaco, but has a smaller population.

A camera onboard the International Space Station witnessed the early stages of a volcanic eruption back on Earth that appeared to blow a gigantic hole in the clouds. The vast mushroom shape, stretching above the Sarychev volcano on the Kuril Islands near Japan, was thought to consist of brown volcanic ash and steam, which caused clouds to evaporate on either side of the eruption, leaving a clear hole in the cloud cover.

Hole in the Sky

Tentacle Terror

Resembling something from outer space, this mass cluster of tentacles shocked vacationers when it swept onto a beach on the Gower Peninsula in Wales, U.K. Measuring 6 ft (2 m) in length and slightly thicker than a telegraph pole, tourists who witnessed the alien-like sea monster thought it was a UFO invasion! Scientists later revealed the writhing creature to be thousands of goose barnacles clinging to a log, the result of bad weather sweeping them up from the bottom of the ocean.

Salted Shores

Situated on the shoreline of San Francisco Bay, California, these stunning red and green salt ponds are a vital habitat for more than 70 bird species. For over a century, around 80 percent of these shallow man-made ponds have been filled and developed for salt mining. The ponds create salt using only the sun and wind, while the input of varying amounts of algae, minerals, microorganisms and brine shrimp create the beautiful colors. These colors also indicate the salinity of the ponds, which produce around 5–8 in (13–20 cm) of salt at the end of their five-year process.

FOREST FACE

From the air it is possible to see a face-shaped forest in Denmark. "The Sun as a Face" was planted in Odense in 2005 as part of the bicentennial celebrations of the birth of fairytale author Hans Christian Andersen.

TIME ZONES

Geographically, China falls into five time zones—but officially the entire country adheres to the same time.

HOUSE RAFFLE

Brian Wilshaw sold 46,000 raffle tickets at $35 each—with first prize in the draw being his $1.5 million estate at Morchard Bishop in Devon, England. Owing to the recession and falling U.K. house prices, he had been losing nearly $20,000 a month while trying to sell his 11.5-acre (4.6-ha) property, which came complete with a five-bedroom house, four holiday lodges, some woodland and a fishing lake.

MOVING CLOSER

New Zealand's biggest earthquake in 78 years—recorded in the Tasman Sea in 2009—has brought the country's South Island a foot closer to Australia. The 7.8 magnitude quake expanded South Island westward by about 12 in (30 cm), making a tiny inroad into the 1,400-mi (2,255-km) gap separating it from Australia.

AWESOME VIEWS

Chicago's Sears Tower, America's tallest building, has installed four glass box viewing platforms to make visitors feel like they are floating above the city—at a height of 1,353 ft (412 m). The Ledge, which can hold a weight of five tons, has glass that is 1½ in (3.8 cm) thick. It protrudes from the 103rd floor of the 1,725-ft-high (526-m) building as an extension to the tower's Skydeck and—for those brave enough to look down—offers unobstructed views of the city's streets and the Chicago River below.

BOTTLE TEMPLE

Around 20 buildings in the grounds of the Wat Pa Maha Chedi Kaew Temple in Sisaket, Thailand, are made almost entirely out of glass beer bottles. Buddhist monks started collecting the bottles in 1984 for their "Temple of a Million Bottles" project and found the medium so favorable that even the temple's mosaics of Buddha have been created with recycled beer-bottle caps.

ICE LAYER

Owing to its massive layer of ice, the continent of Antarctica has an average altitude 1.4 mi (2.2 km) above sea level.

FOG NETS

When dense fog sweeps in from the Pacific Ocean, plastic mesh nets erected on a hillside near Lima, Peru, catch the moisture and provide valuable water to a region that gets little rainfall. The droplets of fog water fall from the nets into gutters and on to collection tanks. Since 2006, the nearby village of Bellavista has received hundreds of gallons of water during the foggy winter months.

ELEPHANT BATTLE

In 1592, King Naresuan of Siam and the Crown Prince of Burma fought a duel while riding elephants. Centuries later, Naresuan's victory is still celebrated as a holiday in Thailand.

JESUS IMAGE

On Google Earth, an image of the face of Jesus can be seen in a Peruvian sand dune. It was formed by the wind buffeting the landscape.

CHURCH STOLEN

A large church in rural Russia was stolen in October 2008. The Church of Christ's Resurrection had stood in the central Russian village of Komarovo for nearly 200 years before thieves dismantled it and took it away brick by brick.

TUNNEL PEOPLE

Hundreds of people have built homes—some complete with double beds, furniture and kitchens—in the dark, damp storm drains that run under Las Vegas, Nevada. Despite the risks to their health from disease and venomous spiders, and a general risk of flooding, the "tunnel people" have set up elaborate camps with beds, bookshelves, wardrobes and even a makeshift shower created from an office water drinking dispenser.

LANDOWNERS

Sixty-nine percent of the land in Great Britain is owned by just 0.6 percent of the population—this is mostly landowning families who have held their land since the 19th century.

WHISTLING ISLAND

On the small island of La Gomera in the Canaries, people communicate with each other from miles apart by using a whistling language. Known as Silbo, the language has a vocabulary of more than 4,000 "words" and is used to send messages across the island's many mountains and valleys. Silbo was once on the verge of extinction, but now children in Gomeran schools are learning it as part of the curriculum.

Wall of Skulls

A tower made from human skulls still stands in the Serbian city of Nis, 200 years after it was first built. Turkish forces built the 10-ft (3-m) tower after they had defeated Serbian rebels in 1809. A total of 952 Serbian skulls became part of the construction, the scalps stuffed with cotton and sent back to Constantinople as proof of the victory. When Serbia was liberated, the chapel was kept as a memorial, and 52 of the skulls remain.

CONTAINER CLASSROOMS

Shipping containers are being used as classrooms to provide education for children who live on the garbage dumps of Manila, the Philippines.

HUSBAND CARRYING

As a part of a fall festival, women in the town of Winesburg, Ohio, compete in a husband-carrying contest.

HEIGHT RESTRICTION

Residents of Munich, Germany, have voted that new buildings must be no taller than 325 ft (99 m), the height of the city's cathedral towers, to avoid spoiling the skyline.

Bionic Fingers

A company from Scotland has invented bionic fingers, which enable people with missing digits to pick up a glass, hold cutlery and even write. The $70,000-fingers are directly controlled by the brain and can write and grip, thanks to a special sensor that allows them to detect when they have closed around an object.

LAKE IN LAKE

The 40-sq-mi (104-sq-km) Lake Manitou in Ontario, Canada, is a lake inside a lake. It is located on 1,067-sq-mi (2,765-sq-km) Manitoulin Island, which in turn is located in Lake Huron.

ROCK BIRD

From piles of more than 1,500 tons of rock, sculptor Andrew Rogers has created a birdlike geoglyph with a 330-ft (100-m) wingspan in You Yangs National Park, Victoria, Australia. Best viewed from the sky, the mythical avian creature, called a Bunjil, resembles an eagle and is the indigenous Aborigines' sky god.

DOUBLY LANDLOCKED

There are only two "doubly landlocked" countries. Liechtenstein and Uzbekistan are both surrounded by landlocked countries.

ROOF GARDEN

The Courthouse Tower in Greensburg, Indiana, has had a tree growing from its roof for more than a century. A small sprig was first spotted there in the 1870s, and two of the trees that subsequently took root in the crevices of the roof are now growing happily 110 ft (33 m) above the ground.

REDUCED ALPHABET

Rotokas, a language spoken by around 4,000 people on the island of Bounganville, Papua New Guinea, has only 12 letters in its alphabet—A, E, G, I, K, O, P, R, S, T, U, V.

TADPOLE DELUGE

In separate incidents throughout Japan, hundreds of dead tadpoles fell to the ground in June 2009. In Nanao, 100 dead tadpoles were found on car windshields and in a parking lot over an area of 100 sq ft (10 sq m), and another 70 were found on a bridge walkway. Experts were mystified by the falls as there were no reports of tornadoes or strong winds at the time.

GALAXY BLING

433 Eros, a banana-shaped asteroid 21 mi (33 km) long, contains precious metals worth at least $20,000 billion, including more gold than has ever been mined by humans on Earth. It orbits the sun, mainly between the orbits of Earth and Mars, and on January 31, 2012, it passed at around 16 million miles (26 million km) of Earth, about 70 times the distance to the Moon.

AGE RESPECT

Each year in September, Respect for the Aged Day is celebrated in Japan and all citizens who have reached age 100 are given a silver cup and a letter from the prime minister.

Spy Tooth

The U.K.'s James Auger has devised a new concept in secret communication— an audio tooth implant. A surgeon implants a device into your tooth, the data is retrieved from a cell phone, radio or computer and the vibration resonates through your jawbone to your inner earbone, meaning that only you can hear the information.

CROSSWORD BLOCK

An apartment block in Lvov, Ukraine, has a crossword puzzle 100 ft (30 m) high filling the whole of one external wall. Clues to the crossword—which is 19 squares across and 34 squares high—are scattered around the city's major landmarks and at night fluorescent letters placed inside every square are turned on to reveal the solution.

BABY BOOM

Cambourne, a small village in Cambridgeshire, England, has a higher birth rate than India, China, Indonesia, Brazil or the U.S.A. Cambourne has just 7,600 residents, but produced 24.1 births per 1,000 women in 2009—almost double the U.K. average. The village has an unusually high concentration of young couples.

HIDDEN MOUNTAINS

Antarctica's Gamburtsev mountain range is located beneath 2.5 mi (4 km) of ice. Only discovered just over 50 years ago, the range has peaks as high as 10,000 ft (3,000 m) and, stretching for 750 mi (1,200 km), it covers as big an area as the European Alps.

HAIR HOUSE

Paula Sunshine built an extension to her house in Bury St Edmunds, Suffolk, England, from human hair mixed with plaster.

HAPPY HARRY

Harry Hallowes, an Irish tramp who squatted for more than 20 years in one of London's most expensive suburbs, was given a plot of land that could be worth up to $6 million. He was awarded squatters' rights to a 120 x 60 ft (36 x 18 m) patch of land on Hampstead Heath, where he has lived in a tiny shack since 1986.

Rat Temple

Rats are not usually welcome house guests, but the hordes of rodents that swarm around the Karni Mata temple in Deshnoke, India, are always treated with great respect. The rats are kept well fed, and any food or drink that has been sampled by a rat is considered blessed. Spotting a white rat bodes particularly well, but if a visitor accidentally kills one of the rodents, he or she is expected to buy one made of gold or silver to replace it. Hindu legend has it that the 14th-century holy woman Karni Mata reincarnated dead storytellers into rats and they are given protection in her temple, which was built in the early 20th century.

ABANDONED APARTMENT

In January 2009, architect Mark Aretz discovered a small, one-bedroom apartment in Leipzig, Germany, that had been untouched since before the fall of the Berlin Wall, nearly 20 years earlier. It had been hastily abandoned by its occupants as the old Communist East German state disintegrated in 1989.

FREE HOUSE

Gerry and Cindy Mann from Battle Creek, Michigan, came up with a novel way of selling their house—they offered a miniature replica of the home for $169,000 with the real house thrown in for free. The dollhouse, accurate in every detail, had been made by Cindy's father, Ron Caldwell, who built it on a 1:12 scale.

REVERSE PLANET

A new planet—twice the size of Jupiter—has been discovered, and unlike any other planet, it travels counterclockwise around its star. The planet, spotted 1,000 light years away in the constellation of Scorpius, has been named WASP-17 because it is the 17th to be recorded outside the Solar System by the Wide Area Search for Planets run by universities in the U.K.

SHIFTING BORDERS

The mountainous border dividing Italy and Switzerland includes glacier ridges. As the glaciers melt, the borders have shifted, prompting the two nations to redraw their borders by up to 330 ft (100 m) in places.

OPRAH'S HEAD

A farmer in Queen Creek, Arizona, has created a crop circle in the image of Oprah Winfrey's head that can be seen properly only from the skies above.

DOUBLE DRAINAGE

The 1,035-sq-mi (2,681-sq-km) Wollaston Lake in Saskatchewan, Canada, drains naturally in two directions. It flows northwest into the Mackenzie River basin and northeast into Hudson Bay.

BRIDAL WAY

Unmarried men in the remote Indian village of Barwaan Kala are building a new road that they hope will bring them brides. More than 120 men in the village, located high in the Kaimur hills, remain bachelors because they say it is difficult for outsiders to reach their home through the rocky terrain.

HARROWING EXPERIENCE

A 3,000-year-old barrel of butter has been found in an Irish bog. Two farm workers harrowing the land discovered a buried oak barrel, cut from the trunk of a tree, full of the ancient butter. Experts say it dates back to the Iron Age.

ROYAL TIME

Until 1936, all 180 clocks in the royal collection at Sandringham House, Norfolk, England, were set on "Sandringham Time," half an hour ahead of Greenwich Mean Time. It was the idea of King Edward VII, who enjoyed shooting game birds on the Sandringham estate and wanted to lengthen daylight hours during the winter.

VANISHING RAIN

Evaporation rates in the desert are often faster than the speed at which rain falls, causing rain drops to disappear before they hit the ground.

DONKEY DELIVERY

More than 3,000 donkeys were brought in to help deliver millions of ballot papers to remote mountain regions of Afghanistan for the country's 2009 presidential elections.

Eye Tech

Filmmaker Rob Spence from Toronto, Canada, has developed a camera to replace the eye that he lost as a child. Rob began working with engineer Kostos Grammatis to create the "Eyeborg," and is now the proud owner of a wireless bionic eye made with one of the smallest digital cameras in the world. The camera is capable of recording and transmitting video directly from his eye socket.

Blue Heaven

In December 2008, a British artist took an abandoned apartment in London and turned it into a glittering cave of crystals. Roger Hiorns created his work, entitled *Seizure*, by pumping 18,000 gallons (70,000 l) of blue, hot copper sulfate solution into the apartment, in order to create beautiful crystalline growths on the walls, floor, ceiling and bath.

The crystals covered absolutely everything, including the bathroom sink.

GREATER WALL OF CHINA

A 2009 study revealed that the 2,000-year-old Great Wall of China is 2,400 mi (3,850 km) longer than previously thought. Using modern mapping technologies, the study uncovered extra sections of the wall that had been hidden by hills, trenches and rivers, making its total length around 5,500 mi (8,850 km).

SALT PALACE

Constructed in 1993, the Salt Palace was built with pure rock salt from Grand Saline, Texas—an area of the U.S.A. that has enough salt to supply the world for 20,000 years.

TOAD KILL

The Australian state of Queensland has an annual one-day holiday for residents to cull cane toads.

REFRIGERATED BEACH

The world's first refrigerated beach has been built in Dubai to prevent tourists burning their feet. A computer-controlled system of coolant-filled pipes under the sand keeps temperatures comfortable at the beach next to the Palazzo Versace hotel.

STARDUST SECRET

Traces of an amino acid called glycine have been discovered by NASA in wisps of stardust from the tail of the Wild 2 comet, suggesting that life could have begun in space before being delivered to Earth by meteorite and comet impacts. Glycine is a basic component of proteins without which life as we know it could not exist.

TALL CACTUS

At a dental college in Sattur, India, there is a 77-ft-tall (23-m) cactus. It was planted in 2002 and has flowers up to 8 in (20 cm) long.

CAVE MOUTH

Predjama Castle in Slovenia was built in the 12th century in the middle of a 400-ft (123-m) overhanging limestone cliff, in the mouth of a cave.

MELON SKIING

At the biennial Chinchilla Melon Festival in Queensland, Australia, competitors go skiing with scooped-out watermelons on their feet. Wearing the melon footwear, they are dragged down a slippery course on a rope. The winner is the skier who stays upright for the longest distance.

SOUL-AR POWER

The above-ground mausoleums in the town of Santa Coloma de Gramenet, Spain, are outfitted with hundreds of solar panels—and they generate electricity for the town.

BIG BALL

A basketball can be seen on Google Earth! Measuring 30 ft (9 m) in diameter and weighing 10 tons, the ball sculpture is located outside the Women's Basketball Hall of Fame building in Knoxville, Tennessee.

STATUE PARADE

At Las Fallas Festival, held each March in Valencia, Spain, hundreds of giant papier-mâché statues—some up to 30 ft (9 m) high—are paraded through the streets and then thrown on to bonfires.

FITNESS CHURCH

Developer and bodybuilder Al Horvath has converted an old church in Barberton, Ohio, into a gym. He created a Superman theme for the church's sanctuary, replaced the pews with rows of workout equipment and added murals depicting such fitness-related biblical characters as David and Goliath and Samson and Delilah.

CHEESE ROLLERS

Competitors in Berne, Switzerland, roll lightweight wheels of cheese around an obstacle course as fast as possible. The race re-creates an old practice whereby wheels of cheese up to 3 ft (1 m) in diameter, 11 in (27 cm) thick and weighing 220 lb (100 kg) were rolled around dairies by hand.

LOW LYING

Although there are nearly 1,200 islands in the Maldives in the Indian Ocean, their combined landmass is only 115 sq mi (300 sq km)—twice the size of Washington, D.C. Most of the islands are less than 5 ft (1.5 m) above sea level, the highest point in the entire archipelago being just 8 ft (2.4 m) above sea level.

FISH RAIDS

Thieves in Britain have been using aerial Internet photography to steal valuable fish. They use the online technology to pinpoint the location of garden ponds that cannot be seen from street level and that contain collections of highly prized koi carp.

SMALL SCREEN

A cinema in Coventry, England, measures just 10 x 8 ft (3 x 2.4 m) and seats only four people. Brian Sexton converted a derelict indoor stall in the city's market into the tiny Market Cinema, complete with small screen.

LONG PROJECT

Romans in the ancient province of Syria (modern-day Jordan and Syria) spent 120 years building a 100-mi-long (160-km) aqueduct, most of which is chiseled from stone at depths of up to 260 ft (80 m).

ONE HOME

Alfonso de Marco of Eastbourne, East Sussex, England, celebrated his 107th birthday in April 2009—in the house where he had lived for the past 100 years. He had moved to Britain from Italy in 1909 as a seven-year-old to live above the ice-cream parlor that his father ran.

Garage Illusion

Thomas Sassenbach, a designer from Cologne, Germany, was tired of the gray, ugly garage doors in his hometown and decided to give them a makeover. His designs are deceptively realistic and intended to make people stop and stare. Now you can persuade your neighbors that you have a Formula-1 racing car, a speedboat, a real horse or a jet fighter in your garage instead of your old car. (They are actually just amazingly painted tarpaulins fixed with Velcro!)

Animal

STORIES

Flea Circus

Flea Circuses have been around for centuries, thrilling audiences with the tiny performers.

Becoming popular in the early 19th century, they held their fame through to the early 20th century, as a main feature at carnivals and circuses. Some modern flea circuses are still in existence today, such as the "Cardoso Flea Circus" in Philadelphia, although they are often more about art than entomology (the study of insects).

Many early trainers dedicated their bodies to their tiny flea performers and gave up their own blood to feed them. However, despite appearances the fleas could not actually be "trained" as such, and were in fact often glued or rigged to the circus machinery. However, with a little illusion, audiences were enthralled and flea circuses became a major draw of a carnival.

A UNIQUE NOVELTY.
Direct from Earls Court Industrial Exhibition, London.

PROFESSOR KONTILI'S
WONDERFUL ROUMANIAN

Flea Circus
MUST BE SEEN TO BE BELIEVED,
PATRONISED BY ROYALTY, NOBILITY, & CLERGY.

Come and see the
LIVELY FLEAS
Dance a Ballet,
Fight a Duel, with
Swords,
Walk the Tight
Rope a la Blondin

Harnessed like
horses and drawing
and driving
Hansom Cabs, Mail
Vans, Funeral Cars
Cabriolets, Milk
Cars, Artillery Fleas
firing a Cannon.

The
Smallest Performers
in the World.
Interesting alike,
to
Old and Young.
Rich and Poor.

BEWARE OF
THE DOG

TO BE SEEN WITHIN.

Cheapest Steam Printers, 38, Church Lane, (cor... ...d, London, E

William Heckler would feed his fleas using his own blood.

A female cat flea tows a miniature 19th-century cart at a circus in Munich, Germany. The common cat flea was a popular choice for the circus as cat fleas are big enough to see.

Famous Fleas

William Heckler started his flea circus in New York in 1900 with his son Roy at the forefront by 1925. When World War II restricted his intake of fleas, Roy started breeding his own. As circus director, Roy would regularly feed his little performers with his own blood, allowing them to help themselves to his "quality human blood" and perform to their maximum potential. Choosing to breed females over males, as they are twice the size, Heckler would train them using a horizontal glass tube to walk or crawl instead of jump. Once they had hit their heads a few times, they knew to stay low!

Rat-busters

The famous exterminator shop Julien Aurouze & Co, located on the rue des Halles in Paris, France, has always specialized in pest control or, more specifically, catching and killing rats. Founded in 1872, the shop window gives an obvious explanation of what they do, with stuffed rats hanging from traps by their mouths, and taxidermied rats scattered all over the displays inside.

TOILET PYTHON

Erik Rantzau found a python almost twice his size coiled up in the toilet bowl of his house near Darwin, Northern Territory, Australia. The 10-ft-long (3-m) carpet python had been seen roaming in the garden for years before deciding to set up home in his toilet.

FROG WEDDING

Two frogs were married in a solemn ceremony in the western Indian state of Maharashtra in June 2009 in an attempt to bring on delayed monsoon rains. Tradition says that if frogs are married off with full Vedic or Hindu rituals, the rain god is pleased and the heavens will open within days.

FLUSHED AWAY

A pet goldfish survived being flushed down a toilet in East Kilbride, Scotland, and was eventually rescued from a sewage plant. The fish was put down the toilet because its owners thought it was dying, but it revived as it made its way through the town's underground waste water network and was spotted flailing about on a mesh filtering screen at the Scottish Water sewage site.

Inside Snout

In 2009, three piglets were born with their nostrils bizarrely inside the upper part of their lip. Half of a litter, born in the village of Jingdezhen, eastern China, had the rare deformity, but they still managed to eat, drink and breathe normally despite having no snouts.

GENTLE GIANT

Sancho, a longhorn steer from a farm in New Holland, Ohio, has horns measuring more than 10 ft (3 m) from tip to tip.

CYANIDE GLANDS

The dragon millipede of Thailand has bright pink coloration and glands that produce cyanide poison.

Whale of a Tongue

When an unfortunate Finback whale washed up dead on a beach in Provincetown, Massachusetts, in 2009, the gases that were given off during the decomposition process caused its tongue to swell up like a giant balloon. Finbacks are the second biggest creatures on Earth after the Blue Whale and this young specimen was 40 ft (12 m) long and weighed about 22,000 lb (10,000 kg).

FIERCE FROG

A species of frog that lived in Madagascar some 70 million years ago was so big and aggressive that it may even have eaten baby dinosaurs. Larger than any frog living today, *Beelzebufo ampinga* was 16 in (40 cm) long, weighed around 10 lb (4.5 kg) and possessed a very wide mouth and powerful jaws.

DOLPHIN RESCUE

In April 2009, thousands of leaping dolphins in the Gulf of Aden prevented Somali pirate speedboats from attacking a flotilla of Chinese merchant ships. When the dolphins, which were swimming next to the Chinese ships, leaped out of the water, the pirates decided to turn back.

Young Angler

Eleven-year-old angler Jessica Wanstall from Kent, England, couldn't believe her eyes when she landed a monster fish twice her size while fishing with her family on a river in Spain in 2009. At nearly 9 ft (2.7 m) long and weighing 193 lb (87.5 kg), the catfish dwarfed Jessica, who weighs only 77 lb (35 kg), and her dad had to help her drag it up the bank in order to take some pictures.

FOXY THIEF

Over several months, a fox in Germany stole more than 120 shoes from homes and gardens near Föhren. A forestry worker found the missing footwear in and around the fox's lair, the tiny tooth marks on the leather suggesting that the vixen may have used them as toys for her cubs to play with.

CLEVER DOGS

Dogs may be as intelligent as two-year-old children. Animal psychologists at the University of British Columbia in Vancouver, Canada, have found that dogs are able to understand up to 250 "human" words and gestures, can count up to five and are even able to perform simple mathematical calculations.

WANDERER RETURNS

A dog that vanished on the Gold Coast in Queensland, Australia, in 2000 was found nine years later and 1,250 mi (2,000 km) away in Melbourne, Victoria. While cleaning terrier-cross Muffy, animal carers spotted the microchip that identified her and enabled her to be reunited with her owners, the Lampard family.

DEEP DIVE

Sperm whales can dive to depths of nearly 2 mi (3 km) and can stay underwater for up to 90 minutes at a time without needing to surface for air.

OCTOPUS STUDY

British marine experts have discovered that instead of eight arms, an octopus really has only six. A new study has revealed that it uses six of its tentacles as arms for eating, but the back two limbs act as legs to help it move across the ocean floor.

BOUNCING FISH

A species of fish has been discovered that bounces on the ocean floor like a rubber ball. The psychedelic dogfish, which was discovered off the coast of Indonesia in 2008, bounces around in a haphazard manner because its tail is off-center and because it propels itself forward jerkily by expelling water from tiny gill openings.

CLOSE CALL

A tiny chihuahua, weighing about 4 lb (1.8 kg), somehow survived and recovered after being trodden on by her best friend—a 1,980-lb (900-kg) Clydesdale horse. Little Berry was playing with her friend Leroy at their home in Geelong, Victoria, Australia, when the giant horse accidentally stepped on the dog's head.

GOOD MEMORY

Elephants can recognize groups of people by their specific smell and color and the style of their clothing.

Frank and Barbara Witte of Fresno, California, have a highly unusual pet. Their Bearded Dragon, Zak-n-Wheezie, has two names because it was born with two heads. Experts predicted that the lizard would not live for long, but Zak-n-Wheezie is still going strong and is possibly the longest living two-headed Bearded Dragon in the world.

Heads and Tail

Sea Pig

This curious creature was caught in deep water by the Cabrillo Marine Aquarium in California. It is about the size of an apple and can be found in most of the world's oceans at depths greater than 330 ft (100 m). It is actually a type of squid, and what looks like hair is actually a crop of tentacles attached to its head. Orange pigments on its body can look like facial features when its body swells with water. Add to this a protruding noselike "siphon," which it uses to propel itself, and you have what is commonly known as the Piglet Squid.

LITERATE DOG

New York animal trainer Lyssa Rosenberg has taught her terrier Willow to read! Willow plays dead when she sees the word "bang," stretches a paw in the air when she sees "wave" and stands on her back feet to beg when she sees the words "sit up." Willow can do 250 different tricks and it took her just six weeks to recognize words and respond to them.

TRACKING DEVICE

A 6-ft (1.8-m) python that was stolen from a research center near Perth, Western Australia, was traced by its last meal. The snake was snatched shortly after it had eaten a woylie, an endangered marsupial that, unbeknown to the unlucky thieves, had been fitted with a tracking device. The device showed up even from inside the python's stomach, alerting scientists and police to the snake's whereabouts.

SYNTHETIC BEAK

A stork with a damaged beak was given a new one in 2009 by a Hungarian bird hospital. The stork, which was thought to have flown into a wall, had its lower beak repaired in an operation, while specialist Tamas Kothay built a new top beak out of synthetic resin.

Pink Dolphin

Never before seen, a bright pink albino Bottlenose dolphin has been catching the eye of sailors on coastal Calcasieu Lake, Louisiana. The dolphin, which has grown up in the area, is perfectly healthy apart from its flawless pink finish. The young creature swims with a small pod of fellow dolphins in the lake and is an unforgettable attraction for those lucky enough to catch a glimpse.

HORSE DRESS

Bavarian designer Hildegard Bergbauer usually creates traditional dirndl dresses for women, but now she has branched out and started making them for cats, dogs and even horses, too!

WOLF DETERRENT

Wolves can be kept at bay using a simple technique of a rope with a red ribbon, or series of red flags, tied to it. The technique is known as fladry and has been used for centuries in Europe.

BALD CAT

A cat who is bald apart from a mass of chest hair has become a tourist attraction at the Exeter Veterinary Hospital in New Hampshire because of his weird appearance. Eight-year-old Ugly Bat Boy, whose breed is not known, was adopted by Dr. Stephen Bassett shortly after he was born bald, probably as a result of a genetic defect.

ELEPHANT SLIPPERS

In a bid to soothe painful abscesses on her front feet, Gay, a 40-year-old Asian elephant at Paignton Zoo, Devon, England, has been fitted with a pair of $750 slippers. To ensure a good fit, keepers had to draw an outline around her two front feet to make patterns that were then sent off to a specialist firm in Australia. Each slipper boot measures about 16 in (40 cm) in diameter and comes with laces that elephants aren't able to undo.

BUNNY BOOM

In June 2009, Nancy Haseman of Rio Rancho, New Mexico, was found to be keeping 334 rabbits in her garden. She said her husband rescued a rabbit 12 years earlier after a neighbor abandoned it, then the couple began rescuing more rabbits. She had tried to keep the males separate from the females but the males kept hopping the fence.

FISH FAST

In some species of whalefish, the males stop eating entirely as they mature, their jaws waste away and they live exclusively on energy stored in their massive, fatty liver.

VENOMOUS MAMMAL

The Hispaniolan solenodon, a small mammal from Haiti and the Dominican Republic, is one of only a couple of mammals that has a venomous bite.

DUNG DWELLERS

Frogs in Sri Lanka's Bundala National Park have set up home in piles of Asian elephant dung. The frogs normally live among leaf litter on the ground, but because that can be in short supply during the dry season, they use elephant dung as an alternative habitat.

FANTASTIC FINBACK

For many years Cambridge University in England has displayed the 70-ft (21-m) skeleton of a Finback Whale at its Zoology Museum. The specimen was found in 1865 on a beach in Sussex, England, and would have weighed 176,000 lb (80 tons).

ZEBRA RIDE

Former racehorse jockey Bill Turner rides a zebra to his local pub in the town of Sherborne in Dorset, England. He bought the zebra from a game reserve in Holland and learned to ride it in just two weeks.

CANINE CASTAWAY

A pet dog that was swept overboard on a sailing trip swam 5 mi (8 km) through shark-infested waters and survived on a remote island for four months by feeding on baby goats. The grey and black cattle dog was reunited with owners Jan and Dave Griffith after being found by rangers on the quiet and largely uninhabited St. Bees Island off the coast of Queensland, Australia.

BEE SWARM

Employees at a game store in one of the busiest shopping areas of New York City were trapped inside for several hours in May 2009 while thousands of bees swarmed outside in the street. After a passerby managed to lure some of the bees into a box, a specialist arrived in protective gear and used the scent of a queen bee to collect the rest of them.

PRESIDENT'S BEARS

U.S. President Thomas Jefferson received a gift of two grizzly bears in October 1807. He was so delighted with the gift that he kept them on the White House lawn for months.

Meat Eater

Intrepid explorers have released details of an amazing new plant species, capable of trapping and devouring a full-size rat, on an island in the Philippines. In a quest to find the plant, which was last recorded in 1907, Stewart McPherson's team climbed a mountain in the middle of a prison, guided by three convicted murderers, and discovered the carnivorous pitcher plants at the summit. The plants are the size of footballs and lined with tentacles that secrete sticky glue to ensnare insects and rodents, before it dissolves them with its acid-like enzymes.

Cow Strange

This six-year-old cow was born with six legs and can be seen in a zoo in Yichang, China. Unsurprisingly, it is a big hit with the visitors. The condition, known as "Polymelia," can affect most animals, and may be caused by a genetic disorder, a deformed twin being partially absorbed in the womb, or environmental issues.

DRUNKEN BADGER

German police were called to deal with a dead badger on the road near the town of Goslar—only to find that the animal was not dead at all, merely drunk! The badger had staggered into the middle of the road after eating overripe cherries that had fermented.

DOLLAR NEST

A mouse made its home inside an ATM at a gas station in La Grande, Oregon, building its nest from 16 chewed-up $20 bills.

FLOOD DIVERSION

During floods, Amazon River dolphins leave the river to swim through submerged forests lying in the flood plains.

EXPENSIVE SHEEP

A young male Texel sheep—a breed highly prized for its lean meat—was sold at a Scottish livestock market for over $350,000 in 2009. The young ram, who could father up to 1,000 lambs per year, cost more than $1,500 per pound, which means that a lamb chop from it would cost about $600!

JUNK FOOD

Zeke, a cat owned by the Scarpino family of Cedar Knolls, New Jersey, had surgery to remove more than a year's accumulation of hair ties, ribbon, twist ties and junk from his stomach—which had grown to five times its normal size.

RAMPANT RABBIT

Benny, a two-year-old giant Flemish buck rabbit owned by Martin and Sharon Heather of Oxfordshire, England, is nearly 3 ft (90 cm) long and tips the scales at over 22 lb (10 kg). His food bill tops $75 a week.

SWIMMING AID

A shark's skin is covered in tiny toothlike structures called denticles, which help it swim with a minimum of friction.

SILK BELL

Europe's water spider spends its entire life underwater and builds a silk diving bell to store oxygen.

Snake Boy

Uorn Sambath from Setbo, Cambodia, has an unusual pet for a boy. He has developed a friendship with a huge 16-ft (4.9-m) python. He gives the serpent hugs and kisses and sometimes sleeps inside the coils of the snake, which weighs over 220 lb (100 kg) and requires three adults to carry. The python first slithered into the boy's bedroom when he was three months old, and now has its own room in the family home.

Cat Nap

Big-cat keeper Riana van Nieuwenhuizen from Bloemfontein, South Africa, shares her home with nine cheetahs, three leopards, two wolves, a jaguar, a lion and three dogs.

Riana hand rears the abandoned or orphaned animals and uses them to raise awareness of endangered species in her country.

Riana bought her first cheetah, Fiela, in 2006 at just six weeks old. Fiela is fully house-trained and allowed to roam free in Riana's house.

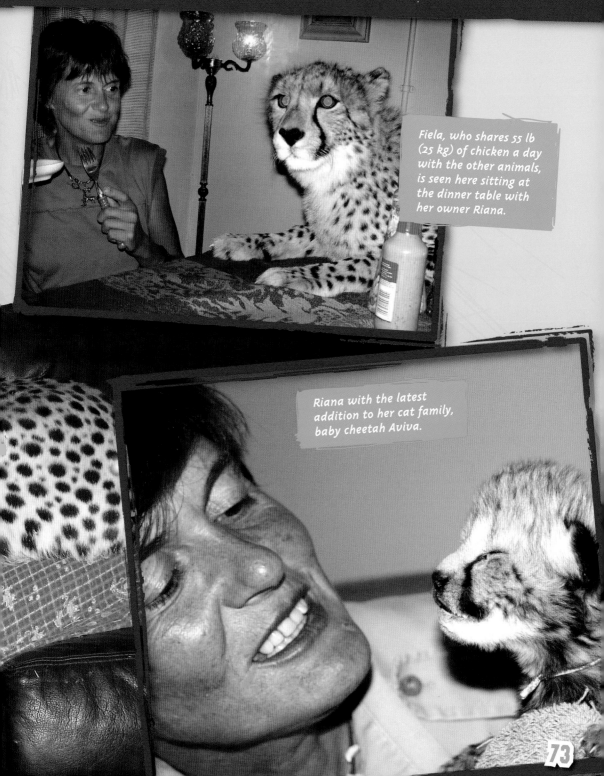

Fiela, who shares 55 lb (25 kg) of chicken a day with the other animals, is seen here sitting at the dinner table with her owner Riana.

Riana with the latest addition to her cat family, baby cheetah Aviva.

73

BEST FRIENDS

Gerald, a 15-ft-tall (4.5-m) giraffe at Noah's Ark Zoo Farm in Bristol, England, had an unusual best friend—a goat named Eddie. The pair were inseparable for more than three years, with Gerald letting his little friend climb on his neck and share his bedding. He even chased away the zebras who bullied Eddie.

LONG REACH

The Giant Pacific octopus has an arm span of more than 14 ft (4 m) across—that's greater than the height of two adult men.

COOKIE BEAR

A black bear was found sitting on a freezer eating cookies after breaking into a bakery in Tobermory, Ontario, Canada, in July 2009.

MANY TEETH

While humans get only two sets of natural teeth to last them their entire life, alligators get between 2,000 and 3,000 teeth during their lifetime.

Albino Turtle

Resembling an uncooked Christmas turkey, this white beast is in fact a rare albino turtle. Found on the banks of the Yellow River in Henan Province, China, in 2009, it measures 16 in (40 cm) in length and weighs 14 lb (6.5 kg). The mutant turtle reportedly acquired its all-white skin, apart from one pink patch, through a genetic mutation caused by pollution.

WINGED CAT

Born perfectly normal, a long-haired white cat in Chongqing, China, began sprouting winglike growths on either side of his spine when he was a year old. Some experts believe the bony "wings" are a freak mutation in the form of a Siamese twin growing inside the cat. Others think the cause may be genetic, the result of chemicals absorbed during his mother's pregnancy.

FELINE PASSENGER

For over four years, a cat in Plymouth, England, has been catching the same bus every day. Casper boards the number 3 bus at 10.55 a.m. outside his home and travels the entire 11-mi (18-km) route before returning home an hour later. He is such a regular passenger that bus drivers look out for him to make sure he gets off at the right stop.

SMOOTH SKIN

Elephants at Belfast Zoo in Northern Ireland have been given a brand of supermarket moisturizer to keep their bottoms smooth. Keeper Aisling McMahon recommended the moisturizing cream she used on her own skin and now the elephants receive regular applications to soften unwanted dry skin around their lower feet and large butt.

One Pig Race

Cushendun Community Fête, in Northern Ireland, enjoyed a fun-filled pig-racing event complete with colorful woolen jockeys in July 2009. Popular in the U.S.A., the races are usually often a main attraction at county fairs. Only juvenile pigs are allowed to participate and they race around a grass or dirt track and even jump over hurdles.

HOPPING MAD

A kangaroo burst through the window of a house and hopped into bed with a startled Australian family in March 2009. Beat Ettlin rescued his children from the kangaroo that stood around 6 ft (1.8 m) tall by wrestling the animal into a headlock and dragging it down the hall and out of the front door.

SWEET TOOTH

A bear with a sweet tooth broke into a San Bernardino County, California, home and ate a 2-lb (900-g) box of chocolates from the refrigerator. He pushed aside vegetables in the fridge and went straight for the chocolates. He also tried unsuccessfully to open a bottle of champagne.

GIANT WORM

The giant Gippsland earthworm, which lives in Victoria, Australia, can reach lengths of 10 ft (3 m). The young are already 8 in (20 cm) long when they hatch and take about five years to reach maturity. When the giant worm was first discovered in the 1870s, its size led scientists to think it was a snake.

BABY SAVED

A dog was believed to have saved the life of an abandoned baby girl in La Plata, Argentina, in 2008 by keeping her warm with her own puppies. Farmer Fabio Anze found the naked baby girl, who was just a few hours old, among his dog China's puppies.

FLYING CHIMP

Bili, a three-month-old bonobo chimpanzee, sat in the cabin with the rest of the passengers for his flight from Birmingham, England, to his new home at Frankfurt Zoo in Germany.

FREAKY PIG

A piglet born in Zhejiang Province, China, in 2009 had two mouths and three eyes. The mother was completely normal, as were the other seven piglets in the litter.

DENTAL CARE

Female long-tailed macaque monkeys near Bangkok, Thailand, have been observed teaching their young how to floss their teeth. The adults were seen using strands of hair to clean between their teeth, and this practice became more regular and more elaborate when the females were with their babies, suggesting that they were trying to teach the youngsters the importance of good dental hygiene.

CAMEL IMPORTS

Camels aren't native to Australia, but the continent has about one million of them roaming its rural interior.

Monkey Business

Visitors at Knowsley Safari Park, Prescot, England, will need to learn to keep their luggage inside their cars after more than 20 resident baboons completely emptied visitors' suitcases in July 2009. The naughty baboons have cleverly worked out how to break into car roof racks leaving visitors no choice but to watch helplessly as their belongings are strewn all over the ground! The incident has occurred so frequently that the Park's General Manager, David Ross, has had to advise cars with cargo cases not to drive through the monkey enclosure.

Angry Hippos

A crocodile was bitten to death after becoming trapped among a gang of 50 angry hippos on the banks of the Grumeti River in the Serengeti National Park, Tanzania. The croc got too close to a female hippo and her calves, and the entire hippo group gathered in a circle to protect them. Instead of backing off, the croc panicked and tried to escape across the backs of the hippos, who responded with a frenzied attack. The croc's armor-plated body was no match for the hippos' huge teeth, which can apply several tons of pressure in a single bite. Fights between hippos and crocs are rare, as they usually show mutual respect, but when a hippo has young to protect, it becomes one of the most aggressive creatures in the animal kingdom.

Short Legs

Fire crews were called out four times to rescue Mayflower, a grey Shetland pony apparently stuck in mud, only to find that the animal simply had short legs! Her unusually short legs and long body mean she is only half the height of other ponies grazing on salt marshes near the River Test in Hampshire, southern England.

MUSICAL ELEPHANT

An elephant at an English safari park entertains keepers and visitors by playing the harmonica. Five, a female African elephant at West Midlands Safari Park, discovered the harmonica after it was accidentally left on the side of her enclosure and soon learned to place the instrument in her trunk and blow out to produce some notes.

DOG'S GUIDE DOG

A blind Border collie has his own guide dog! Five-year-old Clyde is totally blind and relies on another collie, Bonnie, to help him around the dog rescue center in Norfolk, England. Clyde refuses to go anywhere without Bonnie, who stays inches from his side while guiding him on walks or to food and water. She even lets him rest his head on her haunches when he becomes disorientated.

Mistaken Identity

PAINTING POOCH

Ziggy, a Pekingese dog owned by Elizabeth Monacelli of southern California, paints works of art that have sold for up to $250 at auction. He creates his masterpieces by putting his teeth around a paper towel roll, which is attached to a paintbrush. Monacelli plays him special Chinese music to get him in the artistic mood, but even then he manages an average of only three brushstrokes per painting session before curling into a ball and falling asleep.

WHISTLING APES

An orangutan at the National Zoo in Washington, D.C. has amazed keepers by learning to whistle. Thirty-two-year-old Bonnie taught herself after listening to keepers whistling while they worked. She is thought to have taught another orangutan at the zoo to whistle, too.

SURPRISE VISITOR

In March 2009, a sick turtle swam directly to the Turtle Hospital—a turtle treatment facility in the Florida Keys! The 73-lb (33-kg) loggerhead turtle took itself to hospital and was found to be suffering from a bacterial infection.

TALENTED PIG

Sue, a Kune Kune pig owned by Wendy Scudamore from Herefordshire, England, shakes hands by presenting a trotter on command and can perform agility tests as ably as any dog. In fact, Mrs. Scudamore hopes that one day Sue will be able to herd sheep just like the pig in the movie Babe.

LUCKY STRIKE

A chicken in England has laid an egg shaped like a bowling pin! Natalie Wiltshire said the odd egg was laid by one of the 20 chickens she keeps in Willoughby, Northamptonshire.

Reggie, a 3-ft-long (1-m) kingsnake kept as a pet in West Sussex, England, required emergency surgery after attempting to eat his own tail. He mistook his tail for another snake but was unable to regurgitate it because of his backward-facing teeth. He was prevented from choking to death by veterinary surgeon Bob Reynolds, who was able to pry open the snake's mouth, dislocate its jaw and remove the tail before it had been digested.

Snake Attack

A python was caught suffocating an unfortunate cockatoo in Cairns, Australia, in 2008. Artist Cindy Lane was working in her studio when she heard loud squawking, and moving outside she discovered the snake coiling itself around the bird high up in a tree in her backyard. She reported that the python took around two hours to completely swallow its feathered prey.

FLUFFY FISH

A pet goldfish survived out of water for seven hours after apparently jumping out of his tank. Sparkle was found covered in dog hair and fluff behind the tank's stand in North Yorkshire, England, but after being washed under the tap, he started breathing again and made a full recovery.

SUPER RAT

A new species of rat has been discovered in Papua New Guinea that is as big as a domestic cat! Found in the crater of the extinct volcano Mount Bosavi, the Bosavi woolly rat measures more than 32 in (80 cm) from nose to tail and weighs 3 lb (1.4 kg).

SURFING DOG

An eight-month-old Border terrier can ride waves up to 3 ft (1 m) high near his home in Cornwall, England. Trained by owner Tim Kevan, Jack regularly surfs on a 9-ft (3-m) board and can even perform tricks such as a "hang five," where he walks up and down the board while surfing.

Flappy Meal

A Golden Orb Weaver spider managed to ensnare a Chestnut—breasted Mannikin finch in its web in a garden near Atherton, Australia. The giant spider would have then proceeded to inject the struggling bird with venom to prepare it for eating, and wrap the corpse into a food parcel, as it would be too much for the spider to eat in one sitting. Golden Orb Weaver spiders can grow larger than a human hand and usually prey on large insects, so it is highly unusual to see one catching a bird.

SEA BUDGIE

A budgerigar that had escaped from its aviary in the coastal town of Brixham in Devon, England, was found floating half a mile out to sea. The bedraggled bird was plucked from the water by a dive-boat crew and reunited with its owner, budgie breeder Mike Peel.

MOTHER HEN

A hen in China adopted two orphaned puppies after their mother died. Owner Cao Fengying of Jiashan said the hen was best friends with the mother dog, and then looked after the puppies, fighting off other chickens who were trying to steal the puppies' food.

ROLE REVERSAL

Although toads are normally the prey of venomous snakes, some mountain toads in Qingcheng Mountain Park, Sichuan, China, have turned nature on its head by eating one of their chief predators, Jerdon's pit vipers.

SLEEPY CEPHALOPOD

The Australian giant cuttlefish spends an amazing 95 percent of its day resting and hiding in crevices from predators.

CONTACT LENSES

A German company has invented a range of contact lenses for animals that suffer from cataracts, a condition that invariably leaves them blind. Among animals that may be able to be treated are lions, giraffes, bears, sea lions, kangaroos and tigers.

CLONED PET

A Florida family paid $155,000 for a clone of their dead dog. Nina Otto from Boca Raton had the DNA of her beloved golden Labrador, Sir Lancelot, collected and frozen five years before his death in 2008. In 2009, the family collected Lancelot Encore, a three-month-old puppy that was an exact genetic replica of their deceased pet.

Silly Steer

This Belgian Blue bullock was spotted with its head caught between the rungs of a ladder. Inspector Kerry Kirkpatrick, from a Scottish animal charity, was called to the scene and managed to rescue the steer in South Ayrshire, Scotland, by easing the ladder off its head, after which the steer returned safely to the herd.

Mad Menagerie

Todd Ray's "Freakshow" houses one of the strangest collections of live creatures on the planet.

Todd established his menagerie of animals on the beach boardwalk at Venice, California, after retiring from a career in the music industry. His collection contains turtles, snakes and lizards with multiple heads, a dog with five legs, an iguana with two tails, a hairless rat, albino snakes, and many other oddities. Inside the show are less fortunate freaks of the natural world, such as double-headed cows, chickens and even a raccoon, preserved in jars of formaldehyde for curious visitors to see.

Todd holding Myrtle and Squirtle, who share the same shell, outside his Venice Beach Freakshow.

Cheech and Chong, a turtle with two heads and six legs.

Laverne and Shirley the two-headed kingsnake.

Double-headed bearded dragon.

SNAKE BITE

Johannes Swart spent 37 days in a glass box, measuring 16 x 13 ft (5 x 4 m), with 40 highly venomous snakes at a conservation park near Pretoria, South Africa, in September 2009. His stay ended when he was bitten on the foot by a deadly puff adder and had to undergo emergency surgery in the local hospital.

MAN BITES SNAKE

A Kenyan man escaped from a python by biting it after the snake had wrapped him in its coils and dragged him up a tree. During the three-hour struggle, Ben Nyaumbe smothered the snake's head with his shirt to prevent it from swallowing him and then bit the python on the tip of its tail.

SIGN LANGUAGE

A Border collie puppy is learning sign language after it was discovered that she is totally deaf. Pixie is being taught to recognize hand commands by trainer Liz Grewal in Coffs Harbour, New South Wales, Australia.

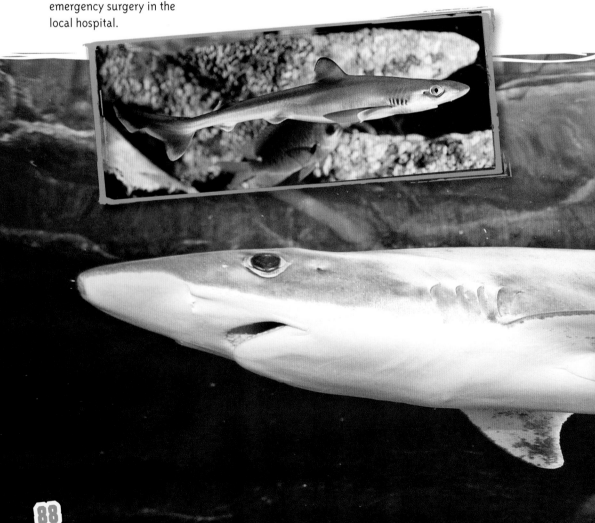

TURTLE RECALL

A runway at John F. Kennedy International Airport in New York City was shut down briefly in July 2009 after about 80 turtles emerged from nearby Jamaica Bay and crawled onto the tarmac. The invasion by the 8-in-long (20-cm) diamondback terrapins caused flights to be delayed for up to 90 minutes.

FEATHERED CRITICS

By rewarding them with food, Japanese scientists believe that racing pigeons can be trained to study paintings and evaluate them—exactly as you might expect from an art critic. The study shows that, with practice, pigeons can learn to appreciate the color, pattern and texture of paintings.

SWALLOWED RING

Anne Moon from Yorkshire, England, lost a $2,250 antique diamond engagement ring in August 2009 when it was swallowed by a piglet. She went to pat Ginger, a ten-week-old Kune Kune pig, at a farm but it clamped its teeth around the ring and refused to let go.

Shark Cesarean

When a pregnant shark at an aquarium in Auckland, New Zealand, was bitten in the side by another shark, visitors watched in amazement as four baby sharks swam out through the gaping wound. Staff described the deep gouge as like the mother shark having a cesarean section. The injured shark needed stitches—but only after four more pups were found alive inside her.

Snake Foot

This snake was discovered in China in 2009 with a single clawed foot growing out from its body. The 16-in-long (40-cm) mutant reptile was found by Duan Qiongxiu clinging to the wall of her bedroom in Suining with its talons. Mrs. Duan was so scared that she beat the snake to death with her shoe. Growing a foot is a very rare mutation for a snake—they more frequently grow two heads—and scientists are working to find out if the foot evolved from changes in the snake's environment.

LIQUID LUNCH

Spiders are unable to eat solid food, so they must liquefy the insides of their prey. They do this by regurgitating digestive juices onto the prey and then crushing it with their jaws and sucking up the juices.

FROG'S LEG

A giant bullfrog that had been attacked by a dog near Johannesburg, South Africa, became the first frog in the world to be fitted with a false leg. In a delicate two-hour operation, the amphibian had his shattered lower leg bone replaced with a one-inch-long (2.5-cm) steel rod.

SWALLOWED WHOLE

An Australian woman was horrified when her pet dog was swallowed whole by a snake in March 2009. Patty Buntine of Katherine, Northern Territory, was worried when Bindi, her three-year-old Maltese terrier cross, went missing. On going outside to investigate, she saw the snake with its belly bulging so much it was unable to move. The dog amounted to around 60 percent of the snake's bodyweight, which meant that the serpent's snack was like a fully grown man swallowing a 16-year-old boy.

NON-SWIMMERS

Although adult hippos can see and breathe underwater and are adapted to aquatic life, they can't swim or even float. Their bodies are too dense for them to have any natural buoyancy, so they move around either by pushing off from the bottom of the river or simply by walking along the riverbed.

WINNING STREAK

Bertie the Labrador dog won his owner Dave Hallett from Sussex, England, $300 in a pub lottery five weeks in a row, beating odds of 282-million-to-one. He predicted the winning bonus ball by putting his nose up against a number on a board.

FALSE FOOT

A three-year-old Asian elephant whose front left foot was caught in a trap is able to walk again after he was fitted with a prosthetic foot. After cutting away 5 in (12 cm) of infected tissue, surgeons in Cambodia made a cast of Chhouk's stump so that a false foot could be created by a prosthetics' team. He needed no anesthetic while the limb was being attached—just a steady supply of turnips and bananas.

Incy Wincy Spider

The tiny "happy-face" spider can be found in the rainforests of only four islands in the world—Oahu, Molokai, Maui and Hawaii. Measuring around 1/5 in (5 mm), no one knows why the colorful patterns on the spiders' backs look like happy faces. One theory is that the patterns evolved to confuse their predators—birds—but the species is nevertheless under threat from a growing number of animals that have been introduced to the islands. Perhaps they need to evolve a scary face!

Porky Puss

In 2009, the People's Dispensary for Sick Animals started a fat-fighting club for animals with weight problems, and Socrates the cat was one of nine chosen animals. The fat cat from Newcastle, England, loves to eat cheese-and-onion potato chips and weighs a massive 22 lb (10 kg). This is more than double his ideal weight and makes him "morbidly obese." The animals in the fitness club are put on a strict diet and exercise regime for 100 days to increase their life "pet-spectancy" and the most improved creature (and owner) wins a vacation.

LUCKY FELIX

In April 2009, Felix, a 12-year-old cat belonging to Andrea Schröder of Cologne, Germany, was found alive despite having been trapped in the rubble of a collapsed apartment building for nearly five weeks.

IN A SPIN

A seven-week-old kitten survived in July 2009 after being trapped in a washing machine for a full cycle, including a spin. Toby is believed to have crawled into the machine at his home in Aberdeenshire, Scotland, before it was switched on, in an attempt to escape the summer heat wave.

EARTHQUAKE PACKS

Pet owners in earthquake zones can buy special kits to ensure their cats and dogs survive. The Japanese-manufactured emergency packs contain a padded jacket and rain hat, special boots to protect paws, a bell in case the pet is lost in rubble, food, water and bowls, and aromatherapy oil to soothe stressed animals.

NO JAWS

Horseshoe crabs have no jaws to chew with. Instead, they shove food straight into their open mouths with a pair of arms.

ADOPTED OWL

An orphaned baby eagle owl was adopted by a springer spaniel at a bird of prey rescue center in Cornwall, England, in 2009. The pair became inseparable and Sophie the spaniel even gave Bramble the owl a daily wash by licking her.

SHARK JUMP

In December 2008, a reef shark at a Bahamas resort jumped from its aquarium, landed on a nearby water slide, slid down to the swimming pool and surprised the staff.

CRANE PURSUIT

Conservationists in Wisconsin help endangered whooping cranes to migrate south for the winter by encouraging them to fly in pursuit of a microlight plane. The hand-reared birds are taught that the microlight, which plays recordings of simulated crane calls, is their parent, so when the aircraft takes off, they dutifully follow the plane for more than 1,250 mi (2,000 km) to the warmth and safety of Florida's west coast.

15,000 FEET

The sunflower starfish grows to a diameter of more than 3 ft (1 m) across and has around 15,000 tube feet on the underside of its body.

CRUEL TWIST

A dog in China became so attached to two red pandas she had adopted that she rejected her own puppy. The rare pandas were abandoned by their mother shortly after being born at Taiyuan Zoo, but were nursed back to health with love and milk from the dog. However, the dog became convinced that the cubs were its own babies and refused to nurse her own puppy.

BOXER DOG

Chela, a dog owned by Peru's national police force, has been taught to box. Trainer Cesar Chacaliaza says the German shorthaired pointer wasn't keen on wearing boxing gloves at first, but she has now learned to jab with her front paws while standing up on her hind legs.

FROG FIND

Half a century after last being spotted, a population of rare California mountain yellow-legged frogs was rediscovered in 2009. The elusive amphibians were located in the San Bernardino National Forest by scientists following the same course as a 1908 expedition.

NUCLEAR HOME

Half of the world's wild two-humped Bactrian camels live in a former nuclear weapons test site in Xinjiang, China.

Chito Loco thinks nothing of frolicking in the water with a 980-lb (445-kg) crocodile. Chito rescued the giant reptile after farmers shot him 20 years ago, and nursed him back to health. The Costa Rican fisherman now puts on a weekly show during which he feeds and even rides the croc, which he named Pocho, who is an impressive 16 ft (5 m) long.

NAME CHECK

Smokey the cockatiel was reunited with his owner after saying his own name on the phone. Having escaped from the home of David Edwards, the missing bird had been found in nearby Wrexham, North Wales. To prove that she was the rightful owner, Mrs. Edwards asked for Smokey to be put on the phone and as soon as he heard her voice, he started repeating his name.

HIGH LIFE

The common swift spends most of its life in flight, nests on vertical surfaces and never willingly touches the ground.

TALENTED TERRIERS

When dog owner Sun Chien of Shenyang, China, suffered a stroke, he built a shopping cart and trained his two terriers—Pong Pong and Wow Wow—to do his shopping. The dogs push the cart, which has holders for money and shopping lists, to the shops by themselves—and if one gets tired, he hops in and lets the other one do the pushing for a while.

LEG TWITCH

A harvestman arachnid's legs can twitch for up to an hour after they have been detached from its body.

Crocodile Man

Giant Limb

Motola, a 48-year-old Asian elephant from Thailand, needed a heavyweight solution when she lost part of one of her legs after stepping on a land mine ten years ago. After trying various prototypes, she was recently fitted with a custom-made permanent prosthetic limb strong enough to hold her weight at the Elephant Hospital in North Thailand. The jumbo operation to fit Motola's new leg required enough anesthetic to knock out 70 people.

SENIOR DOG

Max, a terrier-cross belonging to Janelle Derouen of New Iberia, Louisiana, celebrated his 26th birthday in 2009—making him a staggering 182 years old in dog years.

FREAK EGG

Thelma, a chicken owned by Margaret Hamstra of Lynden, Washington State, laid an oversized egg—8 in (20 cm) in circumference—with a normal egg inside. Both eggs had both a white and a yolk.

PIGEON HONOR

G.I. Joe, a carrier pigeon for the U.S. Army, helped save the lives of 1,000 British soldiers during World War II—and in 1946, London's mayor presented him with an honorary medal for his work.

SHRINKING SHEEP

A breed of wild sheep in Scotland is shrinking in body size as a result of climate change. Since 1985, Soay sheep on the uninhabited island of Hirta in the St. Kilda archipelago have shrunk by five percent, their legs getting shorter and their body weight decreasing. In the past, only big sheep could survive the harsh winters in the area, but scientists say that because of climate change the winters have become milder and grass is now available for more months of the year, enabling smaller sheep to cope.

Fortunate Feline

When Chase, a kitten from Lexington, Kentucky, was hit by a car she lost her nose, eyelids and the skin on her face, as well as one of her legs. Surgeons were unable to rebuild her features, so she was left with pink tissue instead of fur on her face. She was adopted by Melissa Smith, the veterinary technician who helped look after her, and has since become a "therapy cat" in the local area, helping people with disfigurements to improve their confidence. Chase became an online celebrity with her own blog that reassures her fans that she is happy and not in any pain.

Fly-vertising

At the 2009 Frankfurt Book Fair, a German publishing company started a new advertising craze, attaching very small banners to flies and letting them loose around the halls of the fair. Eichborn, whose logo is a fly, decided to attach the lightweight banners saying "The Publisher of the Fly" to 200 flies to promote their advertising stand. The banners were attached using string and wax that would fall off naturally without harming the fly. However, the flies did have some difficulty staying in the air and kept landing on people all over the convention.

BLOWN AWAY

A chihuahua swept up into the air and blown away by a 70-mph (110-km/h) gust of wind was eventually found safe and sound more than a mile (1.6 km) away. Weighing 6 lb (2.7 kg), little eight-month-old Tinker Bell was standing on her owners' platform trailer at a flea market in Waterford Township, Michigan, in April 2009 when she was hurled out of sight by the sudden blast of air.

HOUSE GUESTS

Lesley Coles of Somerset, England, wondered why her shopping bag was heavy—and when she looked inside she found a 3-ft (90-cm) python curled up in the bottom. The snake was thought to have been secretly living in the cupboard of Mrs. Coles' house for up to six months after crawling in through a hole made for the electrical meter.

ARROW SURGERY

A puppy from Kent, England, survived after swallowing a 10½-in (27-cm) plastic arrow that was almost as long as her. Betty, an eight-month-old Staffordshire bull terrier, underwent emergency surgery to remove the arrow, which had become lodged in her body from the esophagus to the small intestine.

PIGEON SMUGGLERS

In March 2009, Brazilian police discovered inmates raising homing pigeons within Danilo Pinheiro Prison, Sorocaba, for the purpose of smuggling in contraband. Guards intercepted two pigeons carrying cell phones and chargers to detainees.

RECYCLED PHONE

In 2009, a pelican at Tautphaus Park Zoo, Idaho, swallowed and later regurgitated a cell phone that a visitor had dropped into the pool.

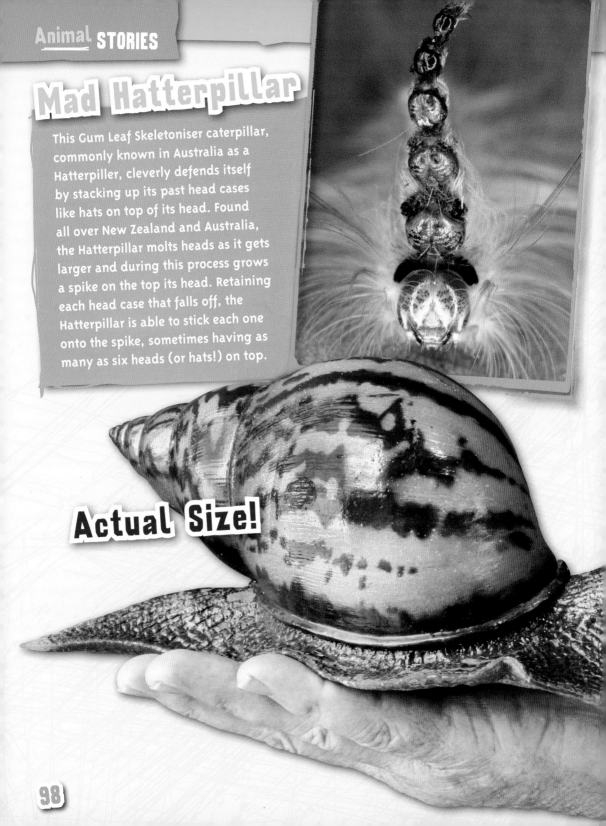

Mad Hatterpillar

This Gum Leaf Skeletoniser caterpillar, commonly known in Australia as a Hatterpiller, cleverly defends itself by stacking up its past head cases like hats on top of its head. Found all over New Zealand and Australia, the Hatterpillar molts heads as it gets larger and during this process grows a spike on the top its head. Retaining each head case that falls off, the Hatterpillar is able to stick each one onto the spike, sometimes having as many as six heads (or hats!) on top.

Actual Size!

FIVE LEGS

Lilly, a chihuahua puppy, was born in Gastonia, North Carolina, with five legs. The extra leg, which had no feeling, hung down between her two rear legs until it was removed at age seven weeks.

WHEEL TRAP

An inquisitive cat that poked its head into the wheel of a car had to be rescued by firefighters after becoming stuck in the small hole in the center. Using specialist cutting gear, it took fire crews from Bury St Edmunds in Suffolk, England, an hour to free Casper the Siamese.

LONG TONGUE

The pangolin, a rare African animal, has a tongue that can extend up to 16 in (40 cm), which it uses to lap up termites and ants.

DANCING COLLIE

Samson, a Border collie dog from Manchester, England, loves disco dancing. He can perform twirls, spins and jumps in time to his favorite music, and can even stand on his back legs to do his own version of Michael Jackson's famous moonwalk.

HOT HIPPO

A hippopotamus that decided to escape the South African heat by climbing into a 10-ft-high (3-m) water tower for a long soak found it couldn't get out again. A farm worker realized the animal was stuck, and in a four-hour operation a team from the Mpumalanga Tourism and Parks Association drained the tank and used poles to nudge the hippo into a steel cage before winching it to safety with a hydraulic crane.

CHEMICAL ALERT

Argentine ants produce chemicals that alert their nestmates to the fact that they are still alive. Once they stop producing it, they are picked up and carried to a garbage pile by the other ants.

Snail Trail

The Giant African Snail is one of the world's most destructive creatures and can grow up to 10 in (25 cm) in length. Found mostly in East Africa, Asia and the Caribbean, they go global by climbing into produce containers and sailing all over the world. In 1966, a boy from Miami, Florida, acquired three of these snails, which his grandma released into a garden. Seven years later, there were 18,000 of them and it took the Florida authorities ten years and $1 million to eradicate them.

Beyond

BELIEF

Raise the Flags

Guinness Rishi from Delhi, India, was featured in *Ripley's Believe It or Not! Seeing is Believing* for a stomach-churning ketchup-guzzling feat.

Now Guinness has undertaken to get his head, face and body permanently tattooed with more than 300 flags in full color, beating his 2009 record of 220. He has 24 flag tattoos on the top of his head, 25 flags on his face and a map of the countries of the world on his stomach. Guinness would like to donate his body to a *Ripley's Believe It or Not!* museum to preserve and put on display when he dies.

Guinness uses his tattoos to promote amity among nations.

Tasty Treats

From smoked rattlesnake to creamed armadillo, there is some crazy canned food available around the world for those with adventurous taste buds. From popular foods, such as cheeseburgers, to more gruesome offerings, such as the cockroaches (shown here) or ants' eggs, there is something to suit everyone—you can even buy a whole chicken in a can, complete with bones and skin!

$500,000 DOG

A woman in China paid over $500,000 for a Tibetan mastiff dog in 2009. Mrs. Wang had spent years scouring China for the perfect specimen, a dog called Yangtze River Number Two. When the pet arrived by plane at Xi'an airport, it was met by banners, a welcoming committee of local dog-lovers and a motorcade of 30 luxury limousines sent by the new owner's wealthy friends.

DIVIDED HOUSE

A couple in Cambodia who separated in 2008 after nearly 40 years of marriage decided to divide their belongings equally—by taking the unusual step of sawing their house in half. The wife stayed in the remaining upright half of the house while her husband carried away his half to a field on the other side of the village where he planned to start a new life.

LIGHT RIDDLE

For five years, farmer Mo Zhaoguang from Nandan, Hubei Province, China, was mystified as to who kept turning on the light in his barn—until he finally realized it was his buffalo. Mo says the buffalo turns on the light when it is hungry or thirsty and then turns it off again afterward to go to sleep.

Raw Talent

Jia Jem decided to make this stylish dress out of raw meats when she had nothing to wear to a friend's party. Jia, from Chicago, Illinois, made the dress out of salami because it's thin and stays in one piece, and bacon because it looks meaty. She started with a basic thick cotton dress, layered the meat on top then covered it with a clear vinyl. The dress took her six hours to make and was refrigerated until it was time for the party.

SOLO SAILOR

Southern Californian sailor Zac Sunderland completed a 13-month, 28,000-mile (45,000-km) solo voyage around the world in July 2009—at age 17. Zac, who was just 16 when he set off from Marina del Rey in June 2008, endured many dramas on his 36-ft (11-m) boat *Intrepid*, not least during the leg from Australia to the Coco Islands when he was followed by pirates and forced to call the Australian authorities to scare them off.

CHARMED LIFE

Ninety-year-old grandfather Alec Alder from Gloucestershire, England, reckons he has cheated death no fewer than 14 times. He has survived several car crashes, a 15-ft (4.5-m) fall from a tree as a boy, war-time bombing, being run over by a tank, and he even walked away after a fighter jet smashed into the side of his house as he slept. Perhaps his narrowest escape came in 1939 when his wedding prevented him from being sent to Dunkirk, where his whole army squadron was killed.

FAITHFUL FRIEND

Buddy, a German shepherd dog, has phoned for help on three separate occasions when his owner, Joe Stalnaker of Scottsdale, Arizona, was incapacitated by seizures. Amazingly, the emergency operators took the calls from the clever hound to save its owner's life.

CAVEMAN RECAPTURED

An escaped prisoner was recaptured in northern Portugal in 2009 after 16 years on the run. The bearded, long-haired fugitive had been hiding out in caves and living mainly on fruit.

TYPO SQUAD

As part of their campaign to eradicate bad spelling and punctuation, Jeff Deck of Somerville, Massachusetts, and Benjamin Herson of Virginia Beach, Virginia, toured the U.S.A. for two months in 2008, removing typographical errors from public signs.

SNAKES BLAMED

A motorist who lost control of his sports utility vehicle in Hartford, Connecticut, in 2009 blamed the accident on two pet baby snakes that he said escaped from his pants pockets as he was driving. He claimed the snakes slithered near the gas and brake pedals and, while he and a passenger tried to catch them, the vehicle veered into some parked cars and overturned.

FREAK DRAW

The same winning numbers were drawn in Bulgaria's national lottery two weeks in a row—at odds of more than four million to one. The freak occurrence saw the numbers 4, 15, 23, 24, 35 and 42 selected, in a different order, by machine, live on TV on September 6, 2009, and again four days later.

TRAIN ORDEAL

An American tourist survived for 2½ hours clinging to the outside of a train as it sped through the Australian outback at up to 70 mph (110 km/h). Chad Vance from Alaska jumped on to The Ghan, which travels from Adelaide to Darwin, as it was pulling out of a station in June 2009. As the express train gathered speed, he squeezed himself into a precarious stairwell until one of the crew members finally heard his cries for help and brought the train to a halt.

DOG BAN

A judge banned a small Pomeranian dog from the resort of Aspen, Colorado, for repeatedly biting. Municipal Judge Brooke Peterson told the dog's owner that if the animal was seen again in Aspen, it would have to be put down. The dog, named Gizmo, had previously been sent to an animal shelter for ten days in a bid to curb its aggressive behavior.

GRATE DRAIN ROBBERY

Between 2007 and 2008, thieves stole more than 2,500 manhole covers and storm drain grates from the streets of Philadelphia, Pennsylvania, to sell as scrap metal.

Red Hot

Brave contestants devour red hot chili peppers in a speed-eating competition in Guizhou, China. Chili peppers are measured in Scoville Heat Units (SHU), which relate to the number of times a chili extract must be diluted in water to lose its heat. The naga morich chili pepper from Bangladesh measures a tongue-numbing 1,500,000 SHU, making it no less than 50 times hotter than cayenne pepper.

All Aboard

India has the world's largest rail network. More than 18 million people travel on Indian trains every day—more passengers than any other country—as a result of which trains are often alarmingly overcrowded. Passengers sit on carriage roofs or cling to the sides, with some trains carrying over 3,000 people—twice the intended capacity.

DANIEL PETERSON KLINGER VAIL GUTHRIE ALFORD

Butt Molds

In the early days of NASA, for reasons of comfort and safety, astronauts on manned space missions sat on couches individually molded to fit their body shape. None of the names on these test seats—pictured at NASA's Langley Research Center at Hampton, Virginia, in 1959—made it aboard the pioneering Mercury spacecraft: They belonged to NASA employees.

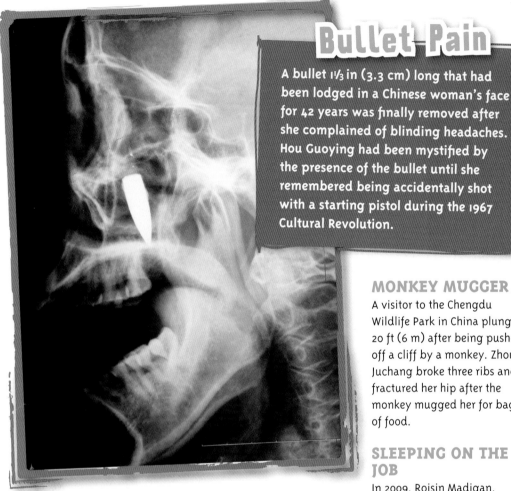

Bullet Pain

A bullet 1⅓ in (3.3 cm) long that had been lodged in a Chinese woman's face for 42 years was finally removed after she complained of blinding headaches. Hou Guoying had been mystified by the presence of the bullet until she remembered being accidentally shot with a starting pistol during the 1967 Cultural Revolution.

MONKEY MUGGER

A visitor to the Chengdu Wildlife Park in China plunged 20 ft (6 m) after being pushed off a cliff by a monkey. Zhou Juchang broke three ribs and fractured her hip after the monkey mugged her for bags of food.

SLEEPING ON THE JOB

In 2009, Roisin Madigan, a student from Birmingham, England, was paid $1,500 to sleep in designer beds every day for a month. She spent eight hours a day in bed to help with a sleep survey being carried out by a luxury bed manufacturer.

FRIDGE PARTY

Paul and Val Howkins from Coventry, England, invited friends and family to a 50th birthday party—for their fridge. They had banners, party poppers and even a cake to celebrate the milestone birthday of the still-working fridge, which they bought for around $100 in 1959.

DILLINGER'S DERRINGER

A small pistol belonging to notorious 1930s U.S. bank robber John Dillinger was sold at auction for $95,600 in 2009. The Remington .41 caliber Double Derringer was said to have been hidden in one of Dillinger's socks when he was arrested in 1934 in Tucson, Arizona.

Sheep Man

"Rham Sam" was a circus sideshow performer in Europe in the 19th century whose body exhibited a mass of sheeplike wooly hair. He is shown here in London in 1890 with lecturer Professor Langdon.

Believe It or Not!

GOAT ARRESTED

A vigilante group in Kwara State, Nigeria, turned a goat over to police in January 2009, convinced that it was a car thief who had used black magic to change his form.

Dream Machine

A Brooklyn-based artist collaborative—Ghost of a Dream (Lauren Was and Adam Eckstrom)—created a life-size replica of a Hummer H-3 from $39,000-worth of losing lottery tickets. Their artwork, titled *Easy Money, Dream Car*, features windshield wipers, tires and body panels made entirely from lottery tickets. The wheel hubs are plastic casts of coin-covered hubcaps to represent the tool people generally use to scratch off the tickets.

HOSPITAL CRÈCHE

The state of Nebraska has a law that allows a person to leave a child of any age at a hospital without risk of prosecution for abandonment. One of the first parents to use it dropped off nine children aged one to 17!

NEW NAME

After a night out, 19-year-old Tom Hayward, a computer-games design student from Leicestershire, England, changed his name by deed poll to N'Tom The Hayemaker Hayward-youliketocomebacktomine. He forgot all about it until he received a formal letter confirming his new name.

LIFELIKE COSTUME

A man dressed as a gorilla for a charity run through England was stopped by police, who had received calls from passing motorists thinking he was a real ape that had escaped from a zoo! Rory Coleman was running to support the Gorilla Organization.

USEFUL BONES

In 2009, seven years after his death, Gordon Krantz, a professor of osteology from Port Angeles, Washington State, received his dying wish that the bones of he and his dog become a museum display when he was exhibited in the Smithsonian Museum of Natural History.

SPACE ODDITY

Canadian circus tycoon Guy Laliberté was blasted into space as a space tourist in 2009, dressed as a clown. The founder of the Cirque du Soleil wore a bulbous red clown nose and took along more red noses for his crew mates on the International Space Station.

RAPID BOUNCE

Ashrita Furman of New York City bounced a basketball 339 times in just 60 seconds in February 2009.

PAMPERED PET

An Israeli woman paid $32,000 so that her boxer dog Orchuk could travel in business class with her from Paris, France, to Tel Aviv. She paid for an entire compartment to carry her, the dog and a veterinarian on the four-hour El Al flight. The Israeli airline had to remove several seats to make way for the dog's cage.

BOG CHAMPION

Bride-to-be Casey Squibb of Dorset, England, went bogsnorkeling on her bachelorette party—and ended up recording the fastest time ever for a woman at the Irish Bogsnorkelling Championships in Castleblayney, Monaghan. She took 22 friends to Ireland and 15 of them entered the race along a 360-ft (110-m) trench. Casey wore a wetsuit and flippers, and a mask with a white lace veil.

EMU CUFFED

Police officers used a stun gun and handcuffs to capture an emu that was running loose on a highway in central Mississippi. Deputies surrounded the bird as it dodged traffic on Interstate 20, but had to resort to a Taser and cuffs to get it off the road.

PETTY CASH

When two women were laid off from their jobs at a ceilings-installation company in Vladivostok, Russia, their former boss paid them the $1,150 he owed them—in 33 heavy bags full of low-denomination coins.

THREE POLES

British explorer Adrian Hayes reached the three extreme points of the Earth—the North and South Poles and the summit of Mount Everest—in the space of just 19 months. He climbed to the top of Everest in May 2006, arrived at the North Pole in April 2007 and reached the South Pole in December 2007—a daunting triple challenge that takes most explorers several years to attempt.

EXPENSIVE HAIRCUT

The Sultan of Brunei, one of the richest men in the world, pays over $13,000 every month for a haircut. The huge fee enables him to fly his favorite barber, Ken Modestou, first-class, from London's Dorchester Hotel to Brunei and to have him stay in a hotel. Modestou normally charges $45 for a trim.

Spider Skin

It might look like this man's skin has been scraped away to reveal a superhero suit, but it is actually a most extraordinary lifelike tattoo by Dan Hazelton from Milwaukee, Wisconsin. The talented skin artist inked the startling design, known as a "tear out," on a tattoo-mad client's chest in 1996. The design took ten hours of work over three sessions.

Wily Coyote

A coyote struck by a car at 75 mph (120 km/h) near the border of Nevada and Utah was found embedded in the front fender eight hours later—still alive! The coyote not only survived the impact and the 600-mi (965-km) journey, it was even well enough to escape from its rescuers.

GARBAGE COLLECTOR

Officials made Merv Jones move out of his home in Lincolnshire, England, while they cleared out 100 tons of rubbish that had been collected over decades and stacked floor-to-ceiling throughout the house. The stench from the waste, which included old ammunition, samurai swords and propane gas canisters, was so bad that it could be smelled more than a mile away.

KEEPING ACTIVE

Xie Long from Chongqing, China, kept fit for 30 years using two old mortars as dumbbells—until a friend noticed the weapons were still live. Police defused the mortars, which could have exploded at any time.

WEDDING TOAST

Opening their presents following their wedding at Howden Minster, East Yorkshire, England, in 2009, Claire and Stuart Linley were amazed to discover that they had been given no fewer than 24 toasters. They kept one and returned the other 23.

YOUNG LECTURER

Aman Rehman of Dehradun in Uttarakhand state, India, started teaching adult students computer-generated animated film at Dehradun's College of Interactive Arts in 2009—when he was just eight years old! The son of an illiterate mechanic, Aman mastered his first animation program at age three and a half and has since made more than 1,000 animated films.

QUIT SMOKING

After smoking for 95 years, 102-year-old Winnie Langley from London, England, finally decided to quit in 2009. Since her first puff in 1914, she smoked on average five cigarettes a day, making a total of more than 170,000.

CLOVER BUNCH

Ten-year-old Mabel South picked more than 120 four-leafed clovers in the garden of her home in Hertfordshire, England, in less than half an hour. The bunch included three five-leafed clovers and one six-leafed clover.

Personal Urns

Cremation Solutions of Arlington, Vermont, offers a unique memento of the dearly departed—an urn shaped like their head. A full-sized head, created from photographs of the deceased and able to hold the ashes of any adult, costs $2,600, and the company can even add a wig to the urn if the customer wishes.

ALCOHOLIC SOAP

A hand gel intended to combat swine flu was withdrawn from use at a British prison in 2009 after inmates realized it contained alcohol and starting eating it. Instead of rubbing the liquid soap on their hands, inmates at Verne Prison, Dorset, England, put their mouths over the dispensers and started consuming significant quantities of the gel, with the result that a number became involved in a drunken brawl.

CANINE TUXEDO

Having first met while walking their dogs on the beach, Harriet and Andrew Athay of Dorset, England, chose their pet dog Ed to be best man at their wedding. Ed wore his own miniature tuxedo, while the couple's two female dogs, Humbug and Goulash, dressed in pink sparkly collars.

UNBELIEVABLE OFFER

A four-star hotel near Venice, Italy, lost $129,000 after mistakenly offering a romantic weekend for just one cent. The Crowne Plaza received over 1,400 room reservations as soon as the offer—the result of a human error at their head office in Atlanta, Georgia—was posted on its website.

WASP DIET

An eight-year-old Indian boy, Ravi Singh, is addicted to eating wasps. He says they have a sweet taste and he enjoys the sensation of the wasp's sting on his tongue. He can eat up to seven at a time and, although five wasp stings can kill a grown man, Ravi's body has developed a resistance to the poison in them.

THRIFTY BRIDE

Heather Saint, a 20-year-old bride from Teesside, England, beat the recession in 2008 by buying her wedding dress on the Internet auction site eBay for just five pence (8 cents).

PENGUIN MAN

For over 35 years, Alfred David of Brussels, Belgium, has lived life as a penguin. Monsieur le Penguin, as he is known, walks the streets in a penguin costume, likes to eat raw sardines and preens himself to keep clean. He believes he has a telepathic connection with penguins, has a collection of more than 3,000 ornamental penguins and has even hosted penguin exhibitions in Belgium and abroad. He wants to be buried in a penguin-shaped coffin and is convinced that he will eventually be reincarnated as a penguin.

CAT CALLS

Police broke into a home in Sussex, England, after a cat dialed the emergency number 999 four times in the space of a few minutes. The owner, who was perfectly safe and well the whole time, said her cat Watson, who enjoys playing with the phone, must have accidentally called the number.

Soft as a Peach

Using 24,000 peaches, this sculpture of Australian actress Jolene Anderson was made and displayed in Sydney's First Fleet Park, Australia, in 2008. An advertising agency constructed the 39-ft (12-m) model to promote a skincare range. With the key slogan "Skin good enough to eat," the work was intended to remind Australian women that their skin is soft and fragile, like a peach. What a shame the peaches will eventually rot!

ZOO QUEST

Marla Taviano and her family from Columbus, Ohio, visited 55 U.S. animal parks in 52 weeks. They began their 22,000-mi (35,405-km) safari at Louisville Zoo, Kentucky, in August 2008 and, after visits to zoos in Dallas, New York and San Diego among others, ended it a year later at their hometown Columbus Zoo and Aquarium.

SHREK WEDDING

Living up to his name, Keith Green married Christine England in Devon, England, in April 2009 dressed up as the movie character Shrek. He and his bride—who was dressed as the ogre princess Fiona also from the movie *Shrek*—spent three hours having their faces and hands painted green.

SILENCE IN COURT!

Annoyed by repeated interruptions in court, a judge ordered the defendant's mouth be taped shut. Judge Stephen Belden, of Canton Municipal Court in Ohio, decided that putting duct tape over the mouth of robbery suspect Harry Brown was the only way to restore order.

SUN INSURANCE

French travel agencies offer insurance to reimburse sun-lovers whose vacations are marred by bad weather. Travelers can claim back up to $550 if they suffer at least four days of rain in any one week.

Carry on Canine

Irish customs officers were extremely surprised to see a Chihuahua dog clearly visible on the luggage X-ray screen at Dublin airport in October 2009. The dog had been smuggled out of Spain inside a passenger's hand luggage. Despite its unconventional method of travel, the dog was reported to be in good health.

Cheese Crawlies

Casu Marzu cheese is a gourmet tradition on the island of Sardinia, Italy. While many cheeses encourage the growth of bacteria, Casu Marzu is not ready to eat until it is fully infested with the maggot larvae of the cheese fly. As the maggots process the cheese, they give it the required moist texture, and then it is eaten, maggots and all. It is only when the maggots die that the cheese becomes unfit for human consumption.

JAWS BURGLAR

Police investigating a series of baffling burglaries through caged windows around Chongqing, China, discovered that the culprit had gained entry by biting through steel bars. When arrested, the man revealed that he could chew any steel bar up to ⅜ in (1 cm) thick by tearing open the welding spots with his powerful teeth.

FAMILY REUNION

Gary Nisbet discovered his long-lost brother when he turned up as his new workmate 35 years after the two boys had been adopted by different families. Lookalike Randy Joubert's arrival at the bedding retailer in Waldoboro, Maine, prompted remarks that the two could be brothers, which they laughed off—until they discovered they were.

Whale Watch

In July 2009, free diver Yang Yun was suffering dangerous paralyzing cramps when a Beluga whale, Mila, heroically guided her to the surface.

Diving 20 ft (6 m) without any breathing equipment, Yun was facing certain death when her legs froze from the Arctic temperatures of the aquarium pool in Harbin, northeast China. Mila cleverly sensed the problem, well before the organizers did, and used her dolphin-like nose to push Yun to safety.

Drinking Hole

A 46-year-old man woke up stuck from the waist down in a gully in Bochum, Germany, after a night of drinking in July 2009. With no knowledge of how he ended up jammed down the drain, the man was finally pulled out by baffled firefighters. Police are still confused as to how the drain cover was removed when he claims he did not touch it!

KNUCKLE CRACKER

Donald L. Unger of Thousand Oaks, California, cracked the knuckles of his left hand—but never his right—every day for more than 60 years to investigate whether frequent knuckle cracking could lead to arthritis of the fingers.

CATTLE OFFER

During U.S. Secretary of State Hillary Clinton's 2009 visit to Kenya, 39-year-old Godwin Chepkurgor, a former Nairobi councilor, offered her 20 cows and 40 goats in exchange for the hand of her daughter Chelsea in marriage.

BULL GUEST

A runaway bull spent an entire night in a hotel room in Jinan, Shandong Province, China. The bull casually strolled into a room at the hotel without being noticed and was not discovered there until the following morning.

WORM CANDY

Annie Munoz from Panama makes candies filled with grasshoppers and mealworms, and lollipops with worms inside.

MOBILE ZOO

Police officers who stopped a motorist in Bari, Italy, found no fewer than 1,700 animals squeezed into the trunk of his car. Inside were more than 1,000 terrapins, 300 white mice, 216 budgies, 150 hamsters, 30 Japanese squirrels and six chameleons.

BOMB ANCHOR

A fisherman in Johor, Malaysia, had been using an unexploded bomb from World War II as a boat anchor for months before he realized what it was.

LLAMA GUARD

Two of farmer Terry McCrone's llamas served as the honor guard at his funeral in Plymouth Township, Ohio.

BLINDFOLD SKATER

Nine-year-old limbo skater Rohan Ajit Kokane squeezed his body under a car with a clearance height of just 6¾ in (17.1 cm) at Belgaum, India, in 2009—while blindfolded.

Smelly Nelly

In August 2009, a baby elephant was walking to work with his trainer in Rayong Province in Thailand when he slipped and fell into a manhole. His owner had taken his eyes off him for just a moment when he turned to find the calf firmly stuck in the 3-ft-wide (90-cm) drain. It took three hours for rescuers to get him out, eventually having to use a bulldozer to widen the hole. The elephant miraculously survived without any injuries.

Mice Kebab

After being killed in the fields of Malawi, mice are boiled, dried, salted and sold by children as lunch to passing travelers. For easy handling, half a dozen of the sun-dried rodent carcasses are inserted in a piece of split bamboo. The heads are left on, so the customer eats everything—including the mouse's hair, bones, teeth, tail and toenails.

DEAD-END JOB

In 2009, a London, England, tourist attraction offered an annual salary of $45,000 to the successful applicant for the post of resident zombie. Job seekers were asked to turn up for the auditions with the London Bridge Experience in blood-soaked costumes and scary makeup.

SUPERHERO GATHERING

To raise money for charity, more than 100 students and staff at Bournemouth University, England, crowded into one room dressed as superheroes, including a number of Batmen and Supermen.

RESTING PLACE

Jack Woodward's last wish was honored when his ashes were buried in the pub where he had spent many hours nearly every day of his life. The former landlord's remains lie beneath a flagstone in the bar at the Boat Inn in the village of Stoke Bruerne, Northamptonshire, England, with a plaque saying: "Stand here and have a drink on me."

BIG BUBBLE

In August 2009, professional bubble maker Sam Heath (aka Samsam Bubbleman) of London, England, made a free-floating, multicolored soap bubble measuring 20 x 5 x 5 ft (6 x 1.5 x 1.5 m). He used a secret mixture—that he has spent 20 years perfecting—and a piece of rope tied between two sticks.

MILK ROUND

Eighty-one-year-old milkman Derek Arch has been delivering milk to homes in the city of Coventry, England, for nearly 70 years. Driving the same van he has had for more than 50 years, he rises at 2.30 a.m. to make his daily deliveries, seven days a week, visiting more than 400 houses and walking 8 mi (13 km) each day.

ELEPHANT HANGED

On September 13, 1916, "Murderous Mary," an elephant from Sparks Brothers Circus, was hanged for killing a handler in Erwin, Tennessee. A crowd of 2,500 gathered to watch as the five-ton elephant was hanged by the neck by a chain attached to a 100-ton derrick car.

TRAPPED UNDERGROUND

A Jack Russell terrier was trapped for 25 days underground in a rabbit warren in 2009—until he lost so much weight that he was able to crawl out. Six-year-old Jake was out walking with his owner Richard Thomas in Haverfordwest, Wales, when he chased a rabbit down a hole. When he failed to reappear, he was feared dead, but nearly a month later a new slimline Jake finally scrambled out, courtesy of his enforced diet.

BACK FROM THE DEAD

Found lying in a pool of blood from a head wound at her apartment in Cernavoda, Romania, 84-year-old Elena Albu was declared dead by a doctor. However, when a forensic photographer took her picture, she opened her eyes and complained of a headache.

THE WRONG NEIL

Neil A. Armstrong, a 38-year-old financial services worker from Symmes Township, Ohio, used to receive dozens of letters and phone calls every year intended for famous astronaut Neil A. Armstrong who lived just 11 mi (18 km) away. When he moved from West Virginia over 15 years ago, Mr. Armstrong said he had no idea that the first man to walk on the Moon lived in the area, but he found himself having to field inquiries from autograph seekers, journalists, even NASA's Johnson Space Center.

FEIGNED DEATH

A 22-year-old Japanese man feigned death for three hours in a failed attempt to avoid being arrested for driving into a police motorcycle. After fleeing the scene of the accident, he collapsed and pretended to be dead even after a catheter was inserted into his urethra by paramedics.

BARE HANDS

On November 21, 2008, expert knife thrower the Rev. Dr. David Adamovich—aka The Great Throwdini—from Freeport, New York, caught a thrown knife, a flying arrow and a fired .22 caliber bullet— all with his bare hands.

Human Kebab

A wayward throw from a classmate left athlete Jian Liao writhing in agony on the track at Guilin, China, as a 5-ft (1.5-m) javelin went through his kneecap. Rescue workers tried to cut the spear off with bolt cutters, but when Jian screamed in pain, they set fire to it instead and burned it in half before they moved him.

BAMBOO BALANCE

Three couples got married on the Xiangjiang River in Zunyi City, China, in January 2009 while balancing on bamboo poles that measured 8 in (20 cm) in diameter. The couples, who wore traditional wedding attire, are all members of the local single bamboo rafting club and chose to get married on the water to demonstrate their skill at the sport.

CLOWN STOLEN

An inflatable clown stolen from a Russian circus in Alice Springs, Northern Territory, Australia, in 2009 was found a few days later on a nearby golf course—along with a handwritten note in which he had made demands for better working conditions.

PRIZED MUSTACHE

Many police departments throughout India offer bonuses and prizes for officers that grow mustaches.

CANINE BRIDE

Two-year-old Sagula Munda was married to a dog at a ceremony in Jajpur, India, in 2009 to protect the boy from ghosts and further bad luck following the discovery of a rotten tooth in his gum.

ROBOT DANCERS

A total of 269 people dressed as robots on the Bournemouth and Poole College campus, in Dorset, England, in July 2009 and gave a five-minute performance of robot dancing.

UNDERPANTS SMUGGLER

In 2009, a man was caught wearing 15 pairs of contraband underpants, four tracksuits and three pairs of pants as he tried to smuggle them into Belarus from Ukraine. He was sweating so heavily and waddling so badly that he could hardly walk, thus attracting the attention of customs officials.

Bug Cuisine

What's bugging you? Taiwanese water bugs on a bed of Japanese udon noodles are a traditional dish in Tokyo.

Sweet Bugs

An Italian museum offered up some bizarre fare for visitors in 2008, including chocolate-covered locusts. The Natural Science Museum in Bergamo held the event to promote "entomophagy," the practice of eating insects, which is common in many cultures around the world. A variety of bug salads were also on the menu, made from crickets, worms and other insects.

Donkey Wreath

Doing all the hard work, a donkey is guided along a road south of Dushanbe, Tajikistan, carrying hundreds of leaves on his back.

MR. BIG

A Chinese man wanted on suspicion of stealing dozens of electric bicycles in Anyang, Henan Province, nearly evaded arrest because police officers didn't recognize him as he had put on 28 lb (13 kg) in weight in a month. He had changed his appearance by remaining in his motel room, getting meals delivered and not exercising.

Riding Recycler

A woman in Shanghai carries masses of Styrofoam for recycling on the back of her bicycle.

PRISONER RETURNS

Jail guards in Camden County, Georgia, caught a prisoner in March 2009 as he was sneaking back into jail after he had escaped to steal cigarettes from across the street.

CROC JAILED

Police in Gunbalanya, Northern Territory, Australia, threw a 6½-ft-long (2-m) saltwater crocodile in jail for three days in October 2009 after it was found loitering in the town.

KITCHEN DIG

To reach an underground river full of fish, Li Huiyan of Chongqing, China, hired 30 villagers to dig a 50-ft (16-m) hole in his kitchen. After digging down to the river, he placed a fishing net across it and hauled out enough fish every day to support his family.

CHAMELEON CHAOS

A fire brigade in Hampshire, England, sent 18 officers, three trucks and a unit wearing special chemical protective clothing to a house in Basingstoke—to clean up a broken jar containing a pickled chameleon that had been preserved in formaldehyde.

Duckling Delicacy

Duckling embryos that are almost ready to hatch are a culinary treat in the Philippines. Known as balut, the popular delicacy is sold by street vendors across the country. Getting the balut eggs to this stage is a painstaking process, as they have to be carefully incubated for 17 to 20 days—until the ducklings are almost ready to hatch—before they are part-boiled and sold. Balut has become so popular you can even get bottled balut, pickled balut and balut omelet.

HUMAN WEIGHTS

In January 2009, a fitness gym in London, England, set up weight-lifting machines using people as weights. The five differently sized human weights—ranging from a 66-lb (30-kg) man to one weighing 340-lb (155-kg)—not only helped gym goers visualize the weight they were lifting, but also shouted words of encouragement.

COMPUTER CASKET

The family of a computer geek have stored his remains inside an old PC. The computer displays a plastic plaque bearing his name, Alan, and the dates of his birth and death. Friends were encouraged to pay their tributes by writing messages on post-it notes and slipping them through the floppy drive slot.

VEGAS CRAZY

Anette and Kenneth Lund from Vejle, Denmark, got married four times in one day in Las Vegas, Nevada. They wed in a hotel, in a limousine with the service conducted by an Elvis impersonator, in a helicopter and while skydiving. They said they plan to get married once a year for the rest of their lives to keep their relationship exciting.

STOLEN SAND

Environmental enforcement officers supported by the Mexican Navy put crime tape around a Cancun hotel beach in 2009 on suspicion that the hotel had stolen the sand for its beach by pumping it illegally from the sea floor.

FAST-FOOD CEREMONY

Paul and Caragh Brooks got married in Normal, Illinois, in 2009 in their favorite restaurant—a branch of the Mexican fast-food chain Taco Bell.

Freed Frog

In 2007, an eight-legged frog was saved from the cooking pot at a restaurant in Quanzhou, southeast China. The one-of-a-kind frog was close to contributing its legs to one of the restaurant's famous frogs' legs dishes, but compassionate staff decided to keep the animal instead of cooking it!

Giant Hand

Liu Hua from Jiangsu, China, had an operation to remove 11 lb (5 kg) of tissue from the index finger, middle finger and thumb of his left hand. Before the operation his thumb measured 10½ in (26 cm) long, his index finger was 12 in (30 cm) and his middle finger 6 in (15 cm)—and his thumb and index finger were thicker than his arms! The total weight of his left arm was a whopping 22 lb (10 kg).

ELECTION DRAW

When a 2009 council election in Cave Creek, Arizona, ended in a tie, the result was decided by invoking a 1925 local statute and drawing from a deck of cards. Adam Trenk was elected after his king of hearts beat rival candidate Thomas McGuire's six of hearts.

SCREAMING CONTEST

Russian Sergey Savelyev can scream at 116.8 decibels — that's about as loud as an ambulance siren. He demonstrated his shrieking ability when picking up $900 for winning an international screaming contest in Pattaya, Thailand, in August 2009.

Hairy Meal

An 18-year-old girl was so addicted to eating her own hair that a massive hairball measuring 15 x 7 in (38 x 18 cm) formed in her stomach. The teen had complained to doctors of abdominal pains and vomiting and that's when they discovered the 10-lb (4.5-kg) mass of dark, curly hair, which filled almost her entire stomach.

FIVE WEDDINGS

Simone and Ryan Feeney from Buckinghamshire, England, got married five times in less than a year. They first tied the knot in March 2008 at the Little White Wedding Chapel in Las Vegas, Nevada, and followed it up over the next ten months with ceremonies in Turkey, Britain, the U.S.A. (again) and Australia.

VISIBLE SHIPWRECK

The wreck of the S.S. Jassim, a Bolivian cargo ferry, which ran aground and sank on the Wingate Reef off the coast of Sudan in 2003, can be seen clearly on Internet aerial photography.

EXTRA HEAD

In July 2009, a baby cow was born at a farm in Rivera, Colombia, with two heads but only one brain. The weight of the extra head meant the calf—named Jennifer—could not stand without help, so farmer Marino Cabrera built a sling to support her.

Dead Art

New York artist Nate Hill scours backstreet trashcans for animal carcasses, which he then sews together in unique, grotesque creations. Nate presented his grandest creation, the A.D.A.M. project, at his apartment in January 2008. A life-size man with fish for shoulders and a deer-fur torso, A.D.A.M. is also part chicken, conch, cow, crab, duck, eel, frog, lobster, rabbit and shark.

RESTLESS GOATS

Some 400 goats on Taiwan's Penghu archipelago are believed to have been killed by lack of sleep caused by late-night noise from a wind farm adjoining their pasture. A local farmer says the constant noise from the eight turbines left his goats exhausted.

PIGEON FANCIER

Former U.S. boxing champion Mike Tyson once booked a hotel suite in Louisville, Kentucky, for his eight favorite pigeons.

UNINVITED GUEST

When Vickie Mendenhall from Spokane, Washington, bought a used couch for $27 in 2009, she found a cat living inside it. The cat had climbed in through a small hole on the underside when the couch's previous owner had donated it to the Value Village store.

SALT HOTELS

Bolivia's Uyuni Salt Flats contain 10 billion tons of salt and are home to several hotels that are built from blocks of salt. Some even have beds made from salt.

POODLE STANDS

A poodle in Xi'an City, China, goes for a walk every day—on two feet. Gou Gou draws large crowds by walking hand-in-paw with owner Wang Guoqiang who taught the dog to walk on its two back legs as a puppy.

STAR WITNESS

In April 2009, Judge James Martz of Palm Beach County, Florida, ordered a parrot to appear in court for a custody dispute involving the bird.

SEA HUNT

A fugitive sea lion tried to escape from Californian police officers in June 2009 by taking control of their speedboat. The animal, nicknamed Snoopy, was picked up by Orange County sheriffs after reports that he had bitten a boy in Newport Harbor. But once on board the patrol boat, the resourceful sea lion apparently managed to start the throttle, steer the boat and even sound the siren.

TOILET ORDEAL

A puppy survived being flushed down a lavatory in June 2009 after his four-year-old owner decided that his pet needed a wash. The week-old cocker spaniel was muddy following a walk, so young Daniel Blair of Middlesex, England, decided to wash it by putting it in the toilet and flushing it. The puppy was rescued by plumbers after being trapped in a waste pipe for nearly four hours.

CANINE COMMUTERS

Stray dogs in Moscow, Russia, use the subway to travel to the city center in search of food. They board the trains each morning and travel back on the subway to where they live in the evening. If they fall asleep and miss their stop, they get off and take another train back to the center.

DOUBLE VISION

A set of identical twin brothers married a pair of twin sisters in a military ceremony in Pechora, Russia, in 2009. Lilia and Liana Kobozevsa were indistinguishable in their matching white dresses, while the only slight difference between Alexei and Dmitry Semyonova was the shade of their dark suits.

Fridge-tastic

An unusual art exhibition in Paris, France, entitled "Energy-Devouring Monsters" featured more than 50 refrigerators. Transformed into colorful works of art by Cuban artists Mario Miguel Gonzalez (known as Mayito) and Roberto Fabelo, the fridges are all classic 1950s models, which were commonplace in Cuban homes until the country replaced all high-energy consuming appliances during an energy crisis in the 1990s. These fridges were saved from the scrapheap and now enjoy a new lease on life in this unique display of icons from Cuba's past.

Goodbye Rocco by Jorge Perruorria is a 1950s fridge made to look like a brightly colored coffin.

Fast Food by Luis Enrique Camejo marries a fridge with the front of a 1950s American car in a comment on the consumerism of that era.

ECHO CHAMBER

Harajuku, a futuristic Protestant church in Tokyo, Japan, was designed in 2005 with a ceiling specially made to reverberate natural sound for two seconds, thereby providing a unique listening experience for worshipers.

FIELD OF GOLD

Armed with a simple $4 metal detector, in 2009 Terry Herbert unearthed 1,500 pieces of medieval treasure from a field in Staffordshire, England, that together are worth millions of dollars. The 1,300-year-old treasure includes beautiful gold sword hilts, dazzling jewels from Sri Lanka and ornate early Christian gold crosses. The gold objects alone weigh more than 11 lb (5 kg) and Herbert's haul filled nearly 250 bags.

CATERPILLAR INVASION

The President of Liberia declared a state of emergency in January 2009 owing to giant armies of caterpillars. In the worst invasion in 30 years, tens of millions of marching caterpillars swarmed over 80 towns and villages, preventing farmers from reaching their fields and causing others to flee their homes.

LOST DEER

While fishing in Chesapeake Bay, Chad Campbell from Washington state and Bo Warren from Virginia found a whitetail deer swimming in 80 ft (25 m) of deep water 1.5 mi (2.4 km) from the nearest coast.

GNOME RESCUE

When an elderly Australian lady died in 2009, the 1,500 ornamental gnomes she had collected over the years faced eviction from their home in Cootamundra, New South Wales, and the prospect of being thrown in a dumpster. However, local people came to the rescue and in a four-hour operation they rounded up the gnomes with a view to finding foster homes for them.

RETURN VISIT

A burglar who stole a man's valuables returned to the house in Pensacola, Florida, a few hours later and took what he hadn't been able to carry on his first visit—a 100-lb (45-kg) plasma-screen TV. A police investigator was at the house by then, but the TV was unattended in the backyard (where the burglar had put it the first time around) so that it could be dusted for fingerprints. Police offered to pay for the TV.

TV ADDICT

A pet rabbit in Xiamen, China, is so addicted to South Korean TV soap operas that she attacks her owners if they change the channel while she is watching. Every night at 10 p.m., the rabbit, Jia Xiaoyu, climbs between the couple to watch an imported drama, but starts biting the pillow and becoming aggressive if her favorite show, *Ms. Mermaid*, isn't on.

PANDA-MONIUM

In June 2009, keepers at Thailand's Ayutthaya Elephant Kraal painted five of their elephants in black and white watercolor paint to make them look like giant pandas! The bizarre move was intended to raise the profile of the elephant—Thailand's national symbol—after the whole country had gone panda-crazy since the birth of a female panda cub at a zoo in Bangkok.

PUSHY PORKER

A pig the size of a Shetland pony terrorized a woman in Murwillumbah, New South Wales, Australia, in 2008. The pig took up residence at the home of Caroline Hayes and refused to leave her alone.

Scrap Yard Monsters

Innovative Irish company RoboSteel weld scrap steel recycled from old cars, motorbikes and airplanes into giant sculptures of film icons and fantasy characters, such as Transformers, Predator and Alien. The team uses thousands of pieces of steel per sculpture, which can take over two months to complete. Each figure is entirely unique and some stand over 8 ft (2.4 m) tall.

Transformer

COFFIN REST

The Wat Prammanee Monastery in Nakhon Nayok, Thailand, offers death and rebirth ceremonies for distressed worshipers, which include a brief rest in a coffin to mark the occasion.

GUCCI POOCHES

Dogs wearing designer outfits ranging from polka-dot bathing suits to glitzy evening wear took to the catwalk during a fashion show in Taipei, Taiwan, in July 2009.

Space Soldier

LUCKY BREAK

After chasing a rabbit over a 40-ft (12-m) cliff on the Isle of Wight, England, Mac the golden retriever escaped plunging to his death when his collar caught on some rocks, breaking his fall.

SAME TIE

Attorney Bob Flournoy of Lufkin, Texas, wore the same U.S. flag tie every day for more than six years. With daily wear, the tie started to disintegrate, forcing Bob to cut portions out and hold it together with Velcro, but by 2007 it was only half its original size and was too fragile even to tie.

TWO NOSES

A rabbit with two noses and four nostrils was discovered at a pet store in Milford, Connecticut, in 2009.

BULLET COLLISION

David Olson of Riverton, Wyoming, found a pair of 9mm bullets that had collided in midair.

Extraordinary

FEATS

Amazon Marathon

British ex-army officer Ed Stafford began the trip of his life in April 2008, when he set out to walk the entire length of the Amazon River in South America, from its source to the Atlantic Ocean.

He became the first man ever to do this and to highlight rainforest deforestation in the process. The river is 4,000 mi (6,400 km) long, but Ed had walked almost 6,000 mi (9,650 km) by the end because the river is so wide and deep in so many places that he couldn't always take the shortest route. By February 2010, Ed had passed the halfway point of his trek, accompanied by a local guide, Cho, and with much of his "walk" spent chest deep in murky water. Hiking through one of the wildest environments on Earth, Ed faced venomous snakes, flooding, electric eels, piranhas and jaguars. He was pursued by armed Peruvian tribespeople and wrongly arrested on suspicion of murder. Traveling light with only a backpack, he was also at risk of scurvy or even starvation, and was often forced to forage in the jungle and catch piranhas for breakfast. He completed his amazing journey in August 2010 after walking for 860 days.

Ed had to be prepared at all times for unwanted visitors or attacks.

DUCK RACE

A staggering 205,000 plastic ducks floated 0.6 mi (1 km) down the River Thames near London, England, in the 2009 Great British Duck Race.

PASSENGER PILOT

Passenger Doug White took over the controls and landed a twin engine plane at Southwest Florida International Airport in April 2009—after the pilot died in mid-flight.

LIMBO SKATER

In July 2009, seven-year-old Abbishek Navale, of Belgaum, India, limbo skated backward under ten multi-utility vehicles (Tata Sumo Jeeps). A few days later, he limbo skated backward a distance of 62 ft (18.8 m), under a series of bars positioned just 8.7 in (22 cm) above the ground. Abbishek, who has also skated 335 mi (540 km) from Bangalore to Belgaum in six days, practices his considerable skills for 2½ hours every day.

Flash Cars

English photographers Mark Brown and Marc Cameron have re-created the familiar shapes of well-known sports cars using only flashes of moving light and a camera. This vivid Bugatti Veyron is part of a collection inspired by various iconic cars, which also includes models from Ferrari, Morgan and Aston Martin.

Fast Fog

This amazing image captures the moment a U.S. Air Force B-2 Spirit Bomber created its own cloud as it approached the speed of sound near Los Angeles, California, in 2009. Despite a wingspan of 172 ft (52 m), the bombers—which cost around $1 billion each when first made in 1989—are designed to be difficult to detect and can travel at 604 mph (972 km/h).

80 PLUS

Two teams of hockey players, all over the age of 80, took to the ice for a seniors' tournament in Burnaby, British Columbia, Canada in 2009. The oldest player to take part was 87-year-old goaltender Jim Martin.

CHOPSTICK CHALLENGE

In March 2009, Ashrita Furman of New York City ate 40 M&Ms in a minute—with chopsticks.

KISSING FRENZY

Twenty young women lined up in Blackburn, England, in 2009 to give 28-year-old local DJ Paul Winstanley 110 kisses in one minute—that's almost two kisses a second.

GIANT CIGAR

Sixty-five-year-old Cuban Jose Castelar, who has been making cigars since the age of 14, rolled a monster 142-ft-long (43.3-m) cigar in 2009—that's ten times the height of a double-decker bus.

Tomato Force

In Guiyang, China, hundreds of people hurled tomatoes at each other at a bizarre promotional event organized by a local shopping center. Inspired by the famous Tomatina festival in Spain, the juicy battle required a massive haul of tomatoes weighing more than 20 family cars and costing almost $15,000.

Tasty De-Light

Constructed by California-based artist Ya Ya Chou, this amazing gummi bear chandelier is made entirely from the famous candy bears and can remain fresh and on display for up to two years! It has been made by stringing hundreds of different flavored gummies together.

This chandelier is just one of a series of gummi-bear sculptures that also includes a bearskin rug and a deer.

DEATH RACE

Among the competitors in the 2009 Canadian Death Race—run over 78 mi (125 km) of mountainous terrain—was a blind woman, 57-year-old Lorraine Pitt from Peterborough, Ontario. Competitors carry their own supplies in the event, held annually in Grand Cache, Alberta. The race begins and ends on a 4,200-ft-high (1,280-m) plateau, passes over three mountain summits as well as bogs, forests and a river, and includes 17,000 ft (5,180 m) of elevation change.

CHAMPION CRAWLER

The city of Vilnius, Lithuania, stages an annual baby-crawling contest where tiny tots crawl along a 16-ft (5-m) carpeted track, encouraged by their parents waving keys and toys at the finish line. The 2009 winner was eight-month-old Kajus Aukscionis, who completed the course in 18 seconds.

POLE RACE

Rune Malterud and Stian Aker of Norway skied nearly continuously for 17 days 11 hours to win the Amundsen South Pole Race, crossing Antarctica to reach the South Pole before five other teams.

HOOP HOPPER

Thirteen-year-old Anna Schmeissing of Chicago, Illinois, can play basketball while hopping on a pogo stick.

FIVE-DAY SPEECH

At the railway station in Perpignan, France, in January 2009, 62-year-old Catalan local-government worker Lluis Colet spoke for five straight days and four nights—a total of 124 hours—about Spanish painter Salvador Dalí and Catalan culture.

WATER JUMP

In July 2009, 13-year-old Charlotte Wharton from Northamptonshire, England, leaped a distance of nearly 100 ft (30.5 m) on water skis. Charlotte, who had been skiing for just two years, soared nearly 50 ft (15 m) high in the air at 30 mph (48 km/h) as she jumped 98 ft 8 in (30.1 m), which is the equivalent of three standard double-decker buses parked end to end.

BIKE STAND

Mr. Liu, a farmer from Jiangxi, China, is able to stand, lie down and even sleep on a motorcycle traveling at high speed. He once drove a motorbike for 3.7 mi (6 km) while standing.

MODEL FLOTILLA

In the course of 75 years, Peter Tamm of Hamburg, Germany, has amassed a collection of 36,000 model ships (each built to 1:1,250 scale), thousands of photographs of ships, a maritime library of more than 100,000 volumes and 15,000 ship menus, some dating back to the 1890s.

FLYING CAR

From 1949 to 1960, Longview, Washington State, engineer Moulton Taylor built six cars that could also fly. His prototype Aerocar had folding wings that allowed the car to be converted into a plane in five minutes by one person. It could drive at 60 mph (96 km/h) and fly at 110 mph (180 km/h).

SUPER SANDWICH

In June 2009, the Bradley County Chamber of Commerce made a 168-ft-long (51-m) BLT (bacon, lettuce and tomato) sandwich at the 53rd Annual Bradley County Pink Tomato Festival in Warren, Arkansas. The sandwich, which took nearly two hours to build, used 300 lb (136 kg) of bacon, 80 lb (36 kg) of lettuce and 60 lb (27 kg) of tomatoes, and oozed 220 fl oz (6.5 l) of mayonnaise.

YOUNG PARAGLIDER

Luan Da Silva from Florianopolis, Brazil, is already an experienced paraglider even though he is just six years old. Both of his parents are paragliding instructors and he made his first flight with his father at age two and his first solo flight a year later. Sitting in a specially weighted harness to stop him from blowing away, Luan loves to leap from the top of a sand dune and soar 65 ft (20 m) into the air.

GIANT DOG

More than 2,000 people ate a 660-ft-long (200-m) hot dog in Santa Marta, Colombia. Twelve of the city's leading cooks used 220 lb (100 kg) of bread, 275 lb (125 kg) of sausages, 250 bottles of sauce and tons of vegetables and cheese to make the dog.

BALL JUGGLER

Dan Magness from Milton Keynes, Buckinghamshire, England, used his feet, legs and head to keep a soccer ball in the air for 24 hours in May 2009.

BAR TURNS

In Yerevan, Armenia, in July 2009, Armenian gymnast Davit Fahradyan completed 354 turns on a horizontal bar.

MOOSE FAN

Al Goddard of Takoma Park, Maryland, has collected more than 1,000 items of moose memorabilia. His collection began in 1975 when he was teaching at a school in Oakton, Virginia, and a student presented him with a stuffed toy moose as a gift.

KITE DISPLAY

Some 4,000 Palestinian children flew kites simultaneously for 30 seconds on beaches of the Gaza Strip in July 2009.

SNOW GOLF

An Italian ski resort stages a golf tournament in up to 3 ft (90 cm) of snow and at an altitude of 5,250 ft (1600 m). Players use brightly colored orange balls on the specially built nine-hole course at the Rein resort in Taufers.

NEW YEAR CAKE

In December 2008, bakers in Bucharest, Romania, made a cake that weighed an amazing 619 lb (280 kg). The tiered cake was covered with fruit and whipped cream and decorated with the Romanian and European flags, along with the words "Happy New Year 2009."

Driving on Thin Ice

Every winter, hundreds of truckers risk their lives by driving monster 18-wheeled rigs weighing over 50 tons across frozen lakes and rivers, and even the frozen Arctic Sea. The ice-road truckers make as many runs as possible (the "dash for cash" as they call it), each run taking over 20 hours. Driving hundreds of miles at a time, over sheets of ice just 28 in (70 cm) thick, truckers drive having had little sleep and in constant fear of the sound of cracking ice beneath their wheels, a sound that could send them plunging to their death.

At temperatures of -58 °F (-50 °C), if a truck falls through the ice and sinks into the water, the driver has less than one minute to get out before freezing to death.

The ice has to be 40 in (102 cm) thick to withstand the largest 70-ton trucks. Speeds on the road are often limited to below 20 mph (32 km/h) to minimize damage as the ice shifts.

Daredevil Falls

Since 1901 a succession of "Niagara Daredevils" have made life-threatening attempts to conquer the rapid waters of the Canadian Horseshoe Falls, the highest drop at Niagara Falls, in various objects.

Most seek fame, fortune or publicity, some seek the thrill, and all of them are fully aware of the risk they take when they plunge over the top. The chances of survival are so slim that the jump is statistically more like suicide, with at least 12 to 15 deaths recorded at Niagara each year. Individuals who made early attempts were aptly named "daredevils" when they survived, with those that died being seen to have committed suicide. Although Niagara Falls are not the highest in the world, they are one of the most dangerous. The flow of water is so powerful that no man has ever been able to completely control it—not even trained engineers.

FORTUNE FALL—1901
In October 1901, Annie Edison Taylor was the first person to drop down the Falls in a barrel—and survive. Annie was looking for some money and attention when she decided to conquer the falls at 63 years old (although she claimed to be in her forties). She emerged from the airtight wooden barrel with only a scratch on her forehead. Despite this, she never really became famous and spent the rest of her life selling souvenirs on the street.

STEEL SQUEAL—1911

In July 1911, Bobby Leach was the second person to take on the Falls in a barrel, but this one was made of steel. Leach was a performer with the Barnum & Bailey Circus and was sure he could complete the Falls even better than Annie had. The drop resulted in him breaking both his knee caps and his jaw. However, he managed to use his experience to tour Canada, the U.S.A. and New Zealand, telling people his story and posing with his barrel. He died later in life after contracting gangrene in his leg when he slipped on an orange peel.

INFLATABLE TALE—1928

On July 4, 1928, Jean Lussier, a 36-year-old from Massachusetts, went over the Falls in an inflatable rubber ball 6 ft (1.8 m) in diameter. Although three of the 32 inner tubes burst, Jean survived.

157

HOT RIDER

In summer temperatures of up to 118°F (48°C), Omar Al Mamari, founder President of the Oman Bike Club, rode a motorcycle 1,281 mi (2,062 km)—from Muscat to Salalah and back—in 24 hours.

KAYAK PLUNGE

Kayaker Tyler Bradt of Missoula, Montana, plunged 186 ft (57 m) in four seconds over the Palouse Falls, Washington State, in July 2009—and emerged with nothing worse than a sprained wrist and a broken paddle. He had visited the spot four times before plucking up the courage to tackle the waterfall, which is so high the spray it generates creates its own rainbow.

GIANT PUZZLE

Indian jigsaw-puzzle enthusiasts created an online jigsaw puzzle with 25,000 pieces. The challenge attracted more than 180,000 participants, each working with 1,000 blocks of 25 pieces to assemble a large image designed by New Zealand jigsaw expert Royce B. McClure. In its physical form, the puzzle measured 36 x 16 ft (11 x 5 m).

MOON PIE

To celebrate the 40th anniversary of the first lunar landing, NASA created a giant moon pie in 2009. The special pie—consisting of marshmallow dipped in chocolate—measured 40 in (101 cm) in diameter, 6 in (15 cm) high and weighed 55 lb (25 kg).

BED JUMP

Over a period of 16 hours in May 2009, around 20,000 people in four cities—New York, London, Paris and Shanghai—jumped on four giant beds. The beds, which took a team of 100 people five weeks to build and incorporated over 200,000 nuts and bolts and six tons of steel, measured 49 x 33 ft (15 x 10 m) and were each topped with 30 double mattresses and a huge super-sized duvet that could cover 65 regular double beds.

PIZZA RUSH

Dennis Tran of Silver Springs, Maryland, made three large pizzas in just over 46 seconds in 2008—that's an average of around 15 seconds per pizza. He had to hand-stretch the fresh dough, apply pizza sauce and top the three pizzas—one pepperoni, one mushroom and one cheese.

SUPER SHOOTER

Thirty-four-year-old novice Jim Collins of Cambridgeshire, England, beat experienced rivals from as far afield as the U.S.A., Australia and New Zealand to be crowned world peashooting champion of 2009. The championships, which were started in 1971 by Cambridgeshire school principal John Tyson, who had confiscated a peashooter from a pupil, require competitors to puff peas from a distance of 12 ft (3.6 m) at a 12-in (30-cm) target. Some entrants even use laser-guided peashooters!

F1 LIMO

Canadian inventor Michael Pettipas has spent two years building a street-legal Formula-1 stretch limousine racing car with seven seats— six for passengers and one for the driver. The 30-ft-long (9-m) car has an 8-liter engine, can do 0 to 60 mph (0—97 km/h) in five seconds and is capable of reaching speeds of 140 mph (225 km/h).

FLOWER GARLAND

In May 2009, residents of San Pedro, the Philippines, strung together a *sampaguita lei*—a flower garland—that measured more than 1¼ mi (2 km) long.

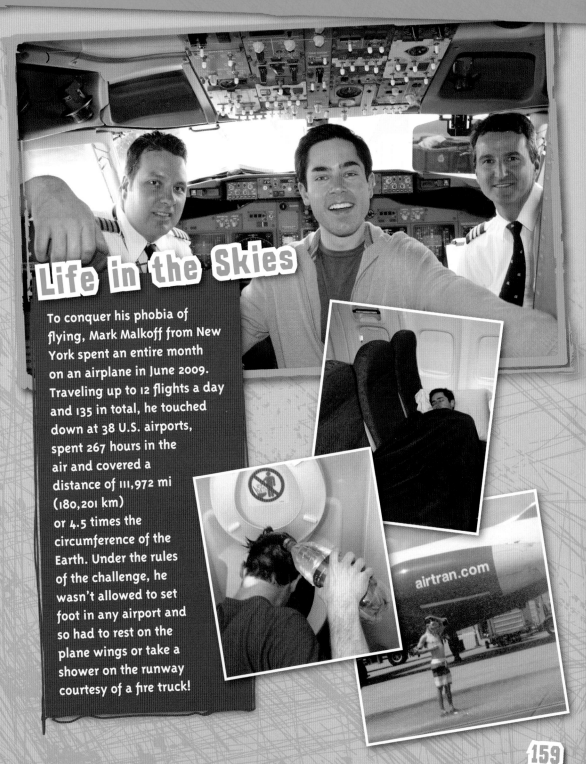

Life in the Skies

To conquer his phobia of flying, Mark Malkoff from New York spent an entire month on an airplane in June 2009. Traveling up to 12 flights a day and 135 in total, he touched down at 38 U.S. airports, spent 267 hours in the air and covered a distance of 111,972 mi (180,201 km) or 4.5 times the circumference of the Earth. Under the rules of the challenge, he wasn't allowed to set foot in any airport and so had to rest on the plane wings or take a shower on the runway courtesy of a fire truck!

Grab Hold

In May 2009, Canadian freestyle motocross rider Jeff Fehr completed a massive jump off a ramp over a cowboy ranch in Alberta, Canada, close to the Rocky Mountains. Fehr pulled the tricky "Superman Seat Grab" move at the top of his leap.

HANDICAP GOLFER

Forty-five-year-old former soldier Alan Perrin, who is almost blind and has only one arm, hit a hole-in-one at his local Exminster Golf Club, near Exeter, Devon, England, in April 2009. He and his golfing partner could hardly believe it when, after several minutes of searching, they finally found the yellow ball in the hole.

VOLCANO BOARDING

In the new sport of volcano boarding, thrill-seekers race at speeds of up to 50 mph (80 km/h) down the sides of an active volcano. Dressed in protective jumpsuits, kneepads and helmets, competitors hurtle down Nicaragua's 2,382-ft-high (726-m) Cerro Negro mountain—which has erupted 20 times since 1850, the last as recently as 1999—on specially constructed plywood boards.

HIGH TEE

A team from Bay College, Michigan, created a wooden golf tee that was over 26½ ft (8 m) tall—80 times bigger than a normal tee. The head measured 35 in (90 cm) in diameter and the whole tee weighed almost a ton.

TENNIS ACE

Over a period of five years, Swiss tennis player Roger Federer reached at least the semifinals of more than 20 consecutive Grand Slam tournaments, and from 2005 to 2007 he reached ten consecutive Grand Slam finals. Between his first-round loss at Wimbledon in 2002 and his defeat in the 2008 Wimbledon final, he won 65 matches in a row on grass.

STRANGE HYBRID

Friends Nicolo Lamberti and Milko Dalla Costa took the chassis of a speedy Ferrari F355 Berlinetta and crossed it with the body of a Citroën 2CV bread van—and created a bread van capable of speeds of 180 mph (290 km/h). After discovering the Citroën in Turate, Italy, the pair spent five years and more than $220,000 putting together their bizarre hybrid.

FIRE WALL

The Marine Corps Air Station in Yuma, Arizona, created a 15-story-high wall of flame in March 2009 that stretched for 10,173 ft (3,100 m)—that's nearly 2 mi (3.2 km) long. The wall of fire was made up of dynamite, electric blasting caps and 20,000 ft (6,100 m) of detonation cord.

Versatile Craft

Welsh engineers have created a boat that can operate above or below the waves. Above water, the Scubacraft is propelled by a 160-horsepower engine; when submerged, it is powered by electric thrusters and can descend to a depth of nearly 100 ft (30 m). As it is not a pressurized submarine, those on board must wear scuba-diving gear when diving below the water.

IRREGULAR BIKE

Guan Baihua of Qingdao, China, spent 18 months developing a bicycle with odd-shaped wheels. The front wheel is a five-sided pentagon, while the back wheel is a triangle. He says the bike is mainly for fun but adds that riders could use it to lose weight because it takes more effort to pedal.

RIB FEAST

Pat "Deep Dish" Bertoletti of Chicago, Illinois, ate 5 lb 12 oz (2.6 kg) of ribs in 12 minutes at the Best in the West Nugget World Rib Eating Championship in Sparks, Nevada, in September 2009.

COCA-COLA ADDICT

For years, Jason Morgan, a 32-year-old truck driver from Neath, South Wales, drank more than 20 pt (10 l) of Coca-Cola every day. He would drink five 64-fl-oz (2-l) bottles daily—equivalent to 26 cans!

Science-fiction Author

Hugo Gernsback was way ahead of his time when he invented these television glasses, for portable TV viewing, which he unveiled in 1963.

Ice Ride

The famous Ford Model T car was converted into an early version of the snowmobile in 1937. The vehicle had caterpillar belts around the regular rear tires, and metal skis were used in place of the front wheels. Such modified classics could reach around 18 mph (29 km/h) in thick snow.

MINI MOTOR

Perry Watkins from Buckinghamshire, England, has created a roadworthy car that is only 39 in (1 m) high and 26 in (66 cm) wide. Remembering the children's TV character Postman Pat and his mail delivery van, Watkins bought a Postman Pat coin-in-the-slot children's ride on the Internet, reinforced its fiberglass shell with a steel frame and mounted it onto a mini four-wheeled bike before adding a 150cc engine, mirrors, windshield wipers and lights.

BIKE JUMP

In Chicago, Illinois, in July 2009, U.S. freestyle motocross star Ronnie Renner launched into a jump that took him more than 63 ft (19 m) above the ground. Riding his motorbike up a 22-ft-high (6.7-m) quarterpipe, he soared 41 ft 5 in (12.6 m) into the air upside down before landing on a ramp, giving him a total height of 63 ft 5 in (19.33 m).

Titanic Tribute

In London, England, in February 2009, fans of the movie *Titanic* donned Victorian costume and sat in old rowing boats as they watched a screening of the blockbuster in a swimming pool complete with dry ice and miniature icebergs. The real *Titanic* was an ocean liner that hit an iceberg and sank on its maiden voyage when crossing the Atlantic Ocean on April 14, 1912, with the loss of 1,517 lives.

DAPPER DAREDEVIL

Dressed in a tweed jacket, and shirt and tie, dapper daredevil Les Pugh of Gloucestershire, England, abseiled down the side of a 160-ft-high (49-m) office block in the town of Cheltenham in April 2009—at age 93!

YOUNG HUNTER

In September 2009, 16-year-old Cammie Colin of Pelion, South Carolina, bagged an alligator 10 ft 5 in (3.2 m) long and weighing 353 lb (160 kg)—in the middle of the night—with a crossbow. Having won a lottery slot for the state's annual public alligator harvest, she shot her prize while out with her family and a guide in an 18-ft (5.4-m) boat on Lake Marion.

MILK DELIVERY

For nearly 100 years, three generations of the Hall family delivered milk to the village of Gunnislake in Cornwall, England, placing an estimated 20 million pints on people's doorsteps. The last in the line, Jo Hall, retired after 55 years in the job, during which time she clocked up 176,000 mi (283,245 km) doing her milk delivery round.

JET PACK

Using a jet pack powered by hydrogen peroxide, Eric Scott of Denver, Colorado, clocked a speed of 68 mph (109 km/h) at Knockhill Racing Circuit, Scotland, in May 2009. Although Scott's jet pack currently carries only enough fuel to fly him for 30 seconds, it was sufficient for him to beat a Ford Focus RS car driven by British Touring Car champion Gordon Shedden in a drag race.

PASTA BOWL

In March 2009, a restaurant in Doha, Qatar, dished up a bowl of pasta measuring 20 ft (6 m) long and 6 ft 6 in (2 m) wide and weighing 9,480 lb (4,300 kg).

Car Crash

Visitors to a square in Berlin, Germany, had to look twice when they encountered a car that appeared to have fallen from the sky and smashed through the pavement. It was actually a convincing sculpture conceived as a publicity stunt by a German website.

BASKETBALL BEGINNER

Despite never having played basketball before, S. Ramesh Babu of Bangalore, India, scored 243 baskets in an hour—that's an average of just over four baskets a minute.

KEEP IT UP

In May 2009, at San Marcos, California, Abraham Muñoz of the U.S.A. ran 3,280 ft (1,000 m) in under five minutes while keeping a soccer ball continuously airborne with his feet.

FOLDING BIKE

Dominic Hargreaves, a graduate from the Royal College of Art in London, England, has devised a bicycle that folds up to be smaller than its own wheels. He sees "the Contortionist" as being the perfect bike for commuters, because when folded it can be wheeled along the street by one handlebar.

FARMING FUNERAL

The coffin of farmer Gordon Hale from Wiltshire, England, was put on a trailer and towed to his grave by the Ford 4000 tractor he had used every day for 38 years. Maintaining the farming theme, mourners wore ribbons of bale twine and the same material was used to form the handles on the coffin.

HIGH ROLLER

Branden Moyen of Shillington, Pennsylvania, has built a model of a roller coaster 36 ft (11 m) tall and 50 ft (15 m) long from around 40,000 pieces of the construction toy K'NEX. The track measures about 400 ft (122 m) in length and the roller-coaster car travels at speeds up to 70 mph (115 km/h) after being slingshotted to the top of the first hill by 25 rubber bands. His model is a 1:10-scale replica of Klinga Da, a giant steel roller coaster at Six Flags Great Adventure, New Jersey.

LONG BIKE

Colin Furze of Lincolnshire, England, spent two months creating a 46-ft-long (14-m) motorbike. He used two Honda 50cc mopeds, which he extended with pieces of aluminum. The elongated bike can travel at speeds of up to 30 mph (48 km/h) but needs six widths of an ordinary road to turn!

SCHOOL RUN

Having missed his bus one morning in January 2009, a six-year-old boy from Richmond, Virginia, took the keys to his family's Ford Taurus car and decided he would drive to school. He crashed into a utility pole on the way, but escaped with only minor injuries.

POPCORN BALL

In 2009, hundreds of volunteers from Sac City, Iowa, used 1,500 lb (680 kg) of popcorn, 2,400 lb (1 ton) of sugar and 1,100 lb (500 kg) of syrup mix to build an enormous popcorn ball weighing around 5,000 lb (2.2 tons). Even though it has a population of just 2,300, Sac City calls itself the "Popcorn Capital of the World" and produces nearly 5 million lb (2.27 million kg) of popcorn every year.

Holy Cannoli!

Speed eater Kevin Basso devoured 17 whole cannoli at the 2009 Little Italy Cannoli Eating Competition in New York City. Kevin finished third, with winner "Crazy Legs" Conti gulping down 20½ of the traditional Italian desert pastries in just six minutes.

Knuckle Buster

Mick Gooch must have the strongest fingers in the world. The martial arts expert from Kent, England, is capable of 17 one-armed, single-finger push-ups on the head of a nail. Mick was inspired by the two-finger push-ups performed by kung-fu legend Bruce Lee, and decided to go one incredible step further, a feat that took years of dedication—and broken knuckles—to master.

ON THE EDGE

In April 2009, 15-year-old Duncan Harris of Normal, Illinois, rode a unicycle on a treacherous 12-mi (19-km) journey along cliff trails at Moab, Utah. He had no brakes except his own legs, no handlebars, and drops of hundreds of feet were just inches away.

COLOSSAL PUTT

Irish TV and radio presenter Terry Wogan holed an incredible 99-ft (30-m) putt at Gleneagles golf course in Scotland during a BBC pro-celebrity match in 1981.

BIRTHDAY FLIGHTS

On his 16th birthday, Errick Smith of Ocean Springs, Mississippi, flew an airplane and a helicopter solo. Errick, who began taking flying lessons at 14, piloted a Cessna 172 aircraft and two helicopters, an R22 and a Schweitzer.

SEVEN MARATHONS

Richard Donovan from Galway, Ireland, completed seven marathons on seven continents in less than six days. He began his challenge in sub-zero temperatures in Antarctica on January 31, 2009, and after running marathons in South Africa, Dubai, England, Canada and Chile, crossed the finish line in Sydney, Australia, just five days, ten hours and eight minutes later. He ran a total of 183 mi (295 km) in 130 hours, enduring extreme temperatures and sleeping only in the economy-class seats of airplanes on his flights between continents.

MUSCLE MAN

At age 80, Abdurakhman Abdulazizov, from the southern Russian republic of Dagestan, can pull a railway carriage by means of a rope tied to his body and lift an iron girder weighing over 220 lb (100 kg) with his teeth.

PIE FIGHT

More than 200 people took part in a mass pie fight on a farm at Genoa, Illinois, in 2009. The fight, organized by farm-owner Molly Holbrook, involved participants hurling chocolate, meringue, pumpkin and custard pies at each other.

Ear Ache

Rakesh Sharma from India strains as he lifts 105 lb (48 kg) with his ears in Punjab, India, in October 2009. He attaches straps and a wooden clamp to his ears before slowly lifting the weights from the ground.

NUGGET DROP

To welcome in the New Year in 2009, a chicken restaurant in McDonough, Georgia, dipped a plaster chicken nugget 6 ft 6 in (2 m) tall and weighing 795 lb (360 kg) into a giant vat of fake sauce.

SPEEDY WHEELIE

Fifteen-year-old Jake Drummond maintained a bicycle wheelie for over 330 ft (100 m) at Oshkosh, Wisconsin, in July 2009—and covered the distance in just over 15 seconds.

Pear of Buddhas

After more than six years of work, Gao Xianzhang from Hebei, China, has managed to modify a crop of pears to look like little Buddhas. In 2009, after a lot of effort and rotten fruit, he perfected a technique and was able to mold 10,000 pears into edible Buddha-shaped fruit. Selling them for $10 each, the pears, which resemble baby Buddhas, are grown in special plastic molds on the tree branches from an early stage.

SOLO VOYAGE

Sarah Outen from Rutland, England, rowed solo across the Indian Ocean in 2009, making the 4,000-mi (6,400-km) journey from Perth, Australia, to the island of Mauritius, off the east coast of Africa, in 124 days. She spent up to 12 hours a day rowing, often in scorching sun and riding 30-ft (9-m) waves.

BRICK SMASHER

Using a combination of speed and power, German martial arts expert Bernd Hoehle smashed 12 freestanding bricks in just eight seconds in Hanover, Germany, in 2009.

SPEEDY JUGGLER

In July 2009, the Czech Republic's Zdenek Bradác, while juggling three balls, made 339 catches in just 60 seconds.

BRAVE SURFER

Aged 18, Bethany Hamilton finished runner-up in the World Junior Women's Surfing Championships in January 2009—despite having lost an arm to a shark five years previously. Bethany was surfing near her home in Hawaii in October 2003 when she was mauled by a 15-ft-long (4.5-m) tiger shark, but within just three weeks she was back on her board.

BASEBALL BASH

Mike Filippone of North Babylon, New York, swung at nearly 7,000 baseball pitches over a period of 13½ hours in August 2009.

BOND FLYER

German Hermann Ramke has spent nine years developing a James Bond-like jet pack that is powered by high-pressure water. The JetLev-Flyer, which sells for around $140,000, has a top speed of 65 mph (105 km/h), can power the rider to an altitude of 33 ft (10 m) and is able to travel nearly 200 mi (320 km) before it needs refueling. A floating pump powered by a 150-hp four-stroke engine sends water through a 140-ft-long (43-m) hose to a pair of nozzles on the jet pack. The jet leaving the nozzles is powerful enough to propel the rider into the air.

PEDAL POWER

Sam Whittingham of British Columbia, Canada, can reach a speed of over 82 mph (132 km/h)—without an engine. Relying solely on human power, his recumbent bicycle clocked a speed of 82.4 mph (132.6 km/h) on a flat section of road at Battle Mountain, Nevada.

CANADA RIDE

Riding about 185 mi (300 km) a day, Corneliu Dobrin of Abbotsford, British Columbia, Canada, cycled 4,475 mi (7,200 km) across Canada in just 24 days in July 2009. He departed from Vancouver and finished his epic ride in St. John's, Newfoundland.

PUMPKIN FACES

In October 2008, Stephen Clarke of Havertown, Pennsylvania, carved jack-o'-lantern faces into one ton's worth of pumpkins in 3 hours 33 minutes 49 seconds at Atlantic City, New Jersey.

BRIDE PARADE

Sporting full bridal regalia, 110 brides and brides-to-be paraded through Bucharest in June 2009 to promote the institution of marriage in Romania.

BABY BIKER

A three-year-old boy in India can ride a full-size motorcycle. Shantanu Khan from New Delhi extended the bike's controls so that son Azeem could reach them. Judges were so impressed they issued Azeem a special license to ride the bike around the neighborhood—but not on main roads.

EPIC VOYAGE

Although paralyzed from the neck down, 37-year-old Hilary Lister from Kent, England, sailed solo around the U.K. in 2009—a total distance of 1,500 mi (2,415 km). She operated the 20-ft (6-m) racing yacht by blowing through straws connected to a computer. Her epic voyage took her three months and she covered approximately 60 mi (96 km) a day. Wheelchair-bound since the age of 15, Hilary, who suffers from Reflex Sympathetic Dystrophy, earned a degree in biochemistry at Oxford University despite having to dictate her papers with an epidural drip in her spine.

BUS RESCUE

When the driver of a New York City school bus full of children suffered a fatal heart attack while at the wheel, 16-year-old Rachel Guzy took control and brought the vehicle to a halt as it sped toward a busy intersection. Driver Ramon Fernandez collapsed and tumbled out of the moving bus, but Rachel, who does not know how to drive, jumped into his seat and pulled the emergency brake, slowing the bus right down before it gently crashed into a van.

Pokémon Craze

Lisa Courtney from Hertfordshire, England, has spent the last 13 years accumulating more than 13,400 items of Pokémon cartoon memorabilia, and she is still adding to her collection. Pokémon was originally a Japanese creation, so 21-year-old Lisa has traveled to the country five times to satisfy her obsession with the cartoon creatures.

Snow Brakes

Extreme driver and keen snowboarder Ken Block drove his $150,000 Subaru rally car up onto the slopes at Snowpark, New Zealand.

After towing several snowboarders around the course at high speed, Californian Block raced professional boarder Torstein Horgmo down a 55-ft (16.8-m) ramp, soaring 70 ft (21 m) over the snow and landing cleanly on the other side.

Block also performs extreme driving stunts away from the slopes, in his Gymkhana videos.

Metal Bender

Joe Price from Gloucester, England, was a champion strongman in the 1920s and 1930s, and could bend a solid metal bar between his teeth. He was reported to have had a chest measuring 58 in (147 cm) in circumference and was renowned for the power of his hands. A blacksmith by trade, Price would train with large sledgehammers instead of conventional weights. In 1932, Robert Ripley released a cartoon that showed Price writing successfully with a 50-lb (25-kg) weight attached to his little finger.

HUGE FUDGE

In June 2009, Lansing Community College, Michigan, created a slab of chocolate fudge that weighed 5,500 lb (2,496 kg). The slab was made from 2,800 lb (1,270 kg) of chocolate, 705 lb (320 kg) of butter and 305 gal (1,155 l) of condensed milk.

BALANCING ACT

Wearing no harness despite being hundreds of feet up in the air, 24-year-old tightrope walker Samat Hasan, from the Xinjiang region of China, climbed 2,300 ft (700 m) along a high wire spanning a valley in Hunan Province in April 2009. The cable was just 1.2 in (3 cm) wide and had a steep gradient of 39 degrees.

GIANT JAMBALAYA

More than 50 volunteers from Gonzales, Louisiana, teamed up in June 2009 to cook a giant jambalaya in a pot that measured nearly 8 ft (2.4 m) in diameter. The pot was so big that it had to be transported by forklift and placed in a specially dug trench. Several people had to stir the dish simultaneously, using 9-ft-long (2.7-m) paddles. The recipe contained 1,200 lb (545 kg) of pork and sausage, 300 lb (135 kg) of onions, 16 cups of red and black pepper, 20 lb (9 kg) of garlic and 100 gal (378 l) of water.

HOMEMADE HELICOPTER

Despite having only a basic school education, 20-year-old Wu Zhongyuan of Luoyang, Henan Province, China, made his own helicopter, which he claims can fly to a height of 2,625 ft (800 m). It took him nearly three months to build his flying machine, which has a motorcycle engine and wooden blades made from an elm tree.

COFFIN MAKER

During a career spanning more than 30 years, carpenter Herbert Weber from Austria's Salzburg province has built more than 700,000 coffins.

FAMILY RUN

Sixteen brothers and sisters from the Kapral family of Oshkosh, Wisconsin, finished the 2009 Fox Cities Marathon— and all in under six hours. Only two of the family members—brothers Vince and Stephen—had completed a full marathon before.

SMART BIKE

A bicycle designed to be as intelligent as a computer was unveiled by Britain's former Olympic champion racing cyclist Chris Boardman in 2009. The bike of the future could never be stolen and would feature puncture-proof, self-inflating tires and a mini computer to count the calories as the pedals turned.

COSTLY CURRY

To coincide with the DVD release of Oscar-winning movie *Slumdog Millionaire*, Bombay Brasserie restaurant in London, England, prepared a curry that cost $3,000 a portion. The dish, called the Samundari Khazana, or Seafood Treasure, contained Devon crab, white truffle, Beluga caviar, quails' eggs, sea snails, and a Scottish lobster coated in edible gold leaf.

Hair Raising

Zhang Tingting, a Chinese strongwoman, successfully pulls six cars a distance of 165 ft (50 m) in Beijing in 2009, using her hair.

Strong Tongue

Habu, known as the "Man with the Iron Tongue," was a 1930s strongman from India who was able to lift up to 105 lb (48 kg) by hooking the weight to his tongue and lifting it from above.

HOT STUFF

In April 2009, Anandita Dutta Tamuly of Jorhat, Assam, India, ate 51 ghost peppers—one of the world's spiciest chilis—in two minutes. She has been hooked on hot peppers since the age of five when chili paste was smeared on her tongue by her mother as a cure for an infection.

FINGER POWER

Kung-fu master Ho Eng Hui pierced four coconuts with just his index finger in a little over 30 seconds in Malacca, Malaysia, in June 2009.

YOSEMITE WALK

Without any safety equipment, American Dean Potter walked an unleashed slackline— a rope length that isn't taut—3,200 ft (960 m) above the floor of Yosemite Valley, California. The only things holding him to the rope during his 100-ft (30-m) walk were his size-14 feet.

Rode Kill

Californian hot-rod artist John Towers has created "Rode Kill," a unique, handcrafted, custom motorcycle seemingly made from a decaying corpse. The bike has incredibly detailed features such as a heart protruding from an exposed ribcage that houses the fuel tank, and super-realistic bones that flex at the elbow with the bike suspension.

Look closer and you will see maggots crawling over the decaying flesh, bloodstained exhaust pipes, and headlight eyes in the skull. John wanted to graphically drive home how dangerous powerful motorbikes can be for inexperienced riders— "Rode Kill" will reach speeds of 140 mph (225 km/h).

PAPER PLANE

Engineer Takuo Toda, chairman of the Japan Origami Airplane Association, kept a 4-in (10-cm) paper airplane in flight for 27.9 seconds at a competition in Hiroshima Prefecture in April 2009.

PRESSING ENGAGEMENT

On January 10, 2009, 86 scuba divers dived 173 ft (52.7 m) to the bottom of a flooded quarry in Monmouthshire, Wales, and ironed clothes on ironing boards at the same time.

WHOLE LOTTA SHAKIN'

In April 2009, Chris Raph of Minneapolis, Minnesota, bar manager at the Shout House Dueling Pianos bar, poured 662 cocktails in an hour, averaging over ten cocktails per minute.

THE EATER

Salim "El Akoul" (The Eater) Haini of Ain Defla, Algeria, eats lightbulbs, candles, nails, newspapers and sawdust. He once ate a staggering 1,500 boiled eggs in under three hours and on another occasion consumed an entire roasted lamb, weighing 77 lb (35 kg), in one sitting.

CREAM TEA

In May 2009, Anne Tattersall from Devon, England, created an enormous cream tea, featuring a scone that weighed 99 lb (45 kg) and measured 3 ft (1 m) in diameter. The scone was baked by Nick, Amy and Mary Lovering and Simon Clarke and was filled with 20 lb (9 kg) of jelly and 35 lb (16 kg) of clotted cream.

MONSTER MUNCH

At Doha, Qatar, in March 2009, a sandwich was made that stretched 5,676 ft (1,730 m)—more than a mile. It contained 1,102 lb (500 kg) of salami and mortadella, 2,205 lb (1,000 kg) of coleslaw, 440 lb (200 kg) of mozzarella cheese, plus lesser amounts of mushroom, onion, garlic and spices.

WHISKY GALORE

Over a period of 35 years, Brazilian whisky enthusiast Claive Vidiz built up a collection of 3,384 different bottles of whisky. Among the many rare bottles he owned was a Strathmill single malt made to celebrate a Scottish distillery's centenary, which was one of only 69 such bottles ever produced.

Giant Gummi

Derek Lawson makes giant gummi bears at Popalop's Candy Shop in Raleigh, North Carolina. Each one weighs a massive 5 lb (2 kg) and measures a whopping 9 x 5½ x 3½ in (23 x 14 x 9 cm), which is 1,400 times the size of an ordinary gummi bear. It takes nine hours to create each bear and make them taste exactly like the original smaller version. The bears are available in a variety of different flavors, including blue raspberry, cola, grape and green apple.

ZOMBIE PARTY

In July 2009, a total of 3,894 people dressed as zombies for the "Red, White and Dead Zombie Party" event in Seattle, Washington State.

WEEKLY COLUMN

At age 102, former 1940s pin-up girl Margaret Caldwell was still writing a weekly column, "Memoirs of a Crone," for the *Desert Valley Times* newspaper in Mesquite, Nevada.

HEROIC REPAIR

In July 2009, after an airplane due to fly from Menorca, Spain, to Glasgow, Scotland, developed an engineering fault, vacationers were spared an eight-hour delay when one of the passengers was able to fix the plane himself.

CHANNEL WINGWALK

In July 2009, Tom Lackey, 89, from West Midlands, England, flew across the English Channel at 1,000 ft (305 m) and more than 100 mph (160 km/h) while strapped to the wings of a vintage airplane. The daredevil grandfather performed his amazing wingwalk over a 22-mi (40-km) stretch of water separating France and England on a plane that was just 20 years younger than him.

TALKATIVE TEEN

Thirteen-year-old Reina Hardesty from Orange County, California, used her cell phone to send 14,528 text messages during the month of December 2008. That worked out at 484 text messages every day—an average of one message every two minutes while she was awake. The online monthly phone-bill statement ran to 440 pages.

COURAGEOUS WALK

Phil Packer, a Royal Military Police Officer in the British Army, was so badly injured in a rocket attack in Basra, Iraq, in February 2008 that he was told he would never be able to walk again. Yet a year later he walked the 26.2-mi (42-km) London Marathon on crutches.

What's your Poison?

In Laos, drinkers can buy a bottle of snake wine—with a real dead snake inside. The poison of venomous snakes is dissolved in the liquor, which is then used for medicinal purposes. Snake products help treat a range of ailments, including arthritis, fever and whooping cough.

Hopping Mad

Pan-fried grasshopper is considered a delicacy in Korea and other parts of Asia. Insect gourmets say it tastes best seasoned with lime or salt, or dipped in garlic butter.

BOTTLE BALANCE

In 2008, Alexander Bendikov of Belarus managed to balance 18,000 matchsticks horizontally on a bottleneck without using any adhesive.

YOUNG HUSTLER

Keith O'Dell Jr. of Gloversville, New York State, plays pool for up to three hours a day—even though he is just two years old.

Amazing

PEOPLE

Twisted Art

Contortionists defy physical boundaries by twisting their bodies into seemingly impossible, backbreaking positions.

A fully grown adult can squeeze his or her entire body through an unstrung tennis racket that is 10 in (25 cm) in diameter or through a toilet seat, or into a glass bottle that is just 2 ft (0.6 m) high. Or they tie their body into intricate knots with their legs wrapped around the back of their neck and touching each other.

The art of contortionism is depicted in ancient Roman, Egyptian and Greek sculptures and has been featured in the Buddhist Tsam dance for centuries. In Mongolia, there are many contortionist schools where children are trained in the art of contortion from as young as five years old. Contortionism is also part of the Hindu discipline of yoga.

In the early 20th-century U.S.A., contortionists were popular circus acts. One of the most famous was "Dad" Whitlark, who could still tie his body into pretzel knots and put his face between his ankles at the age of 76. He could also bend over backward and pick up handkerchiefs from the floor with his teeth.

FRONTBENDING
Frontbenders, like this woman in 1957, twist their bodies into human knots. In this position they can squeeze through small hoops or tight barrels.

MAN IN A BOTTLE
Argentinian contortionist Hugo Zamoratte specialized in squeezing himself into bottles—but he nearly died while practicing his act in a Santiago, Chile, hotel room in 1982. He became stuck in the bottle, the door of which had accidentally locked, and after 40 minutes in a very uncomfortable position he was starting to hallucinate. He was saved by the timely arrival of a bewildered cleaner, who opened the door of the bottle and freed the exhausted contortionist.

Ethiopian contortionist Kiros Hadgu—alias "The Twisted Kiros"—can dislocate both his arms and his legs and even turn his torso through 180 degrees.

Monster Arms

The ironically named Tiny Iron, from London, England, has enormous biceps that measure an incredible 24 in (61 cm) in circumference—that's bigger than most people's thighs—and can smash an egg when flexed! In the past, Tiny put his massive arms to use as a bodyguard, but he is now an actor and wrestler. In order to fuel his 280-lb (127-kg) frame, he eats a heavyweight diet of high-protein chicken breasts for breakfast, lunch and dinner.

WAR WOUND

More than 60 years after being wounded by a mortar shell in World War II, John Ready of London, England, still had pieces of shrapnel working their way out of his skin.

PREMATURE AGING

Werner Syndrome, a rare genetic disease, causes premature aging—wrinkled skin, baldness, cataracts and muscular atrophy—by the time a person reaches their early thirties.

BLACKOUT RAID

Mark Lester from Norwich, England, was spared jail for robbing a supermarket at gunpoint after a court heard that he suffers from a rare medical condition that makes him have blackouts and causes him to forget his actions. After the robbery he told his mother that he had suffered a nightmare about holding up a store with a gun, but when she recognized him from a TV report, she realized it was more than a bad dream.

Swollen Nose

Liu Ge has a nose that is nearly 4 in (10 cm) long and 3 in (7.5 cm) wide—an unwelcome side effect of his job as an official brandy taster in Beijing, China. Liu has been drinking up to half a gallon (2 l) of brandy a day for 52 years and it has left him with a condition called rhinophyma, caused by the constant expansion of blood vessels in his nose.

HOPPING MAD

An 18th-century maidservant from Godalming, England, became a national sensation when she convinced doctors she had given birth to more than 16 rabbits. In 1726, 25-year-old Mary Toft went into apparent labor overseen by John Howard, a male midwife, who recorded that Mary began producing parts of animals, including nine baby rabbits, in one day! Doctors were fascinated by the births, and explained them as "Maternal Impressions," maintaining that her fantasies about rabbits during her pregnancy had created these defects on the human fetus. Mary later admitted staging the births when it was discovered that a porter had smuggled a rabbit into Mary's chamber. The medical profession of the time suffered a great deal of ridicule because they had believed the story.

BAG OF HAIR

Peng Fu, a traveling herbal medicine practitioner from Suining, China, has not cut his hair for over 60 years and carries it around in a bag on his back. When last measured, his hair was 8 ft 10 in (2.7 m) long and weighed nearly 9 lb (4 kg).

METEORITE HIT

In June 2009, 14-year-old Gerrit Blank survived after being hit by a meteorite that crashed into Earth in Essen, Germany, at 30,000 mph (48,000 km/h). The red-hot piece of rock about the size of a pea appeared as a ball of light before bouncing off his hand and causing a 1-ft-wide (30-cm) crater in the ground. The 100 million-to-one strike knocked him off his feet and left him with a 3-in (7.6-cm) scar on his hand. The noise that followed was so loud that his ears were ringing for hours afterward.

SHRAPNEL DISLODGED

A piece of shrapnel that had been lodged in the jaw of Alf Mann from Birmingham, England, for 65 years suddenly dropped out in 2009. Alf had struggled to speak and eat properly since being injured by an explosion during World War II—but one morning he woke to find blood on his pillow, along with the ½-in (1.2-cm) piece of shrapnel.

SPAT BULLET

After Richard Jamison of Bridgeton, New Jersey, was shot in the face in February 2009, he spat the bullet out of his mouth, then went looking for help.

CHEESE ADDICTION

Kate Silk from Manchester, England, is addicted to cheese. She has eaten cheese every single day for over 35 years— since she was two—and cheese is one of only six foods that don't make her sick.

POWERFUL PERFUME

Thirty-four people were hospitalized in Texas in July 2009—by strong perfume. Employees at a Bank of America call center in Fort Worth felt dizzy, nauseous and short of breath after a co-worker sprayed perfume. As panic spread through the building, workers poured on to the sidewalk outside and another 110 people were treated at the scene for chest pains and headaches.

THOUGHT PROCESS

Paralyzed neuroscientist Scott Mackler relies on a computer system that translates thoughts into text, to enable him to continue his work at the University of Pennsylvania. He wears a special cap that picks up the electrical activity of his brain and allows him to select letters just by thinking about them. The computer then turns his sentences into speech.

Sharp Features

Retired bank manager John Lynch of Hertfordshire, England, has over 240 body piercings. He has more than 150 on his head and neck alone and has had to give up flying because he kept setting off airport security scanners. He also has hundreds of tattoos, including an image of Marilyn Monroe that covers most of his torso. He did not get his first piercing until he was in his forties.

Spooky Eyes

Hollywood special-effects artist Kevin Carter creates colored contact lenses, which can make the wearer look as if he or she has been possessed by demons or is an alien visitor from another planet. He spends up to two days hand-painting dye onto each lens with a fine brush, and his scary designs — which also include a shark's open jaws—can sell for up to $750 a pair.

KEPT ALIVE

At Oxford, England, in January 2009, a baby girl was kept alive in the womb of her dead mother for two days until she could be born safely. Jayne Soliman collapsed from a brain hemorrhage and although she was declared brain dead, doctors kept her heart beating for 48 hours until they had safely delivered baby Aya prematurely at 25 weeks by cesarean section.

FACIAL TUMOR

Fifteen-year-old Lai Thi Dao of Vietnam underwent a 12-hour surgery in April 2008 to remove a tumor that accounted for one-third of her body weight. It started out as little more than a cyst on her tongue when she was three, but grew to weigh over 12 lb (5.4 kg) and consumed the lower half of her face.

SIMPSONS SAVIOR

Choking to death on a sandwich, ten-year-old Alex Hardy from Wakefield, England, was saved by his best friend Aiden Bateman who performed an abdominal thrust maneuver—remembering the technique from an episode of *The Simpsons*.

ONE VOICE

British researchers have found a 60-year-old woman who can identify only one voice—that of Scottish actor Sir Sean Connery. She suffers from the rare condition phonagnosia, which leaves her unable to identify anyone speaking on the phone or the radio. She doesn't even recognize her own daughter's voice and resorts to a system of codewords to identify friends and relatives who call.

SLEEP PLUNGE

Marius Purcariu from Arad, Romania, escaped with only minor injuries after falling from a fourth-floor window while he was asleep. He was found wrapped in a curtain on the hood of a car parked beneath his bedroom window. Doctors said that because he was sleepwalking his body was relaxed during the fall, which probably saved his life.

LEAP DAY

The Keogh family have three generations born on 29 February, beating odds of 3,118,535,181 to one. Peter Keogh was born in Ireland on leap day—February 29—1940, his son Eric was born in the U.K. on leap day 1964 and granddaughter Bethany was born in the U.K. on leap day 1996.

ELDERLY GRADUATE

Eleanor Benz, who dropped out of high school to help her family during the Great Depression, finally received her diploma in 2009—73 years later. She left Chicago's Lake View High School at age 17 to take a job, but at her 90th birthday party she was presented with the diploma, gown and cap, complete with a 1936 tassel.

UTENSIL REMOVED

Doctors puzzled by the coughing fits that plagued a man for almost two years found the answer in 2009 by removing a 1-in (2.5-cm) fragment of a plastic eating utensil from his lung. John Manley of Wilmington, North Carolina, said he probably inhaled the piece of plastic while gulping a drink at a fast-food restaurant.

MAGGOT INFESTATION

After suffering from constant nosebleeds for five days, a 70-year-old woman had 40 maggots removed from her nose by doctors at a hospital in Sion, India. A housefly had entered her nose and laid eggs inside it. When the eggs hatched, the larvae started feeding on her flesh, causing her nose to bleed.

Tiny Teen

Eighteen-year-old Jyoti Amge from Nagpur, India, is the smallest woman in the world, standing only 24 in (61 cm) tall and weighing a little over 11 lb (5 kg).

Despite weighing only 9 lb (4 kg) more than she did when she was born, Jyoti says she is no different from other people. She is proud to be smaller, and enjoys all the extra attention she receives. Jyoti travels to the local school on her brother's motorbike along with her sisters. In the classroom she has a custom-made desk next to the other pupils. She has a large collection of dresses like any teenager, and dreams of becoming an actress—she has already starred in a video with Indian pop star Mika Singh.

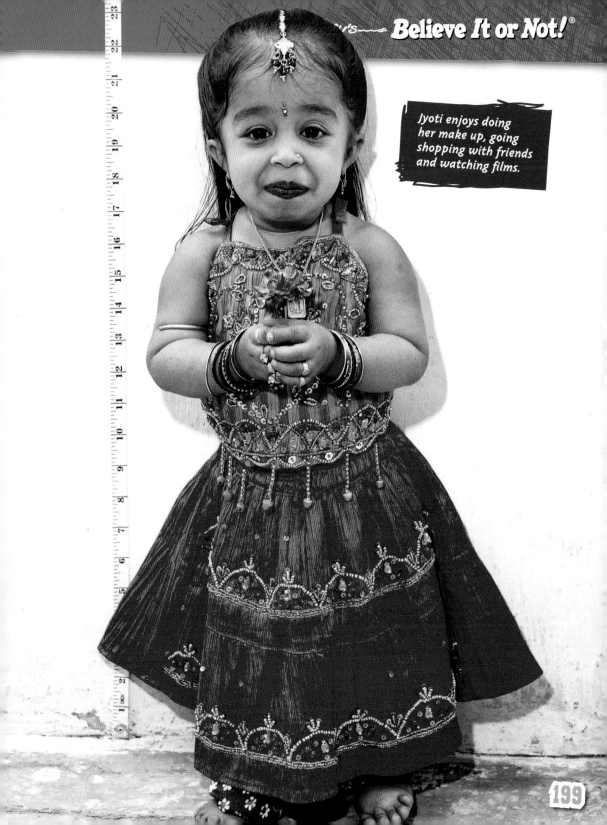

Jyoti enjoys doing her make up, going shopping with friends and watching films.

SAVED BY DIAPER

Eighteen-month-old Caua Felipe Massaneiro survived a plunge from a third-floor apartment window in Recife, Brazil, in 2008 when his diaper snagged on a security spike, slowing his fall.

HAND SEVERED

Mr. Shi of Shenzen, China, lost his hand in 2009 when it was pulled off at the wrist during a beach tug-of-war contest. Doctors successfully reattached the severed hand in a five-hour operation.

First Steps

Jingle Luis from the Philippines took her first unaided steps at age 15 after doctors at a New York City hospital straightened her severely clubbed feet, which were twisted backward and upside down. Dr. Terry Amaral inserted screws into the bones of her feet and turned the screws bit by bit over a period of six weeks so her feet would rotate, a few degrees at a time, into their correct position.

HAIR SALE

To beat the economic crisis, many women in Spain have started selling their hair. Depending on the length and weight, a ponytail can be worth up to $220 when sold to a company that exports natural hair for wigs and extensions.

HAIR DETERRENT

Farmers in Malaysia have been gathering sacks of human hair from barber shops to prevent wild boar from destroying their young oil palms. They spread the hair around the crops, and when a boar sniffs the hair, it thinks humans are present and runs off.

MIRACLE WALKER

A four-year-old boy who was told by doctors that he would be confined to a wheelchair for the rest of his life has miraculously learned to walk by copying a disabled duckling. Finlay Lomax from Plymouth, England, has cerebral palsy, but after his mother took in a day-old duckling with a broken leg, she was amazed to see Finlay standing on his own two feet and mimicking its steps.

All Fingers and Toes

The chances of having six healthy fingers on both hands, or six healthy toes on both feet, are very slim, but K.V. Subramaniyan from Kerala Province, India, has both! K.V., an acupuncture doctor who was once punished at school for saying that humans have 12 toes and 12 fingers, has a genetic condition known as polydactyly. Usually this means that someone has an extra finger or toe that is just a piece of tissue, occasionally containing bones without joints, but K.V. has fully functioning extra digits on both of his hands and feet, which is extremely rare.

SEVERED EAR

Doctors in Cologne, Germany, saved a woman's severed ear by stitching it to her buttocks. Julia Schwarz's right ear was bitten off in a fight, and the surgeons' first attempt to sew it back failed because the side of her head had not healed sufficiently. While waiting to carry out a second operation, they made a small incision in her butt and stitched the severed lobe into the pocket, keeping it there until her head had healed.

PSALM SAVIOR

An Argentinian pastor survived after a book of psalms he was holding deflected a bullet fired at him at close range. Mauricio Zanes Condori was trying to talk two thieves out of robbing his church in Rodeo del Medio in May 2009 when one of the men fired at his chest from a distance of 7 ft (2 m), but the holy book slowed down the bullet and altered its trajectory.

TODDLER CAUGHT

A group of fairgoers in Port Orange, Florida, caught and saved a toddler who was dropped nearly 40 ft (12 m) from a carnival ride in 2008 as her mother dangled helplessly above the crowd. The mother had become trapped when the ride started up unexpectedly just as she and her little girl were getting off it.

MIGHTY ATOM

In 2009, at three years of age, Liam Hoekstra from Grand Rapids, Michigan, could shift furniture, lift 5-lb (2.3-kg) weights, do sit-ups and perform incredible gymnastic feats of strength. Although he is smaller than most children his age, he has a rare condition that causes his body to have very little fat and 40 percent more muscle mass. As he has a fast metabolism, he eats up to six meals a day.

Miracle Mother

On the mountains of Rio Talea in southern Mexico, in March 2000, pregnant Inés Ramirez Perez was forced to cut open her own womb to have her baby after suffering for 12 hours with extreme labor pain. With the nearest clinic over 50 mi (80 km) away and no phone to call her husband at the next town, she was completely alone during the procedure. She gulped down rubbing alcohol to numb the pain and then began to cut using a 6-in (15-cm) slaughter knife. She managed to cut away the skin, fat and muscle before pulling out her baby boy, Orlando Ruiz Ramirez. Inés thinks she operated for about an hour before retrieving her baby and passing out. Her six-year-old son, Benito, returned with help several hours later.

Inés is believed to be the only woman to have ever performed a cesarian section on herself.

Seeing Blue

In 2007, Shannon Larratt from Canada couldn't resist the chance to have the first ever cosmetic eyeball tattoo. The procedure involved injecting ink into the top layer of his eye with a syringe 40 times, which had the effect of turning the white of Shannon's eye blue. Corneal tattooing is a surgical procedure for patients who have suffered severe eye trauma, but doctors do not recommend having it done for cosmetic reasons.

THREE GENERATIONS

In August 2009, three generations of the same family were born within 30 minutes of each other in the same hospital in Dublin, Ireland. Family matriarch Eileen McGuinness, 85, was blessed with her 69th grandchild, her 58th great-grandchild and her first great-great-grandchild in startlingly quick succession. Amazingly, none of the three expectant mothers knew the others were in the hospital at the time they were each preparing to give birth.

BRAIN REWIRED

Even though she has only half a brain, a ten-year-old German girl has near-perfect vision in one eye. Experts were baffled as to how the girl, who was born missing the right side of her brain (which maps the left field of vision) could have excellent left- and right-field vision in one eye, enabling her to see objects on either side. Scans revealed that her brain had rewired itself before she was born. Retinal nerve fibers carrying visual information from the back of the eye that should have gone to the right hemisphere of the brain diverted to the left instead.

SHARK ATTACK

After a Great White shark bit a chunk out of 13-year-old Hannah Mighall's surfboard and dragged her under the water, the teenager's life was saved by her cousin and fellow surfer, Syb Munday, who swam out to her and began punching the shark on the head. The 16-ft-long (4.9-m) predator, which had attacked off Binalong Bay in Tasmania, Australia, let Hannah go. She survived with bites to her legs that required 200 stitches.

NEVER WASHES

A man in India who fathered seven daughters has not washed for more than 35 years in an attempt to guarantee that his next child is a boy. Instead of bathing traditionally and brushing his teeth, 63-year-old Kailash Singh, from a village near Varanasi, has a "fire bath" every evening when he stands on one leg beside a bonfire and says prayers. Apparently a seer had once told him that if he did not take a normal bath, he would be blessed with a male child.

FLU SHOTS

The University of Central Florida administered 2,527 flu shots to staff, students and local residents in eight hours in September 2009.

MEMORABLE BIRTHDAYS

Thirteen months after giving birth to baby Campbell on August 8, 2008 (08/08/08), Alison Miller of Fayetteville, Arkansas, had a second daughter, Molly Reid, on September 9, 2009 (09/09/09).

BROKE FALL

A six-year-old boy survived a 70-ft (21-m) fall from an apartment balcony in Gothenburg, Sweden, in September 2009 when a passerby, who had stopped when he saw the boy fall, managed to catch him.

BABY ALLERGY

Having suffered several blisters and a burning rash after giving birth, Joanne Mackie of Birmingham, England, discovered she was allergic to her own baby. A rare skin disease, pemphigoid gestationis, that developed while she was still pregnant meant that she could not even cuddle baby James or pick him up for the first month of his life because the blisters caused her such pain. To feed him from a bottle, she had to wrap damp towels around her arms.

CONEY ISLAND TRIBUTE

Formerly an island but now a peninsula, Coney Island is located in southernmost Brooklyn, New York City. Its popularity as a resort grew in the 1860s when the Coney Island and Brooklyn Railroad started to serve the area, and by 1880 it boasted rides and freak shows. For more than fifty years, until World War II, Coney Island was the biggest amusement area in the US. On just one day in September 1906, no fewer than 200,000 postcards were mailed from Coney Island.

It housed three major amusement parks—Dreamland, Steeplechase Park and Luna Park. Dreamland was illuminated by one million electric lights, and at night its searchlight beamed 50 mi (80 km) out over the Atlantic Ocean. The brain behind Dreamland was Samuel W. Gumpertz, who scoured the globe in search of human oddities to appear at his sideshows. He made five trips to Asia and five to Africa, bringing back little people, bearded ladies and more than 3,000 peculiar performers.

The sideshow hasn't really died out at Coney Island, but the attention has moved away from "freaks" and oddities of the body and now focuses on performers. "Sideshows by the Seashore," founded by Dick Zigun in 1985, offers such exotic attractions as human blockheads, sword swallowers and fire eaters.

The Barnum & Greatest Show

THE GREAT CONEY ISLAND WATER CARNIVAL

At the height of its popularity in the 1920s, a million visitors flocked to Coney Island every day. They came to ride huge roller coasters, enjoy the thrills of the big wheel and to witness amazing human oddities recruited from Africa, Asia and Europe at the amusement park that became known as "The Playground of the World."

BABY IN A JAR
A baby was preserved in formaldehyde at a Coney Island sideshow in 1944. Coney Island has a long history of baby exhibits, courtesy of the Infant Incubator, a show where newborn infants were displayed under the care of a corps of trained nurses. The incubator babies were miraculously saved from the fire that swept through the island in 1911.

CONEY ISLAND TODAY
"Sideshows by the Seashore" continues the Coney Island tradition of showcasing live bizarre and unusual acts.

PRINCESS LOLA
The fattest lady at Coney, Princess Lola claimed to weigh 558 lb (253 kg) in August 1949.

VIOLETTA, THE LIMBLESS WOMAN
Born in Germany in 1906, Aloisia Wagner entered the world of show business at the age of 15, acquiring the stage name Violetta. Completely self-sufficient despite being born with no arms or legs, she moved around by hopping. Her sideshow performance involved her singing, but also demonstrated her abilities to sew and to light a cigarette using only her mouth.

ELEPHANT FACE GIRL
Anita, billed as "The only human on earth with a nose like an elephant's trunk," performed at the Coney Island sideshow in New York, in 1944. During this time, Coney Island was renowned as the world center of the amusement park industry.

HEADLESS WOMAN
A performance by an apparently headless woman has been a major attraction at Coney Island sideshows down through the years.

UNIQUE BONE

The hyoid bone, just above the larynx, anchors the muscles of the tongue and is the only bone in the human body that doesn't touch any other.

SHIPWRECKED FISHERMEN

After their boat sank in heavy seas off the north coast of Australia in December 2008, two Burmese fishermen survived for almost a month drifting on an ice box in shark-infested waters.

Patient Pinky

Sheng Wang, from Fujian, southern China, left one of his pinky fingernails to grow for 15 years, until it measured an amazing 18 in (46 cm) in length. In 1996, Wang decided to grow the nail for as long as he could to become a more peaceful person and test his patience. He has loved the change so much that he even turned down an offer of nearly $10,000 to remove the nail.

KIDNEY STONE

In January 2009, doctors removed a kidney stone that was the size of a coconut from the body of Sandor Sarkadi in Debrecen, Hungary.

Supple Skin

The "girl with the elastic skin" pictured here was famous for the stretchy skin on her cheeks and neck. Etta Lake, who traveled with the King-Franklin Circus in 1889, could pull the skin an amazing 6 in (15 cm) from her cheek.

VIOLENT SNEEZE

Victoria Kenny from Chichester, England, broke her back—just by sneezing. She sneezed with such force that she ruptured a disk in her spine, which left her paralyzed for almost two years.

TATTOO NERD

Computer nerds have been getting their bodies tattooed with images relating to their laptops. Among popular tattoo requests are a USB cable, the Apple logo and various items of software.

HUMAN TREE

Surgeons operating on a man in Russia in 2009 discovered a tree growing inside his lungs. They think that 28-year-old Artyom Sidorkin had somehow inhaled a seed, which subsequently sprouted inside his lung. The 2-in-long (5-cm) spruce was touching his capillaries and causing him extreme chest pain.

LOUD SNORER

Jenny Chapman from Cambridgeshire, England, snores more loudly than the noise of a jet aircraft. She snores in her sleep at 111.6 decibels—eight decibels louder than the roar of a low-flying jet. She could drown out the sounds of a spinning washing machine, a diesel truck or a speeding express train.

TWO WOMBS

Seeking a hospital diagnosis for a pain in her abdomen, two months' pregnant Lindsay Hasaj of London, England, learned that she had two wombs—a one-in-a-million chance.

Arm Lock

Justin Shaw, a professional drummer from Kentucky, takes pride in his exceptionally long arm hair. The longest hair measures a lengthy 5¾ in (14.6 cm), long enough to stretch around a large grapefruit. Justin has always liked the long blond arm tufts, and has never wanted to cut them short. However, since he moved to Miami, Florida, he has recorded a faster growth in his arm hairs—something he puts down to "getting a lot of vitamin D" in the sunshine—yet he still has no desire to cut them.

SELFLESS SURGEON

Italian surgeon Claudio Vitale finished a brain operation on a patient in March 2009 despite suffering a heart attack partway through the procedure. Dr. Vitale realized his patient would never recover if he halted the operation to seek treatment for himself, so he continued for another 30 minutes in the operating theatre at Cardarelli Hospital, Naples, until the patient was out of danger.

HYPNOTIC DENTIST

In May 2008, Leslie Mason from Essex, England, underwent two hours of root canal work without anesthetic after being hypnotized by his friend John Ridlington. Despite having two upper right molars removed along with their roots, plus two roots from teeth that had been pulled in the 1980s, the patient reported feeling nothing more than "a little sting."

LUCKY STRIKE

When Nada Acimovich of Sljivovica, Serbia, was struck by lightning, her rubber-soled shoes saved her—and the electric jolt cured her deadly heart condition. Her condition, known as arrhythmia, is normally treated with mild electric shocks to reset the heart's rhythm.

MUSCLE BOY

A five-year-old Romanian boy has muscles that are bigger than those of boys over three times his age. Strong boy Giuliano Stroe, who has been training since age two, can perform grueling stunts such as horizontal bar routines, backflips off a table top, and walking on his hands with a weight ball between his legs.

MAIL BOY

Four-year-old Jakob Strauss got trapped inside a mailbox in Feldkirch, Austria. He wriggled in after mailmen had left the door open, and managed to close the hatch behind him. After a passersby heard his cries for help, firefighters used bolt cutters to free him.

IMPROVISED DRILL

Rob Carson, a doctor in Maryborough, Victoria, Australia, used a handyman's power drill to bore into a boy's skull and relieve potentially fatal bleeding on his brain. Nicholas Rossi had seriously injured his head falling off his bicycle, but the small hospital did not have neurological drills, so Dr. Carson sent for a household drill from the maintenance room and called a neurosurgeon in Melbourne to talk him through the complex procedure.

BIG BABY

An Indonesian woman gave birth to a baby boy weighing a whopping 19.2 lb (8.7 kg). The baby, who was 24.4 in (62 cm) long, was born by cesarean section at a hospital in North Sumatra province.

JEEP ADVENTURE

A three-year-old boy was rescued in July 2009 after riding his toy jeep into the Peace River, British Columbia, Canada, and floating nearly 8 mi (13 km) downstream. He was found still sitting happily in his battery-powered jeep in water that was 15 ft (4.5 m) deep.

TOUGH TEEN

Fifteen-year-old Bobby Natoli of Oswego, New York, did 53 chin-ups in one minute in 2008, surpassing the feat of his father, Robert, who had managed 44 the previous year. Bobby also recorded 209 chin-ups in half an hour when he was just 12 years old.

ARM RECOVERED

After 11-year-old Devin Funck from Slidell, Louisiana, had his arm bitten off by a huge alligator in a lake near New Orleans in 2008, wildlife officials shot the reptile and recovered the arm largely intact from its stomach.

EXTENDED LEAVE

Left unable to walk or talk following a road accident that nearly killed him, computer worker Karl McLennan of Aberdeen, Scotland, returned to his job in 2009 after 12 years of sick leave.

GOLFER BOY

After being struck by lightning while playing golf with friends in Cape Cod, Massachusetts, Michael Utley staggered around with smoke pouring out of his mouth, nose and ears. His internal tissues were actually boiling and although his heart stopped, he eventually made an almost full recovery.

SINKHOLE HELL

Jeanne Schnepp, 63, spent nearly a week stuck on a raft in a sinkhole on the Wapsipinicon River in Iowa. She had been fishing from the rubber raft when the strong river current swept her downstream and deposited her in the sinkhole, trapping her between a 12-ft (3.6-m) wall of rocks and a logjam she couldn't climb over. After enduring two thunderstorms, hot days and cold nights, she was finally spotted by an angler.

LONG STRAND

Brian Peterkin-Vertanesian of Washington, D.C., boasts a single red eyebrow hair that measures an incredible 6 ³/₈ in (16.2 cm) long. The hair, which he has named Wally, is so long he can chew on it, although he usually keeps it tucked behind his left ear for safety.

SECRET BABY

Doctors in Qingshen, China, discovered that a 92-year-old woman had been carrying an unborn child in her body for more than 60 years. Huang Yijun, of Huangjiaotan, said her baby had died in her womb in 1948, but she could not afford the money to have the dead fetus removed. Her long-standing secret was finally revealed in 2009 after she hurt her stomach and underwent a hospital scan. Doctors were amazed because normally a dead fetus would decay and cause infection, but Huang had stayed healthy all that time.

EGYPTIAN MUMMY

Mother-of-three Nileen Namita from Brighton, England, has undergone more than 50 cosmetic procedures to make herself look like the ancient Egyptian Queen Nefertiti. Since 1987, Nileen, who believes she is a reincarnation of Nefertiti, has spent over $300,000 on eight nose jobs, three chin implants, one eyebrow lift, three facelifts, six mini facelifts, two lip surgeries, five eye surgeries and 20 minor facial tweaks—to recreate herself in the image of the "Beauty of the Nile."

FOOD FOR THOUGHT

Researchers in Quebec, Canada, have discovered that thinking too hard can make people fat. Blood tests on student volunteers showed that those who had recently taken an exam ate more because the brain workout sent their glucose and insulin levels haywire, making them more hungry.

BODY STRENGTH

At age 83, Sidney Williams of Port Elizabeth, South Africa, can lift up to 353 lb (160 kg) even though he himself weighs only 220 lb (100 kg)—that means he can lift 50 percent more than his body weight.

STRANGER'S DIAGNOSIS

A stranger saved the life of a Spanish bus passenger by telling her that she might be suffering from a rare disease. Montse Ventura was on a bus in Barcelona, when a woman sitting opposite noticed her unusually shaped hands. She urged Montse to have tests for acromegaly, a disorder caused by a pituitary gland problem that causes abnormal growth of hands and feet. Sure enough, when Montse went to the doctor, a small pituitary gland tumor was found and removed.

TOTALLY TATTOOED

Since his first tattoo of a small juggling club on his hip, Australian entertainer Lucky Diamond Rich has had 100 percent of his body tattooed. He even has tattoos on top of tattoos!

SWALLOWED PIN

Doctors in China discovered the cause of an eight-year-old boy's constant coughs and colds—a rusty drawing pin stuck in his right lung. Xiao Ming of Mingguang, Anhui Province, had been suffering from the mystery ailments for a year.

Mini Man

Born in 1992, Khagendra Thapa Magar from the Baglung District of Nepal is one of the smallest known men on earth, standing just 26 in (67 cm). When Khagendra was born, he didn't weigh much more than a can of soda, and now that he is an adult he tips the scales at 12 lb (5 kg), around the same weight as a domestic cat. His tiny size means that he only needs to eat around 3½ oz (100 g) of food each day, the equivalent of two chocolate bars. It is likely that Khagendra's diminutive figure is caused by a pituitary gland problem, but otherwise he is completely healthy and very keen on dancing and karate.

The Coral Man

Lin Tianzhuan from Shuimen, southern China, first noticed the growths on his hands and feet when he was 13, and over the next 25 years they gradually spread and hardened to the point where he could no longer bend his arms or legs.

Dubbed "Coral Boy" by friends and neighbors, Lin became a hermit, hiding himself away at the family home. "If I had to go out I wrapped myself up in blankets because people would scream when they saw me."

Now, after a year of treatment and surgery at a specialist skin clinic, the dark brown shells have been cut away and he has nothing worse than a few discolored skin patches to remind him of his previous horrific condition.

Ice Ordeal

Latvian illusionist Gennady Palychevsky was on the verge of literally freezing to death after spending more than 64 hours as a human ice cube. He survived for nearly three days in the 6-sq-ft (0.5-sq-m) ice cube in Moscow before signaling for help because he was suffering from severe frostbite. Palychevsky, who had trained in ice baths for six months, did not eat or drink while sealed inside his ice tomb.

LUCKY GIFT

Schoolgirl Sophie Frost of Rayleigh, Essex, England, owed her life to the iPod she was wearing when struck by lightning. She survived the 30,000-volt surge only because it traveled through the gadget's wire, diverting it away from her vital organs. She had been given the iPod just four days earlier as a gift from her grandmother.

TWINS PEAK

The Indian village of Kodinhi, Kerala, has more than 250 sets of twins born to just 2,000 families—six times the global average.

HORSE LEGS

Seattle, Washington State, designer Kim Graham has devised the ultimate accessory for people who want to look taller and more elegant—horse leg extensions. Her Digitigrade Leg Extensions, which are shaped like a horse's leg, are made of steel, cable, foam and rigid plastic and add 14 in (35 cm) of height to the wearer. She says it takes only 15 minutes to learn to walk in them, although the wearer should avoid stairs. The standard legs cost $750— with another $200 for spring-loaded hooves to put an extra bounce in your step.

Blood Portrait

A $450,000 self-portrait sculpted by British artist Marc Quinn from his own frozen blood was put on display at London's National Portrait Gallery in 2009. Quinn made his first blood head in 1991, and has subsequently produced a new cast every few years to illustrate how he has aged. He uses 10 pt (4.7 l) of blood for each work, the blood being removed by his doctor, a pint at a time every six weeks.

LAUGHTER LESSONS

After a study revealed that Germans laugh on average for just six minutes a day, an organization of yoga-laughter therapists was set up in Cologne to teach Germans how to laugh. Laughter is considered healthy and the perfect antidote to aging. There are more than 6,000 laughter clubs around the world on five continents and there is even an annual World Laughter Day.

BAT BOY

A blind English boy has learned to "see" the world around him for the first time by using echolocation—the technique used by bats and dolphins. By clicking his tongue on the roof of his mouth, Lucas Murray from Dorset, England, can discover where and how big objects are depending on the echoes that bounce back. He uses the method to play basketball, determining which direction the hoop is in and how far away it is before making his shot.

16 TOES

A baby was born with 16 toes—eight on each foot—in Leizhou, Guangdong, China, in November 2008.

MEMORY MAN

Bob Petrella, a television producer in his fifties from Los Angeles, California, can remember almost everything he has done in life since the age of five. He can recall precise details of virtually all his birthdays, along with every New Year's Eve for the last 40 years and all the conversations he has had on most days for the last 53 years. He has been diagnosed with the condition hyperthymestia (overdeveloped memory), which has been discovered in just four people around the world.

SNOWDRIFT

Fifty-five-year-old Donna Molnar of Ancaster, Ontario, Canada, collapsed in a snowdrift in December 2008 and survived three days of sub-zero temperatures and blowing winds until she was rescued. She was eventually found buried in 2 ft (60 cm) of snow, with all but her face and neck covered.

MADE HIS POINT

To protest a judge's decision that he must sell part of his farm to settle a debt, Orico Silva of Figueira da Foz, Portugal, chopped off his own finger with a butcher's knife on the court desk.

MAGIC TOOTH

After being blind for 12 years following an accident at work, Martin Jones from Yorkshire, England, had his sight restored by having a tooth transplanted into his eye. One of his canine teeth was removed and converted into a holder for a special optical lens by drilling a hole in it. Then the tooth was inserted into his cheek for three months to enable it to grow new tissue and blood vessels before, complete with the fitted lens, being inserted into his right eyeball. Two weeks later, his sight returned and for the first time he was able to see his wife Gill, whom he had married in 2005.

TWO-DAY MEMORY

Andy Wray from Essex, England, has a memory that lasts only two days—so if he is parted from his wife or young daughter for 48 hours or more, he can no longer recognize them. He has dissociative amnesia, a condition that effectively wipes his memory clean on a regular basis. Doctors say it is the result of trauma suffered during his time working as a police officer.

Bare Face

Swiss artist "Dave" created this portrait of President Obama from multiple painted bodies in unison during a performance in Athens, Greece, in 2009. The use of choreography and paint in this way has been described as a new form of art called "fusionism."

Still Live

Retired history teacher Geoff Ostling from Sydney, Australia, is literally a walking work of art. More than 20 years ago, Geoff began working with well-known tattoo artist eX de Merci, choosing the theme of Australian flowers, and they now cover his skin from neck to toe, depicting every flower he could think of. When Geoff dies, he wants to be skinned and the tattoos displayed whole, just as they are on his body, at Australia's National Gallery in Canberra. He has already lined up the help of a taxidermist for when that day comes.

ORGANS REVERSED

An Indian man is thought to be the only living person in the world with *situs inversus*—a condition in which his internal organs are back-to-front. Doctors in Mumbai were about to remove a tumor from the kidney of Ashok Shivnani when they realized that most of his chest and abdominal organs, as well as many blood vessels, were in the mirror opposite position of where they should be in his body.

CHOPSTICK OP

A Chinese kung-fu master, who accidentally swallowed a chopstick during a training stunt, forgot that it was lodged in his stomach for 20 years until it suddenly started to cause him pain. Forty-year-old Wing Ma finally had the 7-in-long (18-cm) chopstick removed in 2009 during an operation in eastern Wuhan.

IMPALEMENT

Doctors in China removed a chopstick that was lodged 0.15 in (4 mm) into the brain of a 14-month-old boy. Li Jingchao, from Shandong Province, was playing with chopsticks when he fell on one and it went up his nose and into his brain.

STRETCH BRIDE

Suffering from a rare kind of dwarfism, Tiffanie DiDonato of Jacksonville, North Carolina, underwent bone-lengthening procedures so that her body could be stretched an incredible 14 in (35 cm), from 3 ft 8 in to 4 ft 10 in (1.14 m to 1.45 m), in time for her wedding day. Surgeons broke her bones and then inserted a device that slowly pulls them apart. The bone then grows and fills in the gaps so that each day her legs would be stretched another 0.04 in (1 mm). Diastrophic dysplasia (dwarfism) had caused Tiffanie to stop growing at age eight.

NASTY SHOCK

A Chinese boy survived a 10,000-volt shock in March 2009. He Haoyang had been playing with wires in a field in Sichuan Province when they suddenly broke. He escaped with just burns to his hands because he managed to run a few steps away from the accident site, where the grass was left completely burned.

TOO PASSIONATE

In December 2008, a man in Zhuhai, Guangdong, China, kissed his girlfriend so passionately that it popped her eardrum and she went deaf in that ear.

MID-AIR DEATH

A novice skydiver landed safely in 2009—even though the instructor to whom he was strapped had died of a heart attack in midair. When they jumped out of a plane above Chester, South Carolina, soldier Daniel Pharr was making his first-ever jump, while 49-year-old instructor George Steele was a veteran of more than 8,000 jumps. However, thousands of feet above the ground as they were finishing their free fall and just moments after their parachute had opened, Steele died. Pharr came down about a third of a mile from the intended drop point despite being able to reach only one of the parachute's steering toggles behind the dead man, forcing him to descend in circles.

SOLITARY TREE

On vacation in Tenerife, 66-year-old grandmother Maureen Evason from Plymouth, England, was saved from a fatal fall off a 150-ft-high (45-m) volcanic ridge when her head became wedged in the only tree on the mountain. Her head was stuck for three hours between two branches, which provided a natural neck brace to immobilize her body and prevent spinal injuries.

Ripley's Heroes

Showcasing some of the most bizarre and weird folk that Robert Ripley found on his travels, a vast modern collection of wax heads are central to the world of Ripley's.

Located in Ripley museums all over the world, the heads are made by a dedicated team of sculptors, makeup experts, costume designers and hair specialists. The team spends its days surrounded by oddities in the Ripley's art department in Florida. They make the eerily lifelike heads by painstakingly sticking each strand of hair to the sculptures and painting each individual wrinkle, believe it or not!

SARA DISK WEARER OF AFRICA
The Ubangi women of the Sara tribe in Chad, Africa, wear wooden plates in their lips to make them unattractive to raiders.

PADAUNG WOMAN OF MYANMAR
The women of the Padaung tribe add a gold ring around their necks annually, to a maximum of 20 rings, which can make their necks 15 in (38 cm) long.

JO-JO THE DOG-FACED MAN
Born in Russia, Fedor Jeftichew suffered from hypertriclosis, or "Werewolf syndrome," and his body was covered with hair up to 8 in (20 cm) long. He became known as Jo-Jo the Dog-faced Man when he became a famous sideshow performer.

HUMAN LIGHT

Our bodies emit tiny amounts of light a thousand times weaker than the human eye can perceive. The light levels are at their highest in late afternoon and at their lowest late at night, and the brightest light is emitted from the cheeks, forehead and neck. It is the result of bioluminescence, a side effect of metabolic reactions within all creatures.

PICKLED LEG

Song Weiguo of Jiangyan, China, has preserved his amputated leg in formaldehyde for more than 20 years to warn others of the perils of drunk driving. Having drunk a pint of strong liquor, he lost his left leg in a motorcycle crash in 1989 and now puts the severed limb on display every year on the anniversary of the accident.

Folds of Skin

Arthur Loos, who performed at the Ripley Odditorium in Chicago in 1933, had huge folds of skin hanging down from his face. He suffered from neurofibromatosis, which causes extreme skin abnormalities.

Webbed Wonder

Although normal in birds, reptiles, amphibians and some mammals, syndactyly—or webbed toes—is a rare condition in humans, occurring in about one in 2,500 births. Usually the second and third toes are joined by skin and flexible tissue. The cause in humans is unknown, but it is sometimes hereditary. Famous people with webbed toes include actors Dan Aykroyd and Ashton Kutcher and former Soviet leader Joseph Stalin.

GRIZZLY ATTACK

In May 2008, Brent Case of Saanich, British Columbia, Canada, managed to drive more than 15 mi (24 km) to find help after a grizzly bear mauled him so badly that he lost part of his scalp. During the attack, he thought that the bear was literally eating his brains.

DOUBLE WOMB

Sarah Reinfelder of Sault Ste. Marie, Michigan, who has two wombs, gave birth to twin daughters in February 2009— one from each uterus.

TRAPPED UNDERGROUND

After the Xinqiao coal mine, in southwestern China's Guizhou Province, was flooded in June 2009, three miners survived for 25 days while they were trapped underground by licking water off the walls.

EXTRA DIGITS

Kamani Hubbard was born in San Francisco, California, in January 2009 with 24 fingers and toes. The 24 were made up of six digits on each of his hands and feet, and were perfectly formed and fully functioning.

VISION RESTORED

A 70-year-old man who had been "as blind as a bat" for his entire life suddenly acquired perfect vision after suffering a massive stroke. Retired architect Malcolm Darby from Leicestershire, England, had worn thick glasses since the age of two, but when he came to after surgery to clear the blood clot that had caused his stroke, he found that for the first time in his life he could see clearly without them.

Big Deal

A German art collector paid $215,000 to buy this vibrant tattoo of the Virgin Mary—even though it was tattooed on somebody else's back. The work, by Belgian artist Wim Delvoye, is on the back of Tim Steiner from Switzerland, who is now an exhibit himself. Steiner has to show the piece three times a year, and is also bound by an agreement that means the tattooed skin will be returned to its new owner after his death. It's not the first time prized tattoos by Wim Delvoye have been for sale. A French man tried to give a Paris museum his tattoo in his will, and a British man attempted to sell his own piece of skin art in an auction—both have failed to find a buyer so far.

STAYIN' ALIVE

A Massachusetts woman revived her husband from cardiac arrest by administering CPR to the funky beat of the Bee Gees' disco classic "Stayin' Alive." After he collapsed during a walk, she remembered a public service announcement by the American Heart Association. It advised people untrained in CPR to help heart attack victims by compressing their chests 100 times a minute and to use "Stayin' Alive," which has 103 beats a minute, as a handy guideline.

SOB STORY

For nearly 20 years, Patricia Webster of Kent, England, suffered from crocodile tears syndrome, a rare medical condition that made her cry uncontrollably whenever she ate food. As a side effect of the condition, nerve fibers that should be used for salivation become damaged and regrow into the lacrimal gland, located under the eye, which controls the flow of tears. So when Patricia chewed and swallowed food, she could not keep herself from crying—until her condition was cured using Botox injections.

SPECIAL BRANCH

John Nash, a rookie police officer from Rochdale, England, fell while pursuing a suspect, but didn't realize he had impaled his eye socket on the branch of a bush until after he caught and arrested the perpetrator. The 6-in (15-cm) piece of wood snapped off, but it had pierced his eyelid, smashed a cheekbone, forced itself under his eyeball and had come to rest against his brain.

STRONG GIRL

Jacqueline Wickens from Elko, Nevada, lifted 308 lb (140 kg) in Anaheim, California, in December 2007—even though she was only 13 years old.

KNUCKLE CRACK

The sound caused by a person cracking their knuckles comes from gas bubbles forming and collapsing with a snapping noise within the joints.

RARE TWINS

In a one in a million chance, an American mother gave birth to twins who have different fathers. Mia Washington from Dallas, Texas, gave birth to Justin and Jordan within seven minutes of each other, but in a remarkable twist of fate, they turned out to be half-brothers. Miss Washington admitted having an affair and conceived two babies by different men at the same time.

Unbelievable

ART

Invisible Man

Chinese artist Liu Bolin uses only paint and a setting of his choice to create these stunning pieces of art.

A rare image of the artist himself, Liu Bolin.

Sichuan, Central China

Known as the "Invisible Man," Liu manages to camouflage himself completely into the background by painting the precise colors and details that he sees onto his clothes, without any digital trickery. Using hundreds of different settings in cities all over the world, Liu is so expert at camouflaging himself that passersby normally don't even notice he is there. An assistant helps Liu to paint his body—he must stand completely still throughout—and it can take up to ten hours to get each image perfect.

TELEPHONE

TELEPHONE

TELEPHONE

Famous Face

A bakery in St. Petersburg, Russia, makes amazing, intricate and realistic cakes of anything you can imagine. The famous bakery, Zhanna, creates sponge-based masterpieces of such subjects as a treasure chest with flowing jewels to a construction site with bricks and cranes, ensuring every tiny detail is re-created in icing. The cakes are completely edible and not one piece of plastic is involved.

DON'T JUMP!

A life-size plastic art installation in Vienna, Austria, showed a smartly dressed businessman clutching a briefcase and apparently about to jump from the top of a four-story real-estate company building. The work of artist Ronald Kodritsch was inspired by the international financial crisis of 2009.

SKULL SAUNA

Dutch artist Joep van Lieshout has built a 15-ft-tall (4.5-m) human skull featuring a built-in sauna. The white "Wellness Skull" is made of wood and synthetic material, and when the eight-person-capacity sauna is in use, steam emanates from its eye sockets. The skull also houses a bathtub and shower on either side of its neck.

TILL RECEIPT

A $100 grocery receipt listing 36 white shopping items including boil-in-the-bag rice and toilet roll was exhibited at a prestigious gallery in London, England, in 2009 by Pakistani-born artist Ceal Floyer. The conceptual artwork, entitled *Monochrome Till Receipt (White)*, was displayed at Tate Britain and was valued at $45,000.

COIN FLAG

Inspired by the realization that people don't bother to pick up small-currency 10-won coins on the streets of Korea, Jin Jeong-gun decided to collect as many coins as possible and turn them into a giant mosaic of the Korean national flag. Over a period of 14 years he collected 110,000 coins and then spent four months arranging them into a flag measuring 20 x 13 ft (6 x 4 m). Jin had previously made a pagoda from 2,000 discarded 10-won coins.

SOUND OF MOOSIC

An Austrian farmer plays the accordion to his herd of dairy cows to keep them calm and improve their milk yield. Franz Koeberl and his family stage live concerts for the animals in the hills around the farm at Birkfeld and have discovered that the livestock prefer classical music, especially Strauss. The concerts have proved so successful that Koeberl has even compiled a CD of his cows' favorite tunes.

TANGO EXTRAVAGANZA

After six months of practice, some 200 children (100 pairs) danced tango simultaneously in Medellin, Colombia, in July 2009.

LEGO JESUS

A church in Sweden marked Easter 2009 by unveiling a life-size LEGO® statue of Jesus Christ. Over a period of 18 months churchgoers at the Oensta Gryta Church in Vaesteras donated nearly 30,000 LEGO® bricks to build the statue, which reached 5 ft 10 in (1.78 m) high and was based on a Danish sculpture depicting Christ's resurrection.

DRUM ENSEMBLE

A total of 582 drummers beat the same rhythm together for five minutes at the National Indoor Arena in Birmingham, England, in July 2009. Among them was Don Powell, drummer with the 1970s U.K. band Slade, who said: "It isn't difficult getting everyone playing at the same speed—getting them to stop at the same time is the problem!"

EXTRA-LARGE WAIST

In 2009, Tunisian fashion designer Larbi Boukamha created a pair of pants that were equal to the height of a 22-story building. He worked eight hours a day for two whole months to make the oversized pants, which measured 164 ft (50 m) in length, had a waist of 118 ft (36 m) and used a mile (1,600 m) of fabric.

TRICKS OF THE EYE

Californian artist John Pugh specializes in trompe l'oeil—or "trick of the eye"—art, deluding the viewer into seeing 3-D scenes that are actually painted on flat surfaces. On the side of an intact building in Los Gatos, he created the illusion of earthquake damage, depicting crumbling walls that revealed a Mayan temple. Another work, featuring a huge wave about to crash onto a sidewalk in Honolulu, Hawaii, was so lifelike that a passing fire crew stopped to try to rescue some children in danger—only to find that neither the wave nor the children were real.

DJ MARATHON

A German DJ broadcast nonstop for more than a week in April 2009. Dominik Schollmayer presented his morning show on Hit-Radio Antenne in Hanover for 169 consecutive hours.

LINE DRAWING

Sethu Subramaniyan of Bangalore, India, spent six months illustrating a portrait of Qaboos Ibn Sa'id, the Sultan of Oman, drawn in one continuous, unbroken line beginning and ending at his signature with no overlap.

METAL ARMADILLO

Known as "Scrap Daddy" for his work with waste materials, Mark Bradford of Houston, Texas, created the sculpture "Carmadillo," a shiny 50-ft-long (15-m) armadillo built from a pickup truck and a van.

GUM LADY

Artist Ally Rosenberg from Prestwich, England, has created sculptures of an old woman from chewing gum and an old man from used teabags. To obtain the raw materials for the model of the old woman, Ally challenged 50 friends to chew 1,000 pieces of gum in two weeks.

ELEPHANT HEDGE

After falling in love with wildlife on a safari in Kenya, Gavin Hogg decided to transform the box hedgerow of his home near Brecon, Wales, into a herd of elephants. Using a trimmer, shears and a pair of scissors, he painstakingly carved out seven adults and three babies in a 100-ft-long (30-m) trail of green elephants.

PRETTY SHED

Artist Sarah Hardacre from Salford, England, knits cozies for trees and has covered an entire garden shed in her knitted squares.

PRINCIPAL'S PORTRAIT

Fifty-five years after being kicked out of school and told he would never amount to much, a successful artist was commissioned to paint a portrait of the principal who expelled him. David Ingham was thrown out of Ermysted's Grammar School, North Yorkshire, England, as a 12-year-old by Marcelus Forster. However, in 2008 he was approached by the school to paint him.

ORNATE HUBCAPS

Ken Marquis of Wilkes-Barre, Pennsylvania, collects art created from car hubcaps. As part of his Landfillart project, artists from 51 countries plus every state in the U.S.A. have sent him their individually decorated hubcaps. Some have painted animals onto their hubcaps, while others have added jewelry, wings and even an hourglass.

TOILET HORROR

A Japanese company has printed a horror story on toilet paper. Drop, a nine-chapter novella by Koji Suzuki, is set in a public restroom and takes up about 3 ft (1 m) of toilet roll. It can be read in just a few minutes.

Art Angel

See if you recognize any favorite toys in this statue made entirely out of plastic playthings. Artist Robert Bradford, who lives in Cornwall, England, collects thousands of discarded toys and uses them to create life-size action figures. "Toy Angel" stands 6 ft 6 in (2 m) tall and took two months to complete. The artist has also modeled a toy soldier of a similar size, as well as buildings and various animals.

Leandro Granato can achieve amazing symmetry and precision when creating a work by squirting paint from his eye.

Eye Opener

Leandro Granato, an artist from Buenos Aries, Argentina, paints pieces of art using only his eye as a paintbrush. First, he puts the paint into his nose, next he forces the paint up through his eye and finally he squirts it onto a canvas. Leandro achieves this by using his nose sinus cavities, which empty into the eye through small vents. When Leandro puts pressure on his nose, the paint can escape into his eye. Leandro is lucky it doesn't take the other possible exit—through his ears!

MASS MARIACHI

Nearly 550 mariachi musicians gathered in the Mexican city of Guadalajara in August 2009 to perform a repertoire of songs. Guadalajara is home to mariachi music, featuring bands of violinists, guitarists and trumpeters, who wear silver-studded outfits and wide-brimmed hats.

HAIRY DOG

In May 2009, London's Royal College of Art unveiled a sculpture by Gareth Williams of a dog created using human hair clippings from his own head and stuck together with used chewing gum.

SHOE TUBS

A collection of bathtubs has been created by Italian designer Massimiliano Della Monaca to look like women's shoes. Water flows from a jet at the heel of the shoe for hair washing, while the plug is located down at the toe end. One of the tubs was styled on a pair of heels worn by the doll Barbie.

CLOSE-KNIT COMMUNITY

Twelve women have spent 23 years knitting a perfect replica of their home village of Mersham in Kent, England. They have created more than 60 woolen properties, including a church, two pubs, a shop, a school, a large manor house and dozens of cottages with gardens full of flowers.

Magic Sticks

A dedicated *Harry Potter* fan has created his own incredibly detailed copy of the child magician's school, Hogwarts, from 602,000 matchsticks. Patrick Acton of Gladbrook, Iowa, spent two years creating the matchstick masterpiece, which is held together by 15 gal (57 l) of glue and rises over 7 ft (2.4 m) tall and 10 ft (3 m) wide. He managed to replicate every minute detail of the fictional school, from the tiny mullioned windows to the chimes on the clock tower.

LONG TRAIN

For her wedding to Zhao Peng in Jilin, China, Lin Rong wore a dress with a train that stretched more than 1.3 mi (2.2 km) behind her. The gown, which cost nearly $6,000 and took guests over three hours to roll out, was the groom's idea. As an added romantic gesture, it had 9,999 red silk roses pinned to it.

BICYCLE SYMPHONY

Argentinean composer Mauricio Kagel wrote a symphony to be played on bicycle bells. His work "Eine Brise" ("A Breeze") is a 90-second outdoor piece, described by the composer as a "fleeting action for III cyclists."

MASSED CHOIR

More than 160,000 people assembled to form a massed choir in India in May 2009. The vast ranks of singers chanted hymns in honor of a Hindu deity in the southern city of Hyderabad.

FRY ART

Ocean City, New Jersey, stages an annual French fry sculpting contest. Competitors take paper plates full of deep-fried potatoes and mash or arrange them together to create oily, high-carbonate models of everything from crabs to log cabins.

Massive Model

Former oil-rig worker David Reynolds from Southampton, England, drew on his experience at sea to build a scale model of a North Sea drilling platform from more than four million matchsticks. David took 15 years to complete his creation, working for up to ten hours a day, on one section at a time. By the time the 21-ft-long (6.4-m) platform was finished, it weighed 2200 lb (1000 kg) and stood 12 ft (3.65 m) high.

Catch of the Day: the everyday items Tom used to make his fish

Nintendo game sleeve
Window screen
Cassette tape
1 broken clothes hanger
Woman's dress shoe
Daughter's piggy bank
Plastic toy
Tote
Decorative ribbon
Tabs from clothing tags
Pieces of plastic from a clothes hamper
Fabric from dress pants
1 brass button
Sequins
3 plastic utensils
8 bottle caps

Milk jug
Pieces of serving platter
Coffee container
Cut plastic cup
Häagen Dazs® ice-cream lid
Ball-point pen cap
Magic marker
Tape glue
Handle to paintbrush
Pen top
Ruler
Film canister
Compact disks
Square stencil sheet
Scrap wood

Screws
Hot melt glue
Rubber raft
Plastic pail
Gutter mesh
Prescription pill container
Children's sneaker
Buttons from clothing factory that went out of business

Trash Trout

Tom Deininger from Boston, Massachusetts, created this beautiful sculpture of a rainbow trout using only items found lying around his house (see list, above). Artist and environmentalist Tom recycled everyday items to make his fish and applied absolutely no resins or paint to the work— the trout is quite simply a product of Tom's trash!

HEAVY METAL

A busker in Cambridge, England, sings and plays his guitar while squeezed inside a small metal trash can. Charlie Cavey discovered his unusual musical venue after watching garbage men emptying the trash. At 5 ft 9 in (1.75 m) tall, he decided he could fit inside it and, although he finds his job cramped, his singing style has proved a complete hit with passersby.

PLASTICINE GARDEN

British TV presenter James May created a garden for the 2009 Chelsea Flower Show—out of plasticine. Flowers, vegetables, bushes, a lawn and even a pond were all made from plasticine, which was supported with wires to prevent it from wilting.

WHALE OF A TIME

Homeowner Nicki Leggett from the town of Whitstable in Kent, England, took three years of careful pruning to shape a garden hedge into the shape of a whale.

FRIENDS MARATHON

TV fan Steve Misiura from London, England, watched every episode of *Friends* in a marathon 84-hour session. He watched all 238 episodes of the hit U.S. sitcom back-to-back for 3½ days, during which he experienced nausea, stomach aches and even hallucinations.

BYRON'S JOKE

English romantic poet Lord Byron (1788–1824) received numerous fan letters from women enclosing locks of their hair—but the hair clippings he sent back for them to swoon over were not from his own head, but from his pet Newfoundland dog.

Yolk Art

Dutch artist Enno de Kroon has come up with a novel way of recycling old egg cartons—he uses them as canvases for his paintings, and sells them for around $1,000 each.

Enno's art studio in Rotterdam, the Netherlands, is full of discarded cardboard egg boxes ready to be painted with vibrant portraits. The lumpy shape of the cartons makes the resulting paintings change shape according to the angle from which you view them. Enno, who is inspired by famous early 20th-century cubist artists, such as Picasso, has dubbed his creations "Eggcubism." The paintings often look best when viewed from a strange angle, not straight on like a regular 2-D painting. Enno's intention is that his egg cartons reveal different faces that appear to follow the viewer around the room.

Enno uses acrylic paints on regular cardboard egg boxes, using the dimpled surface to help give his characters expression.

Enno's unconventional style means that the paintings are distorted when viewed head on.

The face appears only when the egg tray is viewed at a particular angle.

As well as portraits, Enno paints still-life pictures, such as this bowl of fruit, onto his egg cartons.

Tooth Pick Tail

Greg Lewis from Chesterfield, Virginia, creates stunning sculptures from everyday materials that nobody would think of using for art. Named *Hatteras*, this mermaid figure took three years to build and consists of 67,000 toothpicks. Greg has developed a technique that enables him to mold sharp toothpicks into smooth and incredibly lifelike shapes that at first glance appear to be carved from solid wood.

LIVING STATUES

As part of a new artwork designed by artist Antony Gormley, members of the public stood on an empty plinth in London's Trafalgar Square for an hour at a time, 24 hours a day for three months in 2009. Some 2,400 people took turns to occupy the 22-ft-high (6.7-m) plinth. One man dressed as a panda and carried a sign bearing his cell-phone number so that passersby could call him, and another landed a job after displaying a giant copy of his resumé.

SAME ROLE

English actor David Raven played Major Metcalfe in the Agatha Christie stage play *The Mousetrap* for 4,575 performances between July 22, 1957, and November 23, 1968.

SAND ARTIST

Ukrainian artist Kseniya Simonova draws powerful images of World War II in sand. Drawing with her fingers, she uses an illuminated sand table to show how ordinary people in her country were affected by the German invasion.

Fabric Faces

Bela Borsodi can make weird and wonderful faces out of any old clothes. The Austrian-born artist, based in New York, has developed a style of intricate fabric origami, folding leather jackets, jeans, shirts and other items so that they form individual quirky faces.

MODEL TOWN

A romantic English couple have spent 20 years building a 20-ft (6-m) model town based on the area of west London where they first met. Stanley and Christine Buck have constructed their replica of Greenford in the garden shed of their new home in Cambridgeshire. The model has cafés, shops and a cinema—with billboards advertising the movies the couple watched on their first dates in the 1950s.

Crafty Castle

When Wataru Itou became bored during his university entrance exams in 2005, he decided to build a paper city using just paper, a knife and glue. Now a student at Tokyo University of the Arts, Wataru spent four years folding, cutting and sticking hundreds of pages of craft paper together to create this 7.9 x 5.9 ft (2.4 x 1.8 m) masterpiece, which includes a castle, a cathedral, an airport and a theme park. Wataru bizarrely plans to set fire to it eventually!

RECYCLED CREATURES

London Zoo's Recycled Sculpture exhibition featured a polar bear made from plastic bags, a shark from discarded automobile hubcaps and a dinosaur from old tires.

LEGO HOUSE

British TV presenter James May built a full-size LEGO® house—featuring a working toilet, a hot shower and lighting—from 3.3 million plastic bricks. Around 1,000 volunteers helped him build the 20-ft-high (6-m), two-story house in Surrey, England. He even lived in the LEGO® house for a short while.

FASHION RATWALK

For 2009 London Fashion Week, French designer Charlie Le Mindu created a headdress made from dozens of real mice and rat carcasses. The headdress covered the entire face—leaving just a gap for the wearer's eyes—and was adorned with dead rats' tails hanging down the front.

RHYMING TWEETS

Romanian website developer Andrei Gheorghe has created a poem by pairing up random rhyming Twitter posts. The finished piece is more than 350,000 verses long.

Lint Lady

Heidi Hooper, from Massachusetts, uses dryer lint to create images of animals. The lint is taken from the cotton fiber in towels, chenille from throw blankets and feathers from down comforters that have been through the dryer. Unfortunately, the lint cannot be dyed to a specific color, as it is basically dust, so it can be a difficult task creating a color palette. Heidi will sometimes buy towels in the colors she wants to make her work a little easier.

FARM SOUNDS

For his composition "Earth Machine Music," Finnish classical musician Kimmo Pohjonen incorporated the sounds of farm animals and machinery. The noises of cows and sheep, plus the whirring of tractors and milking machines, all feature in the piece, along with more traditional instruments.

Rock 'n' Roll Reel

Music fan Erika Simmons from Atlanta, Georgia, has found a way to re-use all her old cassette tapes, by making them into pieces of art. Using an unspooled cassette reel per piece, Erika has created perfect portraits of music legends such as Jimi Hendrix, Bob Dylan, Jim Morrison, Amy Winehouse and the Stone Roses' Ian Brown. With the works, entitled *Ghosts in the Machine*, Erika encourages the viewer to question if the music is on the cassette tape, in the head of the musician, or perhaps both.

A portrait of Ian Brown, lead singer of the 1980s British band the Stone Roses, created from the unspooled reel of one cassette tape.

VETERAN CARTOONIST

In 2009, Martin Filchock of Williamson County, Tennessee, was still working as a cartoonist at age 97. He was still producing and selling his work in his 75th year of cartooning.

LONG PLAYER

The recording of "You've Lost That Lovin' Feelin'" by The Righteous Brothers has been played so frequently on radio stations across the world that it amounts to the equivalent of more than 45 years of continuous airplay.

DALEK MODEL

Brian Croucher of West Sussex, England, spent more than two years building a full-size model of a Dalek from the British TV science fiction series *Doctor Who*—out of 480,000 matchsticks. The sinister 5-ft-3-in (1.6-m) alien is the latest in a line of Brian's matchstick creations. He has also built a 5-ft-long (1.5-m) boat, a full-size rocking horse and a grandfather clock.

Phonebook Faces

Queral from Philadelphia, Pennsylvania, creates portraits that pop out of the page at you. When he worked with conventional paints, he always tried to give real presence and texture to the faces in his portraits, but in doing so he was using a lot of expensive paint, so he began to look around for a different medium. When the year's new phonebooks started to arrive in the neighborhood, Alex realized that they were like soft blocks of wood, and as there were a lot of spares lying around, he had an idea to use them in place of a regular canvas. He found his first phonebook in a recycling bin and recycled it into art, carving three-dimensional faces into the books rather than building them up with paint.

Trashy Lingerie

Daring designer Ingrid Goldbloom Bloch from Massachusetts fashions stylish and colorful underwear from trash, such as soda cans, and although they might look incredibly uncomfortable, they are put together in an ingenious way. Ingrid is inspired by the beauty of everyday objects and uses various scrap metals in her art. If you look closely at these underpants, you can see that they are made from tiny slivers of cans carefully threaded through a wire frame.

VOLUMINOUS VASE

The Monte Palace Tropical Gardens, near Funchal, Madeira, has a vase that is 17½ ft (5.4 m) tall and weighs 1,225 lb (555 kg). The huge vase was made in South Africa.

TWITTER NOVEL

Unable to find a publisher for his first novel, *The French Revolution*, Matt Stewart of San Francisco, California, put the entire book on the social networking device Twitter—140 characters at a time. It took around 3,700 "tweets" to transmit all of the 480,000 characters in the book.

JUNK MAIL

Free Paper, an art exhibit by Annette Lawrence of Austin, Texas, was created entirely from a year's worth of unsolicited junk mail. She cut the pieces of paper into strips 2 in (5 cm) wide and displayed them in 12 neat stacks.

HAIR WEAR

Ioana Cioanca from Bistrita Nasaud, Romania, has made an entire wardrobe of clothes from her own hair. Now 72, she grew her hair from the age of 16 until it reached a length of 40 in (1 m) and could be woven. She has already turned her hair into a hat, a shawl, a skirt, a blouse, a raincoat, a pair of gloves, a purse and a handbag.

SINGLE HANDED

French composer Maurice Ravel (1875–1937) wrote the "Piano Concerto For The Left Hand" in 1930 for his friend, the Austrian musician Paul Wittgenstein, who lost his right arm during World War I.

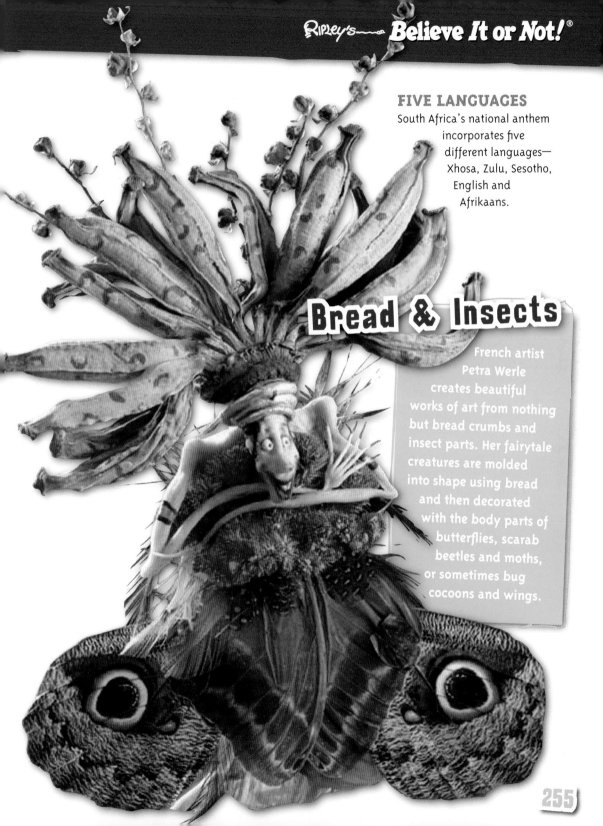

FIVE LANGUAGES
South Africa's national anthem incorporates five different languages—Xhosa, Zulu, Sesotho, English and Afrikaans.

Bread & Insects

French artist Petra Werle creates beautiful works of art from nothing but bread crumbs and insect parts. Her fairytale creatures are molded into shape using bread and then decorated with the body parts of butterflies, scarab beetles and moths, or sometimes bug cocoons and wings.

Mona Easel

The most famous painting in the world, the *Mona Lisa*, is an unmistakable piece of art, but would you recognize her if she were made out of computer parts?

Instead of using traditional paint and watercolors, these resourceful artists have used anything but. From vegetables to Rubik's cubes, these bizarre portraits show Leonardo da Vinci's masterpiece as you have never seen it before.

MONA TOAST
Using 1,426 pieces of toast, Tadahiko Ogawa from Kyoto, Japan, burned slices of bread and scraped them carefully to create the shaded effect of Leonardo da Vinci's masterpiece in 1983.

MOCHA LISA
Made entirely from cups of coffee, this portrait, which measures 20 x 13 ft (6 x 4 m), took three hours to complete, and used 3,604 cups of coffee and 564 pt (267 l) of milk. Displayed on the floor at the Rocks Aroma Festival in Sydney, Australia, in 2009, the portrait has a sepia effect that was cleverly created by pouring varying amounts of milk into each cup.

MONA'S CUBE
Known as Rubikcubism, the "Invader" is a mystery street artist who re-creates famous masterpieces, historic events and celebrities out of Rubik's cubes. This Mona Lisa impression took two days to create. With only six colors to choose from, each of the 800 cubes had to be twisted so that one face showed the correct color to complete the masterpiece.

Tree People

Deep in a natural eucalyptus forest in Victoria, Australia, a sculptor spent 59 years creating more than 90 amazing artworks in the trees. William Ricketts started his incredible project in 1934 and worked on it until his death in 1993, carving mysterious figures that seem to occur naturally in trees and rock, but are actually ceramic sculptures blended into their surroundings. The local authorities eventually protected the land for the public and Ricketts lived in the forest well into his nineties.

Green Piece

Artist Tim Knowles from London, England, has an unlikely assistant—he lets trees do the work for him. With an easel set up under the tree and pens attached to the branches, the paintings take shape of their own accord when the wind blows. According to Knowles, each different species of tree has a distinctive style—hawthorn produces spiky shapes, while the weeping willow makes softer sweeps across the paper.

HIDDEN PIG

The hidden image of a butchered pig in a Dutch artwork was discovered by a U.S. restorer in 2009—350 years after the artwork was painted. *Barn Interior*, a 17th-century painting by Egbert van der Poel, was presented to Calvin College in Michigan in 2007 and the college in turn sent it to Chicago, Illinois, conservator Barry Bauman for cleaning. Bauman noticed that a ladder on the left side of the painting had been heavily painted over and that the paint was flaking. Underneath he found the pig, hanging dead from the ladder.

LEGO CELLO

New York artist Nathan Sawaya has built a life-size working cello from thousands of LEGO® bricks. The cello, made from brown, black and yellow bricks, sounds different to normal cellos, which are usually made from spruce and maple wood.

BACON BOOKMARK

A copy of Len Deighton's World-War-II book *Blood, Tears and Folly* was returned to a library in Worthing, West Sussex, England, with a piece of bacon as a bookmark.

FAMILY TREE

Peggy and Peter Newman from Somerset, England, have spent 25 years and around $150,000 displaying their family tree in a series of amazing 1:12 scale model houses. Each house in the collection, which spans five centuries and 13 generations of relatives dating back to the reign of King Henry VIII, took Mr. Newman six months to carve by hand and is accurate down to the last brick.

Birds on a Feather

An artist in North Wales uses discarded swan feathers as a canvas for his intricate paintings. After collecting the feathers from a local swannery, Ian Davie cleans them and straightens them out with tweezers to make the perfect canvas. He then uses acrylic paint to protect the feathers, painting on fine details with a tiny ooo-size brush. Each work takes about a week to create and can sell for $900.

TOILET BREAK

A website tells movie-goers with weak bladders when is the best time to go to the toilet during a particular film. Runpee.com picks the quiet moments in current movies when you can be absent for up to four minutes without missing much. It can even provide a summary of what you missed on your iPhone.

MASS DANCE

A total of 7,770 people assembled at the Cebu City Sports Center in the Philippines in 2009 for a dancesport class.

RAPID TAPPER

Tap dancer Jo Scanlan of Swindon, England, can perform more than 780 taps in one minute—that's over 13 taps a second!

MOON ROCK

A book published to mark the 40th anniversary of the first Moon landing contained pieces of genuine Moon rock that crashed to Earth as meteorites. Publishers Taschen America produced 1,969 copies of the book—to represent the year of the landing—but only the final 12 contained a piece of rock. Titled *Moonfire*, the tome was based on accounts of the Apollo 11 mission by U.S. writer Norman Mailer. It was signed by Buzz Aldrin, the second man to walk on the Moon, and went on sale for $1,000.

BEAD FLAG

Jeyaraman Ravi, an Indian expatriate living in Abu Dhabi, United Arab Emirates, spent 14 months creating a flag by threading together 288,400 beads. The flag measured 10 x 5 ft (3 x 1.5 m) and weighed 22 lb (10 kg).

HELP YOURSELF

In November 2008, popular London artist Adam Neate left 1,000 pieces of art across the city for people to take for free. Over the years, Neate has scattered more than 6,000 of his works, which are printed on cardboard, around the British capital.

Lemon Crush

Andrew Davidhazy, a high-speed photographer from Rochester, New York City, captured the exact moment a high-powered bullet hit a lemon. Andrew, a professor of imaging and photographic technology at Rochester Institute of Technology, photographed the exploding fruit using a 400-speed film, and a precise burst of light from the electronic flash. The flash lasts just 2 millionths of a second and was perfectly synchronized to the firing of the rifle by an electronic circuit.

Cracking Up

Edgar Mueller's paintings are often the size of a whole street. The artist creates illusions of depth and movement so convincing that viewers feel as if they really could fall into the giant ice crevasse created at East Pier in Dun Laoghaire, Ireland, in 2009. The artist worked with assistants from sunset to sunrise for five days to finish *The Crevasse*, which covered 2,690 sq ft (250 sq m) or about the same size as a tennis court.

Jaw Dropping

Polly van der Glas makes items of jewelry that are embedded with human teeth! She has created a knuckle-duster ring set with four teeth, a sterling-silver single tooth signet ring and a single incisor necklace. The Australian artist, who also collects hair and fingernails, says that most of the teeth she uses are donated by friends and family. The molars are then sterilized before being turned into jaw-dropping jewelry.

ICE FIGURES

In an attempt to draw attention to global warming, Brazilian artist Nele Azevedo carved 1,000 miniature figures out of ice and displayed them on the steps of the Concert Hall in Berlin, Germany, in September 2009. He then watched as they quickly melted in temperatures of 73°F (23°C).

REGENCY TRAIL

In September 2009, more than 400 fans of 19th-century English novelist Jane Austen walked through the streets of Bath, England, wearing Regency period costume.

GREAT TOME

The Great Encyclopedia of Yongle, compiled in China during the Ming Dynasty, took four years to complete (1403–07) and spanned 11,095 books.

TOOTHPICK CITY

For more than four years, Stan Munro of Syracuse, New York State, used over 4 million toothpicks and 45 gal (170 l) of glue to create "Toothpick City II—Temples and Towers," an exhibition featuring toothpick models of some 40 famous buildings from around the world. The landmarks—all created to a precise 1:164 scale—include London's Tower Bridge, the Vatican and a 19-ft-tall (5.8-m) model of the Burj Khalifa tower in Dubai.

PAINFUL MEMENTOS

After splitting up with her boyfriend, artist Olinka Vistica from Zagreb, Croatia, decided to open The Museum of Broken Relationships in Berlin, Germany, to house mementos of breakups. Exhibits include a wedding dress, engagement rings, love letters, a fax, a pair of inline skates, a toy tiger and gall stones. Also on display is an ax used by one woman to break up her ex-girlfriend's furniture, along with the smashed furniture.

BLOOD MONEY

Instead of paying cash, music fans in Poland were able to buy tickets to a 2009 concert by British-Polish duo John Porter and Anita Lipnicka by donating blood.

TOWER HERMIT

In 2009, artist Ansuman Biswas from London, England, lived as a hermit for 40 days and 40 nights in the Gothic tower of Manchester Museum in Manchester, England. Each day he studied one object from the museum's collection of 4.5 million artifacts and posted his thoughts about it on an Internet blog.

BLOOD SAMPLE

A large-format book measuring 20 x 20 in (50 x 50 cm) published by Kraken Opus about Argentinean soccer legend Diego Maradona offered a sample of the player's blood and hair to the first 100 buyers.

VIDEO PROPOSAL

When movie buff Pete Simson wanted to propose to his girlfriend Hannah McDonagh, he hired out a theater in Bristol, England, to screen his own five-minute-long spoof video. Hannah was expecting to see an arty film but instead saw her boyfriend on screen in his underpants miming to Daniel Bedingfield's song "If You're Not The One." At the end of the screening, he got down on one knee and proposed to Hannah to a round of applause. She said yes!

Tiny Dancers

Mexican artist Enrique Ramos will paint on just about anything. He has painted on spider webs, snake skins, vampire bats, grains of rice and, in 2009, he started on cockroaches, ants and crickets, which are called "chopolinas" in his home state. Influenced by the death of Michael Jackson, Ramos created these crickets to show the evolution of the famous singer between 1982 and 2009.

Pulp Art

Two artists from Rapid City, South Dakota, have developed a unique technique that enables them to mold paper into amazing sculptures.

Allen Eckman and his wife Patty create incredibly detailed figures inspired by the old American West. The sculptures are all made entirely from paper, and many stand life-size. Each element of the artworks is molded separately, so the largest pieces can take several months to complete. Ripley's asked Allen how he puts together one of his artworks...

Fancy Dancer, Northern Plains, 4 ft (1.2 m) tall.

"First we sculpture Little Bird—and here you can see the mold complete with hands, ears and eyeballs being extracted. This will now be cast in pulp, dried in the mold and then posed in its final position."

"Here I am adding more finely cut dry, hard paper, which serves as the hair. It is applied in layers in the same way that hair grows."

"After the figure is formed, I add the posed hands. Here I am placing the eyes and ears on the head. Before I add the hair, I will chase and sculpt for smoothness, then clothe the figure."

"The Little Bird at Oak Creek figure finished."

GORILLA HEAD

Scottish artist David Mach created an amazingly lifelike sculpture of a gorilla head— from 30,000 matchsticks. It took him three months to complete the head, which is 15 in (38 cm) high and has flared nostrils and a fierce open mouth, by painstakingly gluing each match onto a mold. He re-creates animals' features and different skin shades by using matchsticks with different colored tips. His works, which have also included grizzly bears and rhinos, sell for up to $50,000.

GIANT ACCORDION

Italian Giancarlo Francenella built an accordion more than 8 ft (2.5 m) high and weighing about 440 lb (200 kg). It has 45 treble keys and took 1,000 hours to make.

PHOTO MOSAIC

In June 2009, a giant photo mosaic that measured 175 x 125 ft (53 x 38 m) and covered an area of 21,875 sq ft (2,030 sq m) was unveiled in the Philippines. Printed on tarpaulin, the mosaic was made up of more than 1,000 photographs taken by artist Revoli Cortez of Filipine president Gloria Macapagal-Arroyo.

REVERSE GRAFFITI

A British street artist known as Moose has pioneered a new art form called "reverse graffiti." He uses scrapers, pressure washers and scrub brushes to create clean designs in dirt-covered canvasses, such as tunnel walls and city sidewalks.

HEAVY ALBUM

In Orlando, Florida, Dodge created a photo album that measured 9 x 12 ft (2.7 x 3.6 m). Produced to celebrate the launch of the 2008 Dodge Grand Caravan, the album featured 20 pages of photographs tracing the history of the Dodge minivan and was so heavy that it required at least two adults to turn each page.

Master of Light and Shade

Artist Benjamin Shine in London, England, created this portrait of Dutch master Rembrandt van Rijn using just one piece of black tulle fabric measuring 26 x 10 ft (8 x 3 m). Benjamin used a technique of intricate pleating and pressing of the material, and took more than 200 hours to achieve the final result. Rembrandt, known as the master of light and shade, was a perfect subject for Benjamin as he, too, displayed varying tones of light and shade in his portrait through the tulle fabric.

Buffalo-gum

Using only chewed bubblegum, Maurizio Savini creates beautiful sculptures such as this pink life-size buffalo made from thousands of pieces of gum. Since "American Gum" arrived in his home country, Italy, Maurizio has been creating various pieces of edible art using the colorful gums. His works, such as his collection of suited businessmen suspended in gymnastic poses, have sold all over the world for as much as $65,000 each.

SISTINE STITCH

Canadian Joanna Lopianowski-Roberts from San Francisco, California, has created an accurate version of Michelangelo's Sistine Chapel ceiling using simple cross-stitch. Measuring 40 x 80 in (1 x 2 m), the project took Joanna a total of 3,572 hours, working for more than one hour a day for eight years.

GHOSTLY GALLERY

Green-Wood cemetery in Brooklyn, New York City, has a collection of art painted by some of the 600,000 people buried there. Works on display include an 1820s portrait of politician DeWitt Clinton by George Catlin, both of whom are buried at Green-Wood.

PAPER DRESS

In September 2009, a woman got married in Kunming, Yunnan Province, China, wearing a dress made entirely out of paper. Designer Zhu Zhu took two and a half months to make the cotton paper dress for the bride, her best friend Sha Sha.

TRAIN WUNDERLAND

Since 2000, twin brothers Frederick and Gerrit Braun from Hamburg, Germany, have been building a model train set that has more than 6 mi (10 km) of track. Built from 4 tons of steel, their "Wunderland" has over 160,000 model people, 700 locomotives, 10,000 carriages and wagons, 2,800 buildings, 900 signals and three-quarters of a ton of artificial grass. It has six regions, including the U.S.A. and the Alps—featuring models of the Grand Canyon, Las Vegas, Mount Rushmore and a 20-ft-high (6-m) replica of the Matterhorn mountain.

OVERDUE BOOK

A man returned a book to a library in Derby, England, 46 years after he had borrowed it. David Hall took out the book *Engineering Workshop Practice* for his father in 1963. In the intervening years it had built up a fine of nearly $4,000, but the penalty was waived.

FLOOR LICK

Korean-born artist Hoon Lee staged an exhibit at the Bemis Center for Contemporary Arts in Nebraska that consisted of him licking yellow cake frosting off a floor area of 2,500 sq ft (230 sq m).

IMITATION OF LIFE

New York artist Alyssa Monks creates amazingly detailed paintings that look just like photographs. She takes about 1,000 photos—usually of people she knows—for a small series of paintings, using the images to play with the color and make the result look as realistic as possible. She employs no tricks, just intricate brushwork, and for a painting of a woman in a shower, she even re-created the steam effect and the droplets of water by hand.

Creating a Buzz

Belgian photographer Nicholas Hendrickx has been creating a buzz in the art world with his wacky pictures of flies. Inspired by the sight of a fly landing on a flower in his garden, he decided to employ live insects as photographic models in his shots. With his bedroom as a studio, Hendrickx uses tiny props to photograph flies apparently playing musical instruments, riding bikes or relaxing on a beach. "It took quite some time," he admits. "Some flies were great to work with, while others were very frustrating. I guess it's normal—flies and humans aren't made to work together. Flies are made to annoy us with their buzzing and pooping on stuff."

JUMBO JEANS

In June 2009, workers in Zagreb, Croatia, created a pair of jeans the size of six tennis courts. Stitched together from 8,023 pairs of jeans that had been donated for charity, the giant denims boast a leg length of 150 ft (45 m) and a total width of 110 ft (34 m).

PIANO MAN

Colin Huggins takes his full-size upright piano to the parks, street corners and even subway stations of New York City—to play music for fun. The crazy piano guy, as he is known, amazes commuters by transporting his 250-lb (115-kg) piano down to subway platforms in the elevator.

CREMATION CREATIONS

Val Thompson from Tyne and Wear, England, paints beautiful works of art using the ashes of loved ones her clients have lost. By mixing the cremated remains with paint, she not only acquires additional texture on the canvas but is also able to create a unique, personalized and lasting tribute.

PAINTED EGG

In 2009, the Romanian city of Suceava unveiled a huge glass-fiber decorated Easter egg that stood 23 ft 8 in (7.25 m) tall, had a diameter of 15 ft (4.6 m) and weighed 1.8 tons.

JACKSON GLOVE

A bejewelled white glove worn by Michael Jackson the first time he performed the moonwalk, in 1983, sold at auction for $350,000.

ORIGAMI GIRAFFE

Himanshu Agrawal of Mumbai, India, spent 12 hours folding a sheet of paper 35 x 35 ft (10.6 x 10.6 m) into the shape of a 20-ft-high (6-m) origami giraffe. The giraffe, designed by American origamist John Montroll, required more than 100 moves and 70 creases in the paper, and the finished article was mounted on a bamboo structure.

HOTEL DISPLAY

In January 2009, a British couple visiting New York City were put on display to passersby in a mocked-up hotel room. In return for a complimentary stay at Manhattan's Roger Smith Hotel, Duncan Malcolm and Katherine Lewis agreed to occupy a replica of one of the hotel's rooms on the ground floor of a nearby building, where for three hours every afternoon for five days, they kept the curtains on the room's large glass windows open so that thousands of pedestrians and motorists could watch their every move.

WHITTLED CHAIN

Skilled wood-carver John Selvey of Port Orange, Florida, has created a chain made from 10,034 hand-carved wooden links that measures an impressive 407 ft (124 m) long. John spent 825 consecutive days carving his chain from 2-ft-long (60-cm) pieces of wood.

"THRILLER" STEPS

To mark what would have been Michael Jackson's 51st birthday, on August 29, 2009, more than 12,000 people gathered in Mexico City to retrace the dance steps from his 1983 video "Thriller."

FINGER PAINTS

In August 2009, 6,000 children in Belfast, Northern Ireland, used finger paints to decorate a 22,496-sq-ft (2,090-sq-m) canvas with the picture of a house.

WOOLY BRAIN

Psychiatrist Dr. Karen Norberg of the National Bureau of Economic Research in Cambridge, Massachusetts, spent a year knitting an anatomically correct replica of the human brain. The two sides of the 9-in (23-cm) woolen brain—one-and-a-half times life size—are joined together by a zipper and Karen used different colors of wool to represent the various areas of the complex organ. She said that using wool rather than clay helped her achieve the desired "rippling" effect of certain parts of the brain.

SHOCK WAVES

As part of his show "Let There Be More Light," London, England, artist Paul Fryer designed a pair of two, fully functioning, 16-ft-high (5-m), aluminum tuning forks, which, vibrating at 72 Hertz, sent shock waves through visitors' bodies.

MULTI-TALENTED

Kim Noble from London, England, paints in the style of as many as 20 different people. She suffers from a rare personality disorder called Dissociative Identity Disorder (DID), as a result of which 20 people live inside her, ranging from an anorexic teenager called Judy to a man named Ken. Many of her personalities paint and each has its own individual style of painting. In just two years, Kim's personalities produced more than 200 canvasses.

Toilet Paper People

French artist Junior Fritz Jacquet uses a particularly unglamorous object for his work—cardboard tubes from the inside of toilet paper rolls. Inspired by the traditional Japanese paper-folding art of origami, Junior molds and folds the 4-in (10-cm) tubes into characters that each display distinctive facial expressions. He then colors the masks with different paints before selling the pieces for around 60 euros each.

275

Extreme

ENDEAVORS

World Beater

Aged just 17, Mike Perham from Hertfordshire, England, completed a single-handed, round-the-world sailing voyage in August 2009.

The intrepid teenager set off from Portsmouth, England, in November 2008—then aged only 16—on board a hi-tech 50-ft (15-m) racing yacht hired especially for the challenge.

The circumnavigation took Mike down the west coast of Africa and south of Australia, where damage to the yacht's rudder forced him to wait for repairs before setting off into the treacherous Southern Ocean. Here, the boat battled through freezing seas and 50-ft (15-m) swells. Fifty-knot (57-mph) winds knocked the boat flat to the waves before the heavy keel

pulled it upright. Mike was forced to climb the 70-ft (21-m) mast in the middle of the ocean to fix rigging in the knockdown, and had to dive under the boat to cut free snagged ropes. The yacht then sailed up the coast of South America and through the Panama Canal before the final leg of the journey took Mike across the Atlantic, landing at Portsmouth in August: nine months and 24,233 mi (39,000 km) later. The light, hi-speed racing yacht was cramped, noisy and uncomfortable, making it very hard to get rest. Mike slept for about five hours out of every 24, snatching 20-minute naps while the boat was kept on course by an electronic autopilot. With nobody else on deck, there was a danger of colliding with vessels at night and ramming surface hazards such as shipping containers and marine debris. Mike was harnessed to the boat at all times in case he was swept overboard.

At home in his cabin—containing bunk, galley, supplies and navigation equipment—Mike catches up on studying for his driving test.

The boat rode ocean waves the size of five-story buildings.

When Mike and his boat were in South Africa for repairs, he met 75-year-old Japanese sailor Minoru Saito, who was in the middle of his eighth circumnavigation of the globe. During his lifetime, Minoru has sailed almost 310,685 mi (500,000 km), the equivalent of sailing to the Moon.

Mike lets off flares to celebrate his return to England after nine months at sea.

Walking in the Air

In August 2009, aged just eight years old, Tiger Brewer from London, England, stood on the top of a biplane flown by his grandfather at 100 mph (160 km/h). His wing-walking feat took place at a height of 1,000 ft (304 m) above Rendcomb airfield in Gloucestershire, England, and followed a family tradition—Tiger's grandfather, Vic Norman, manages SuperAeroBatics, the world's only formation wing-walking team.

LOBSTER ROLL

Using 48 lb (22 kg) of lobster meat and 4 gal (15 l) of Miracle Whip, the city of Portland, Maine, in June 2009 baked a lobster roll that measured 61 ft 9 in (18.8 m) long.

MASS ASCENT

In 2009, a total of 326 hot-air balloons took to the skies simultaneously at the Lorraine Mondial Air Balloons rally in eastern France.

REAL GLOBETROTTER

Marques Haynes of the Harlem Globetrotters played basketball for more than 50 years, making his final appearance in 1997 when he was in his early seventies! He played more than 12,000 games in 97 countries, traveling more than four million miles (that's about 160 times around the world). He learned his famously fantastic dribbling skills from his sisters and could dribble the ball six times a second, his hand just a few inches above the floor.

SPEARGUN

In March 2009, Emerson de Oliveira Abreu of Brazil accidentally shot himself in the head with a speargun. Despite the spear going 6 in (15 cm) into his skull, he survived.

WORM CHARMERS

Ten-year-old Sophie Smith of Cheshire, England, coaxed 567 worms up from the ground in 30 minutes to win Britain's 2009 World Worm Charming Championships. Techniques used to encourage worms to the surface included a man playing the xylophone with bottles and a woman who tap-danced to the theme from *Star Wars*.

BOOK TOWER

In June 2009, John Evans of Derbyshire, England, balanced 204 books on his head in a pyramid-shaped tower that was 4 ft (1.2 m) high and weighed 284 lb (129 kg). The contents of a can of hairspray were used to stop the books from slipping off his head.

Balloon Burst!

Jemal Tkeshelashvili from Georgia in the former Soviet Union is able to inflate a hot-water bottle extremely quickly until it bursts, using only his nose. He is so fast that he managed to burst one of the bottles in only 13 seconds at an unusual contest in Tbilisi, Georgia. Jemel also competes as a strongman, and can pull a Boeing Airliner with just his bare hands.

GENETIC MIRACLE

In a genetic phenomenon that is at least a one in 500,000 chance, a British couple have given birth to their second set of twins where one daughter is white and the other black. In 2001, when Dean Durrant and Alison Spooner from Hampshire, England, were told they were having twins, they were stunned to discover that one daughter, Lauren, took after her mother with blue eyes and red hair, while her sister Hayleigh resembled her father who is of West Indian origin. Then, in 2008, history repeated itself when Leah was born white like her mother and her twin sister, Miya, had her father's darker skin.

GOLF MARATHON

Tom Bucci of Latham, New York, played 1,801 holes of golf in a week at the Albany Country Club in June 2009. Despite losing 75 minutes to a thunderstorm, Bucci played 15 rounds (270 holes) every day, averaging 90 strokes per round, including 32 birdies and his first-ever hole-in-one.

FAT REMOVAL

A half-ton teenager from Houston, Texas, had 70 lb (32 kg) of fat cut off in an operation. Billy Robbins, who at his heaviest weighed 840 lb (380 kg), underwent the radical procedure to prevent his heart from giving out.

EMERGENCY LANDING

A small airplane bound for Santa Barbara Airport, California, was hit by three cars after making an emergency landing on a nearby highway. The Piper PA-24 Comanche, with two people on board, touched down a mile from the airport on U.S. Highway 101 after running out of fuel. Although nine people were involved in the accident, nobody was hurt.

ENORMOUS ECLAIR

In February 2009, the Swallow Bakery of Chichester, West Sussex in England, made a chocolate eclair that was nearly 12 ft (3.6 m) long. The monster eclair contained 2.2 lb (1 kg) of chocolate and 8 pt (3.8 l) of double cream. It took bakers Lou Allen and Michaela Heard four hours to construct the pastry, followed by another hour filling it with cream before spreading the chocolate on top.

ARCTIC MARATHON

Wearing only shorts and a pair of sandals, Dutchman Wim Hof completed a 2009 marathon in sub-zero temperatures 200 mi (322 km) north of the Arctic Circle. His body was exposed to temperatures of -13°F (-25°C) as he finished the 26-mi (42-km) trek in 5 hours 25 minutes.

PAPER BALL

To illustrate the importance of recycling and the enormity of waste, Enrique Miramontes and Ricardo Granados—two friends from San Diego, California—spent more than six years creating a giant ball of discarded paper that weighs 200 lb (91 kg) and is 3 ft (1 m) high. In that time Miramontes alone has spent over $3,000 on masking tape and over 2,000 hours layering the pieces of paper on top of each other. He had the idea as a 16-year-old high school student when a friend threw a rolled up ball of paper at him in biology class.

MASS CRUNCH

More than 39,000 baseball fans ate potato chips simultaneously in the middle of the second inning of a game between the New York Mets and the Cincinnati Reds at Citi Field, New York, in July 2009.

NEEDLE REMOVED
Doctors in China removed a syringe needle from 55-year-old Lao Du 31 years after another doctor had broken it off in his butt cheek.

MASS KISS
On Valentine's Day 2009, nearly 40,000 people (20,000 couples) gathered in Mexico City's main square and kissed for ten seconds.

ELVIS WARDROBE
Vince Everett of London, England, owned more than 3,000 items of Elvis Presley memorabilia, including 14 of Elvis' jackets.

Dart Wall

German 13-year-old Maiko Kiesewetter scaled a 16-ft (5-m) high wall using regular-sized playing darts in his hometown of Hamburg in November 2009.

BLIND BOXER

Bashir Ramathan of Kampala, Uganda, has been blind for over a decade but has recently resumed his career as a professional boxer.

HOME RUN

From 1943 to 1955, the University of Kentucky basketball team had an unbroken 129 home game winning streak.

Splash Landing

After his incredible shallow-water plunges were featured in *Ripley's Believe It or Not! Prepare to be Shocked*, daredevil diver Darren Taylor, also known as Professor Splash, from Colorado has now dropped into just 12 in (30 cm) of water from an even greater height of 35 ft 9 in (10.9 m), emerging soaked, but unharmed. Although his "bellyflop" technique might look painful, by stretching as he falls, Professor Splash reduces the impact on his body when he hits the water.

History Hot Spot

Robert Powell was the most famous of the early fire-eaters. He performed in London in the 18th century, charging a shilling for entry to his shows, at which he would eat hot coals and melted sealing wax, and lick a naked flame with his tongue. He also used to take a large bunch of matches, light them and hold them in his mouth until the flame was extinguished, and he sometimes filled his mouth with red-hot charcoal.

Playing with Fire

Both fire-breathing and fire-eating carry major risks—simply inhaling while swallowing fire can lead to a severely burned mouth and even death. These methods each require different skills. A fire-breather uses his or her mouth to spray a flammable liquid over an open flame, creating a large, spectacular ball of fire from the mouth. A fire-eater places flaming objects into the mouth and extinguishes them.

A Close Shave

In late-1930s U.S.A., Dr. Mayfield, a popular fire manipulator, came to the forefront of the fire-performing world when he appeared at Ripley's Odditoriums. His act involved shaving himself with a "blazing blowtorch" before putting the torch into his mouth and extinguishing it.

BUSY DAY

On August 4, 1982, Texan-born outfielder Joel Youngblood got hits for two different Major League baseball teams in two different cities on the same day. In the afternoon he played for the New York Mets at Wrigley Field, Chicago, Illinois, against the Chicago Cubs. Then, after he had been traded, he appeared in a night game for the Montreal Expos in Philadelphia, Pennsylvania.

HUMAN WHEELBARROWS

In Singapore in April 2009, no fewer than 1,378 students from Temasek Polytechnic took part in a mass human wheelbarrow race. At the same event, students formed an unbroken human wheelbarrow chain comprising 74 people.

SOLAR FLIGHT

The Cardozo family from Wiltshire, England, traveled 1,242 mi (2,000 km) from Monte Carlo to Morocco in an electric paramotor (a motorized paraglider) powered by the sun. The paramotor worked using lithium polymer batteries, which were charged in rotation using 12 solar panels on top of a support vehicle. The family's journey across the Mediterranean took 15 days and they traveled at altitudes of up to 5,000 ft (1,500 m).

PIZZA DELIVERY

In November 2004, Lucy Clough from Sussex, England, hand-delivered a pizza from London to Melbourne, Australia—a journey of 30 hours and a distance of 10,532 mi (16,950 km).

BLOOD LOSS

Named after a French neurologist, "Cotard delusion" is a rare mental disorder in which a person believes he or she is either dead, does not exist, is putrefying or has somehow mislaid his or her blood and internal organs.

Spiderman

Jyothi Raj has incredible climbing abilities whereby he is seemingly able to glue himself to walls without any harnesses or assistance, and even manages to hang upside down using only his feet!

Jyothi, a construction worker from Karnataka, India, spends his days climbing up and down building sites usually on bamboo scaffolding, which can be very dangerous. He started practicing free climbing every day until he was able to cling to the walls, using just his hands, at 90-degree angles and even upside down. He claims he has never used safety equipment to climb and isn't afraid of falling. Every Sunday, Jyothi comes to the famous fort at Chitradurga to entertain his fans. Reaching heights of up to 300 ft (90 m), Jyothi has scaled every wall possible at the fort and is ready to move on to bigger buildings and mountains. Claiming he hasn't had an accident in four years, his ultimate goal is to be like Alain Robert, the famous French free climber known as the "Human Spider," who has climbed many of the world's tallest structures, some of them over 650 ft (200 m) high.

Jyothi Raj believes he was given the gift of climbing and is happy to teach his skills to anyone who wants to learn, provided they use harnesses.

WHEELY ODD

Many times world beard champion Elmar Weisser of Baden, Germany, has styled his long beard into designs of Berlin's Brandenburg Gate, London's Tower Bridge and a bicycle. It takes up to five hours to style his beard for each competition.

Eye-catching

Yang Guanghe has a painstaking talent for using his eyelids to move heavy objects. In 2009, in Guangzhou, China, he dragged a car using ropes attached to his lower eyelids.

MAGIC MINK

In 2008, 73-year-old Ken Mink made the basketball team at Roane State Community College in Harriman, Tennessee—52 years after his last college game. The veteran even made two free throws as King College's B team were beaten 93—42.

CADDIE TREK

In July 2009, Billy Foster, the caddie for English golfer Lee Westwood, walked the 88 mi (142 km) from the Scottish Open tournament at Loch Lomond to the following week's British Open at Turnberry.

MINCE DISH

The town of Ehden, Lebanon, produced a giant circular kibbeh—a dish of minced meat and cracked wheat—covering an area of 215 sq ft (20 sq m). The dish required 265 lb (120 kg) of mince, 21 gal (80 l) of olive oil, 175 lb (80 kg) of cracked wheat, 11 lb (5 kg) of salt and 2 lb (1 kg) of pepper.

CALAMARI KING

Patrick Bertoletti of Chicago, Illinois, ate 6 lb 10 oz (3 kg) of deep-fried calamari in ten minutes at Mallie's Sports Grill World Calamari Eating Championship, held in Southgate, Michigan, in May 2009.

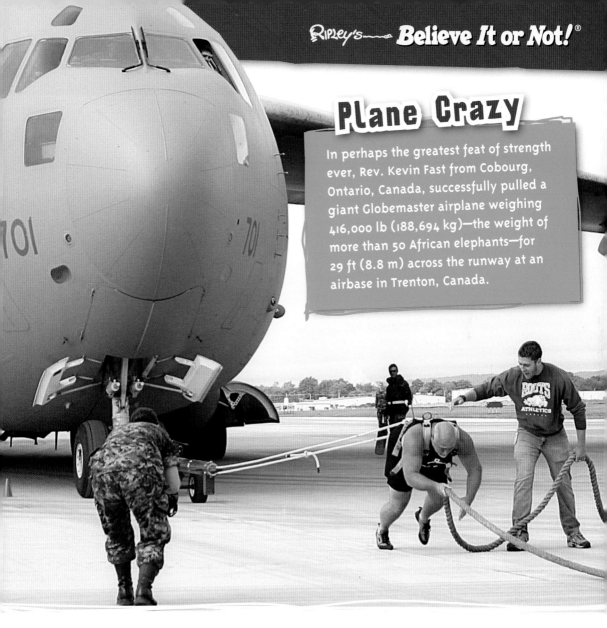

Plane Crazy

In perhaps the greatest feat of strength ever, Rev. Kevin Fast from Cobourg, Ontario, Canada, successfully pulled a giant Globemaster airplane weighing 416,000 lb (188,694 kg)—the weight of more than 50 African elephants—for 29 ft (8.8 m) across the runway at an airbase in Trenton, Canada.

TOILET LINE

In an event organized by the United Nations' children's agency UNICEF to raise awareness for the need for clean water, 756 people lined up to visit a toilet in Brussels, Belgium, in March 2009.

GOAL RUSH

During a 2008 Olympic pre-qualifying tournament, the Slovakian women's ice-hockey team defeated Bulgaria 82 goals to 0, scoring at the rate of more than one goal a minute.

ROPE TRICK

Damian Cooksey of East Bay, California, landed a frontflip on a 1-in-thick (2.5-cm) slackline—a rope that is not taut. In 2007, in Munich, Germany, he walked 506 ft (154 m) on a slackline without falling off.

RICH CAKE

In July 2009, 170 Palestinian bakers from ten pastry shops in Nablus on the West Bank created a giant syrupy Kunafa cheesecake that measured 243 ft (74 m) long, weighed 3,883 lb (1,765 kg) and was big enough to feed more than 100,000 people. The bakers used 1,540 lb (700 kg) of semolina flour, the same amount of cheese and 660 lb (300 kg) of sugar to produce the cake at a cost of around $15,000.

Living the High Life

Heinz Zak is not your ordinary thrill-seeker or adrenaline junkie. Although he risks his life on a regular basis hundreds of feet up in the air, Heinz says that he performs such perilous feats to achieve a state of inner peace and tranquillity. "Highlining" is an extreme form of "Slacklining," which involves a strip of nylon 1 in (2.5 cm) thick strung relatively loosely high above wild terrain or water. This means that the line flexes and even bounces, making the sport different from traditional tightrope walking. Intense focus allows Heinz to walk calmly across the line. Since the 1980s, he has traveled the world searching for the perfect place to practice his death-defying feats.

PET AIRWAYS

The maiden flight of an airline service that caters solely to pets took off from Farmingdale, New York, in July 2009. With Florida-based Pet Airways, founded by Alysa Binder and Dan Wiesel, pets travel in the airline's main cabin, but owners are not allowed onboard—even in the cargo hold. The company was founded in 2005 and the couple spent the next four years replacing seats with pet carriers in their fleet of five planes. Up to 50 animals at a time are escorted to the airplane by pet attendants, who give the animals a "potty break" just before takeoff and check on them every 15 minutes during the flight. At each of the five U.S. airports it serves, the company has even created a Pet Lounge for its animal passengers—or "pawsengers" as it calls them— where they can wait and sniff before flights.

AROUND BRITAIN

Starting and finishing in London, English comedian Eddie Izzard ran 1,105 mi (1,778 km) around Britain from July 26 to September 15, 2009— the equivalent of running 43 marathons in 51 days.

Bride to Bee

When Li Wenhua and Yan Hongxia, workers at Nanhu forestry commission in Ning'an, China, decided to tie the knot, they made sure they invited some of their coworkers—in the form of tens of thousands of honeybees. A carefully placed queen bee attracted the entire swarm, forming living-insect material for an alternative pair of wedding outfits. The number of people stung at the wedding is unknown.

STEAM POWER

A steam car reached an average speed of 139.8 mph (225 km/h) on two runs over a distance of a mile at the Edwards Air Force Base, California, in August 2009—the fastest speed recorded by a steam car in 103 years! The 25-ft-long (7.6-m) British-built car, driven by Charles Burnett III, reached 151 mph (243 km/h) on its second run and has been dubbed "the fastest kettle in the world."

CLEVER GIRL

Born in 2006, Karina Oakley of Surrey, England, had an IQ of 160 at just two years old—the same as eminent scientist Stephen Hawking and Microsoft chairman Bill Gates. Karina, whose IQ is 60 points above the British average, was asked to complete a 45-minute test in several different categories, including verbal ability, memory, numbers and shapes.

UNEXPECTED PASSENGER

A delivery man driving a small van near Peddie, Eastern Cape, South Africa, in May 2009 collided with a bull and had to drive around 9 mi (14 km) to a local police station—with the animal still wedged in the vehicle's roof rack.

CHAMP CHESTNUT

Joey Chestnut of San Jose, California, swallowed 68 hot dogs in ten minutes to capture his third straight Fourth of July hot-dog eating contest at Coney Island in 2009. His winning technique is to grab two hot dogs at a time, force them into his mouth and, with a minimal number of chews, gulp them down. He then dips the buns in water and simply lets them slide down his throat.

NONAGENARIAN SKYDIVER

In April 2009, George Moyse of Dorset, England, went skydiving for the first time—at age 97. Strapped to an instructor, he jumped out of an airplane at 10,000 ft (3,048 m) above Salisbury Plain, Wiltshire, and carried out a free fall for the first 5,000 ft (1,525 m) at speeds of nearly 120 mph (193 km/h).

STILETTO SPRINT

At a race in Nanning, Guangxi Province, China, all the runners wear high heels—both men and women! Male runners must wear shoes with heels at least 3 in (8 cm) high, while women have to run in 4-in (10-cm) stilettos because they are more used to wearing high heels.

SAUSAGE SUPPER

In 2009, cooks from Vinkovci, Croatia, used a 8-ft (2.5-m) pan to prepare a sausage that was 1,740 ft (530 m) long and fed around 3,000 people. The sausage was made with 880 lb (400 kg) of pork (from 28 pigs), 88 lb (40 kg) of paprika, 22 lb (10 kg) of salt, 11 lb (5 kg) of garlic and 5 lb 8 oz (2.5 kg) of spices.

BRIDGE FLIP

Australian motorcycle stunt rider Robbie Maddison performed a no-handed backflip while jumping the 25-ft (7.6-m) gap between the raised spans of London's Tower Bridge in July 2009. He raced up one side of the raised bridge, flew through the air 100 ft (30 m) above the water and made the backflip before landing on the south side of the bridge.

CYCLING TOUR

Over a period of nine years, Keiichi Iwasaki from Maebashi, Japan, has cycled more than 28,000 mi (45,000 km) through 37 countries. He originally set out on his Raleigh Shopper bicycle in 2001 to tour Japan, but enjoyed himself so much that he caught a ferry to South Korea and has not returned home since.

Wild Roller

Extreme inline skater Dirk Auer from Germany reached incredible speeds of more than 180 mph (290 km/h) while being dragged behind a high-powered motorbike at a racetrack in Germany. Dirk has also skated on the roof of an airborne plane and down a roller coaster.

PADDED BRA

Brazilian Ivonete Pereira's life was saved in April 2009 when a robber's bullet struck a wad of cash hidden in her bra. The 58-year-old had stuffed the bills in her bra because robbery had become rife in her local area.

PIE FIGHT

More than 250 people turned up to take part in a mass custard-pie fight at Colchester, Essex, England, in 2009. Around 650 pies—filled with 53 gal (200 l) of custard—were thrown during the battle.

ONE-ARMED PLAYER

Despite being born without a right hand and forearm, Poland's Natalia Partyka competes in table tennis competitions for able-bodied athletes and even represented her country at the 2008 Beijing Olympics.

PANCAKE BLAST

With their pancake-in-a-can product, workers from the Batter Blaster company made an amazing 76,382 pancakes in eight hours at Atlanta, Georgia, in May 2009. The team used more than 30 grills on the challenge.

GLASS CHIN

While shaving in 2009, Thomas Entwistle from Bolton, Greater Manchester, England, discovered a piece of glass from a Ford Cortina windshield embedded in his chin— 30 years after the accident that put it there.

IRON MAN

Japanese athlete Keizo Yamada, known as the "Iron Man," ran three marathons in 2009—at 81 years of age. He finished the Tokyo marathon in 5 hours 34 minutes 50 seconds and kept fit by jogging 12 mi (20 km) every day.

MELON SMASH

At the 2009 Chinchilla Melon Festival, held in Queensland, Australia, local melon picker John Allwood smashed 47 watermelons with his head in one minute.

TURKEY TREAT

A farm in Devon, England, created a roast dinner consisting of a huge turkey stuffed with 11 smaller birds— a goose, a chicken, a pheasant and eight young ducks. Weighing 56 lb (25 kg), the True Love Roast was big enough to feed 125 people.

ECO TRAVELERS

Eco-friendly Tom Fewins and Lara Lockwood of Oxfordshire, England, traveled more than 44,000 mi (70,800 km) around the world in 297 days—without once boarding an airplane. They made their way through 19 countries—including Russia, China and the U.S.A., using 78 buses, 61 trains, 34 cars, 18 boats, 6 bicycles, 2 mopeds and 1 elephant. They say they each generated fewer than 6,600 lb (3,000 kg) of carbon dioxide on their journey, one-third of the amount they would have generated if they had traveled by airplane.

CHESS MASTER

In February 2009, over a period of 14 hours, Bulgarian grandmaster Kiril Georgiev played 360 games of chess simultaneously. He won 284 games, drew 70 and lost only six.

MISSING TRACK

Driving his train along the track in Hungary's Somogy County, Farkas Kolos suddenly realized that the track ahead had completely disappeared. He slammed on the brakes and managed to bring the train to a halt just short of where the track ended. Police confirmed that 2 mi (3.2 km) of track had been stolen.

HUMBLE COLLECTORS

Herb and Dorothy Vogel have amassed a world-class art collection comprising nearly 5,000 pieces—on ordinary working-class salaries. A postal worker and librarian respectively, they live in a one-bedroom Manhattan apartment, but their collection, which is worth millions of dollars, is so important that it was accepted as a gift by the National Gallery of Art in Washington, D.C.

LONG NOTE

Vocal coach, songwriter and music producer Richard Fink IV of Bergen, New York State, held a single vocal music note for a breathtaking 1 minute 43 seconds in September 2009. He prepared for the challenge by doing regular yoga exercises and extra running.

DEFYING GRAVITY

Bryan Berg of Spirit Lake, Iowa, created a gravity-defying sculpture of London landmarks Big Ben tower and the Houses of Parliament, without using any glue or sticky tape, from more than 600 decks of playing cards. It took him more than five days to complete the structure that stood 12 x 7 ft (3.6 x 2.1 m) in Las Vegas, Nevada.

Heat Seeker

As unusual hobbies go, it's a dangerous choice. Keith Malcolm from Aberdeen, Scotland, dresses in several layers of flame-retardant clothing before he's doused in gasoline and set alight like a human torch. He then runs as far as he can before the flames overwhelm him and firefighters put him out. In 2009, Malcolm sped 259 ft (79 m) for charity.

In 2008, Chayne Hultgren swallowed 27 swords at once, more than anyone had ever swallowed before.

Space Cowboy

Chayne "Space Cowboy" Hultgren, a street performer from Australia, is one of the most extreme sword swallowers around. He has swallowed a sword with a 49-lb (22.4-kg) weight suspended from it, and was the first man to swallow a sword underwater—in a tank full of live sharks. Chayne was born with an internal deformation of his digestive system so his stomach sits unusually low. This means that the Space Cowboy can swallow the entire length of a 28½-in (72-cm) sword blade— a blade longer than any other swallower can manage—so that it reaches an inch (2.5 cm) below his belly button. To conquer the extra long sword, Chayne can rearrange his internal organs, elongate his body and change the shape of his stomach.

X-ray photographs were taken as Chayne Hultgren swallowed a sword, proving beyond a doubt that there is no illusion involved. He also hammered a 5-in (12.7-cm) nail into his nose at the same time—this is also clearly visible on the X ray.

Ripley's Sword Frights

Sword swallowers have performed at Ripley museums since 1933, when the very first "Odditorium" opened at the Chicago World's Fair. In 1939, Ripley performer Edna Price swallowed electrified neon tubes, and was believed by Robert Ripley to be the first woman to do so, and other entertainers wowed the crowds with their death-defying blade guzzling.

John "Lucky" Ball learned sword swallowing at the age of 12, becoming one of the most accomplished sword swallowers of his generation. He is pictured here swallowing a corkscrew at a Ripley's Odditorium, a feat more dangerous than a straight sword. "Lucky" Ball could swallow more swords than anyone else at the time, and on one occasion he downed 16.

Edna Price, seen here swallowing neon tubes, came from a sword-swallowing family. Her Aunt Maude died in 1920 after swallowing a sword for the King and Queen of England. Edna would swallow up to 12 practice swords at the same time, removing the blades one at a time. She would have her swords chromed each year to protect against nicks and scratches.

Alex Linton was originally from Ireland. His father was also a sword swallower. At the climax of his act, Linton would throw his final sword into a block of wood on the stage to make sure the audience knew it was real, and sharp!

Joseph Grendol swallowed seven swords simultaneously at the Chicago Odditorium in 1934. He could also swallow watches, golf balls and coins before regurgitating them. Probably his greatest stunt was placing a bayonet on the butt of a rifle, swallowing the bayonet up to the rifle butt, and then shooting the rifle!

Water Home

Cem Karabay, a diver from Turkey, spent five and a half days nonstop living underwater. Surviving on meals put together by an expert nutritionist, and lots of liquids, he managed to eat, sleep, drink and exercise in his tank measuring 16 x 10 x 10 ft (5 x 3 x 3 m), located outside a shopping mall in Istanbul. His diving teacher, Namik Ekin, had previously lived underwater for 124 hours, but Cem's impressive 135 hours and 2 minutes beat his time. After almost a week underwater, Cem had high blood pressure and an eye infection, but he emerged with a greater desire to go back—the next time for ten days!

PIZZA LINE

In May 2009, Scott Van Duzer and nine other cooks prepared more than 1,800 pizzas to form a pizza line measuring 1,777 ft (540 m) around an entire city block in Fort Pierce, Florida. It took 1,250 lb (570 kg) of flour, 600 lb (270 kg) of mozzarella cheese, 70 gallons (265 l) of tomato sauce and 400 tables to form the line.

TOILET LANDING

A pilot escaped unhurt in May 2009 when his small airplane's crash landing was cushioned by a pile of portable toilets. After taking off from an airfield near Tacoma, Washington State, the Cessna 182's engine failed at a height of about 160 ft (50 m). As it dropped from the sky, it hit a fence, flipped over and landed upside down on top of portable toilets stacked in a storage yard.

CHURCH AVOIDANCE

A seven-year-old boy trying to avoid going to church on a Sunday morning took his father's car for a drive around Plain City, Utah. Police officers chased the boy at speeds of 40 mph (65 km/h) before he stopped in a driveway.

Keel Walk

SNAKE WOMAN

In 2009, surgeons in China removed a tumor from a woman's leg that weighed three times more than she did. The non-cancerous growth started out as a birthmark on the body of Wang Houju from Linxi, Shandong Province, but steadily wrapped itself around her leg and up to her waist, earning her the name of "Snake Woman." Eventually, it weighed more than 220 lb (100 kg), whereas the rest of her body tipped the scales at just 70 lb (32 kg).

DOWNHILL SKIER

Austrian Alpine skier Balthasar Egger traveled approximately 232 mi (374 km) downhill on skis in 24 hours at Heiligenblut, Austria, in March 2009.

FACE TRANSPLANT

Surgeons replaced 80 percent of the face of Connie Culp from Unionport, Ohio, in a 2008 operation, using the bone, muscles, nerves, skin and blood vessels of another person. It was the world's most extensive face transplant surgery ever.

English sailor Alex Thomson decided that he wanted to see the sea from a different angle, so he clambered out onto the keel of his 60-ft (18-m) racing yacht when it was fully keeled over and sailing hard off the south coast of England. The experienced ocean racer, who braved the waves in a smart suit provided by his sponsor, said that it was "pretty dangerous but a real buzz."

Man vs Beast

Spanish bull-leapers in Valencia (known as "recortadores") carry on a tradition that goes back to 1500 BC. They face a bull as it charges and, at precisely the right moment, jump over the speeding horns—toes pointed, arms aloft. Spectators watch as the competitors somersault, twirl and twist through the air, for up to four hours at a time, at every moment risking death or serious injury. The bull always remains unharmed.

INSECT DIET

A mountain hiker survived five days after a bad fall on a mountain by eating centipedes, ants and even a poisonous wolf spider. Derek Mamoyac from Philomath, Oregon, was descending 12,300-ft (3,750-m) Mount Adams in Washington State in October 2008 when he fell and broke his ankle. Despite his injury, he continued his descent by crawling or, if that became too painful, shuffling on his backside. When his food supplies ran out, he ate insects to keep up his strength.

MOVING HEART

When April Pinkard's doctor examined her to treat a rare medical condition, he couldn't find her heartbeat—because her heart had moved to the other side of her chest, occupying an empty space where a damaged lung had once been. Her heart kept floating around her body until April from Live Oak, Florida, was finally given breast implants to keep it in place.

TREE PLANTERS

On a single day in July 2009, a team of 300 volunteers planted more than half a million mangrove trees in the Indus River delta region of Sindh province, in southern Pakistan.

DELAYED DEATH

Fifty-four-year-old Craig Buford of Fort Worth, Texas, died on December 29, 2008, from complications of a gunshot wound he had sustained 35 years earlier.

UNDERSEA MAIL

In 2009, a Norwegian mayor sent a letter to an English town through a 725-mi (1,166-km) underwater gas pipeline running beneath the North Sea. Bernard Riksfjord, mayor of Aukra in western Norway, dropped the letter into the Langeled pipeline on August 19, 2009, and five days later the letter, propelled forward by pressurized gas, popped out in the town of Easington, County Durham.

DREAM DRIVE

Graham and Eirene Naismith of London, England, sold their house, gave away their furniture and spent ten months driving 31,116 mi (50,076 km) all the way to Australia and then around the entire circumference of the country— with three children under eight. Driving a Toyota Land Cruiser, the family traveled through 19 countries and crossed three continents.

GROUP SHOWER

One hundred and fifty strangers in swimsuits showered together in a specially constructed 40,000-sq-ft (3,716-sq-m) structure at Gurnee, Illinois, in 2009. The huge shower, designed to hold around 600 people elbow to elbow, had 40 shower nozzles and took 7½ hours to build.

SPEED VIOLINIST

Nikolai Rimsky-Korsakov's famous violin piece "Flight of the Bumblebee" normally takes 80 seconds to play, but German violinist David Garrett can play it in just 66 seconds, averaging more than 13 notes per second.

SCREAM COMPILATION

In 2009, New York City artist LeRoy Stevens compiled an album of musical screams. He spent six months visiting every record store in Manhattan asking workers to nominate their favorite musical scream. The result—"Favorite Recorded Screams"—is a three-and-a-half-minute compilation of 74 howls, screeches, grunts and yells from songs by such artists as the Who, Slayer, the Pixies and Björk.

BASKETBALL SPIN

Cheshire Jets basketball team from Chester, England, gathered more than 100 people to spin basketballs on their fingers simultaneously in July 2009.

REVERSE WALK

In 2008, Bill Kathan of Vernon, Vermont, walked backward from one rim of the Grand Canyon, down to the basin and back up the other side in 15 hours.

CENTENARY JUMP

Peggy McAlpine from Stirling, Scotland, celebrated her 100th birthday, in October 2007, by paragliding from the top of a mountain range in Cyprus. Peggy, who is partially sighted and has lived through the reign of five British monarchs and more than 25 prime ministers, leaped from a 2,500-ft (760-m) peak in northern Cyprus for a 15-minute tandem flight.

TIMELY TWINS

Twins Tarrance (born 11.51 p.m., December 31, 2008) and Tariq (born 12.17 a.m., January 1, 2009) Griffin of Pontiac, Michigan, were born fewer than 30 minutes apart but on different days and in different months and years!

STRAIT CROSSING

Ben Morrison-Jack and James Weight kite-surfed across the Bass Strait in September 2009 from Tasmania to mainland Australia—a distance of 155 mi (250 km).

HAIR RAISING

A bullet fired at the head of Briana Bonds of Kansas City, Missouri, in February 2009 was caught in her tightly woven hair weave. The wig saved her life and amazingly she escaped unharmed.

CAN CONSTRUCTION

A structure built from more than 54,500 cans of food was unveiled in Wellington, New Zealand, in 2009. The work occupied around 3,875 sq ft (360 sq m) of the city's Civic Square and took more than 24 hours to assemble. The cans were then distributed to needy local families.

LONG SERVICE

At age 95, Angelo Cammarata retired following more than 75 years as a bartender at his family's café in Pittsburgh, Pennsylvania. He served his first drink as a 19-year-old just minutes after Prohibition ended in 1933 and, except for a 30-month break during World War II, he tended the bar right up until 2009.

SEOUL SINGER

A South Korean housewife sang nonstop for more than 76 hours at a karaoke bar in Seoul in February 2009. Kim Sun-Ok sang a total of 1,283 tunes over a three-day period before finally giving up because her family was concerned about her health.

OBAMA SKETCH

George Vlosich III from Lakewood, Ohio, has drawn an incredibly detailed picture of Barack Obama (complete with the presidential seal), Abraham Lincoln, and the Stars and Stripes—on an Etch A Sketch®. It took him 80 hours to draw using the toy's two dials—all in one unbroken line. He has previously created Etch A Sketch® portraits of such superstars as The Beatles, Tiger Woods, Will Smith, Elvis Presley and boxing legend Muhammad Ali.

YOUNG ARTIST

Kieron Williamson of Norfolk, England, had an exhibition of watercolor landscape paintings displayed at a Cambridgeshire gallery in August 2009—even though he was just six years old. Remarkably, he had not drawn a thing until he was five.

Bed Rock

A 1980s' invention allows mountain climbers with particularly strong nerves to sleep thousands of feet up vertical cliff faces. The Portaledge is a small portable tent, suspended by only ropes and fabric attached to temporary anchor points jammed in rock cracks. The tents look perilous but are reported to be surprisingly stable; some climbers even take the risk of lighting gas stoves inside to cook food and melt snow. It is recommended that Portaledge occupants remain harnessed to the cliff face when asleep, in case they have a habit of falling out of bed.

HAIR LINE

Over 30,000 women and more than 100 long-haired men from Myanmar donated their hair to pay for repairs to a road leading to the remote Buddhist pagoda of Alaungdaw Kathapha. Nearly 1,750 lb (800 kg) of hair was collected, with some locks measuring up to 4 ft (1.2 m) long. The hair was then sold to traders in China for use in wigs or dolls, while the money raised improved access on the pagoda road.

AGED TORTOISE

Jonathan, a tortoise living on St. Helena Island, is estimated to be over 176 years old. The earliest photo of him, standing beside a Boer War prisoner, dates back more than 100 years.

Strong Sandow

Eugene Sandow, real name Friedrich Muller, was born in 1867 in Konigsberg, Prussia. He was the first popular male strongman. Performing mostly in circuses and sideshows, he was famous for his bulging muscles and for breaking chains around his chest until his death in 1925. He notoriously wore a skimpy costume.

Unbeaten Beauty

Sandwina was known as "The Strongest and Most Beautiful Woman in the World." She would bend rods and straighten horseshoes to the delight of large audiences who saw her perform with the Ringling Bros. and Barnum & Bailey Circus in the early 20th century. She was born Katie Brumbach, one of 14 children, and performed with her parents Philippe and Johanna Brumbach. Her father would offer 100 marks to any man who could defeat her in wrestling—no one ever won the prize! Sandwina defeated the strongman Eugene Sandow (left) by lifting a 300-lb (135-kg) weight over her head—Sandow managed only to lift it to his chest. It was after beating Sandow that Katie adopted her stage name, "Sandwina."

BEARD DAY

To mark the 200th anniversary of the birth of evolutionary biologist Charles Darwin, who was born on February 12, 1809, England's Bristol Zoo allowed free admission on February 12, 2009, to anyone sporting a beard—real or fake.

Man of Strength

Chad Netherland is a black-belt martial artist who performs all kinds of daredevil feats.

In 2009, in one strike, Chad destroyed sixteen 75-lb (34-kg) blocks of ice that were 6 in (15 cm) thick, right, breaking a total of 1,200 lb (544 kg) of ice—enough for a group of adults to stand on. Chad, from Myrtle Beach, South Carolina, learned everything he does from his father, who was also a world-class martial-arts expert. He has smashed 50 blocks of ice in 19 seconds live on television and stopped two light aircraft from taking off for over a minute with only his arms. In 2003, he laid on a bed of 12-in (30-cm) nails, left, while concrete blocks weighing 848 lb (385 kg) were smashed with a sledgehammer on his chest!

Chad suffered no ill effects after being pinned to a bed of 12-in (30-cm) nails by 848 lb (385 kg) of concrete until each block was smashed with a sledgehammer on Sixth Avenue, New York.

Giant Leap for Mankind

Who was the first man in space? Believe it or not, it was not an astronaut, it was test pilot Joe Kittinger. In 1960, he was assigned to discover whether an astronaut could survive an aborted mission, even 20 mi (32 km) above the Earth. Kittinger rose to 102,800 ft (31,330 m) by balloon, and then jumped out. He was so high that initially he felt no wind resistance. He fell for 4 minutes 36 seconds, reaching a maximum speed of 614 mph (988 km/h), before opening his parachute at 18,000 ft (5,500 m).

BIG APPETITE

A former basketball player-turned-street-performer, Zhao Liang, from China's Henan province, stands nearly 8 ft 1 in (2.45 m) tall—and feeds his enormous appetite with a dinner of eight burger-sized steamed buns and three plates of food.

VARIED JOURNEY

Edwin Shackleton, an 82-year-old retired aircraft engineer from Bristol, England, traveled on 100 types of transport in just over six months. He started on New Year's Day 2009 with a car journey and clocked up number 100 in July 2009 in a hot-air balloon. On his way to his century, he traveled in such diverse modes of transport as a microlight, a fire truck, a garbage truck, a rickshaw, a police car, a chairlift, a quad bike and a sled.

MICHIGAN SWIM

By completing a 26-hour, 34-mi (55-km) swim across Lake Michigan in 2009, Paula Stephanson of Belleville, Ontario, Canada, became only the second person to swim across all five Great Lakes. Her first Great Lake swim was across Lake Ontario in 1996 at age 17.

YOUNG CLIMBER

Six-year-old Tom Fryers from England has already climbed 214 peaks in England's Lake District—the equivalent of climbing five Mount Everests. Tom scaled his first peak when he was just three and has since covered 480 mi (772 km) and climbed more than 150,000 ft (45,720 m), including the two highest mountains in England—3,209-ft (978-m) Scafell Pike and 3,162-ft (964-m) Sca Fell.

POLICE BALL

A 267-lb (120-kg) matzo ball was unveiled on the streets of New York City in August 2009. Baked by Noah's Ark Original Deli, it was 3 ft (1 m) high and made from 1,000 eggs, 80 lb (36 kg) of margarine, 200 lb (90 kg) of matzo meal and 20 lb (9 kg) of chicken base. The ball was transported in a 24-ft (7-m) freightliner with a police escort.

HISTORIC FLIGHT

In 2009, to mark the centenary of French inventor and pilot Louis Bleriot becoming the first person to fly an airplane across the English Channel, another Frenchman, Edmond Salis, repeated the 22-mi (35-km) crossing in a restored Bleriot XI—the same model used by his predecessor on that 1909 flight.

Totem Teeth

Strongman Al Fraser from New York is seen in this photograph, taken in 1939, lifting three tables and a chair, all stacked on top of one another and weighing a total of 150 lb (68 kg), with his mouth and teeth.

Don't Look Down

This picture is the right way up! In the skies over Illinois in 2009, a fearless group of 108 daredevils jumped from a plane at 18,000 ft (5,486 m), reaching speeds of 180 mph (290 km/h) as they plummeted head first toward the ground in tight formation. After 40 seconds of individual free fall, the jumpers made the risky mid-flight maneuvers required to get themselves into position, and held on tight, completing the formation only a few seconds before breaking apart for landing.

DEXTROUS FEET

Forty-nine-year-old Jana Blazova of Presov, Slovakia, learned to use her feet to write and embroider despite being paralyzed by cerebral palsy in childhood.

HAVING A BALL

Rikki Cunningham played billiards nonstop for 72 hours in Greensboro, North Carolina, in August 2009. During that time, he competed against 80 different opponents.

SOLO TEAM

Bob Holmes of Rumney, New Hampshire, has played almost 17,000 volleyball games as a one-man team—and has beaten police departments, professional sports teams and a team consisting of more than 1,000 people. He has faced over 400,000 opposing players in that time, but has suffered fewer than 400 defeats.

REPEAT OFFENDER

A man in Boynton Beach, Florida, received more than 50 traffic citations from police in one day on February 5, 2009.

FEMALE FORMATION

Jumping from nine planes at a height of 17,000 ft (5,180 m), 181 female skydivers from 31 countries joined together in formation above Perris, California, in September 2009.

PANCAKE STACK

Sean McGinlay and Natalie King of the Hilton Grosvenor Hotel, Glasgow, Scotland, took 22 hours to build a pancake stack that stood 29 in (75 cm) high. The tower of 672 pancakes used 100 eggs, more than 17 pt (8 l) of milk, 11 lb (5 kg) of flour and 6 lb (3 kg) of butter.

LATE FLIGHT

On May 6, 2009, Lillian Gardiner of St. Marys, Ontario, Canada, took her first ever plane ride—at the age of 105.

GREAT CATCH

Fishing on Lake Minnetonka, Minnesota, in 2008, Jeff Kolodzinski caught 1,680 fish in 24 hours.

Eccentric

TALES

Lava Junky

Patrick Koster will do anything to get a good picture—even sleep on the edge of an active volcano!

Lava from Kilauea pouring into Pacific Ocean, Big Island, Hawaii. The lava can explode on contact with the sea, throwing lava unpredictably into the air. Another danger here is the appearance of plumes of toxic gas, which contain hydrochloric acid, volcanic ash and needle-sharp lava pieces.

The Dutch engineer began photographing natural phenomena over ten years ago. He became obsessed with capturing the violent power of volcanoes, calling himself a "Lava Junky," and even proposing to his wife next to a simmering crater.

To get the best shots, Koster risks inhaling toxic gas, suffocation from hot ash and lethal volcanic bombs—lumps of molten rock violently ejected from erupting volcanoes, not to mention the unstoppable flow of super-hot lava surging past his camera. Despite the dangers, Koster wears regular clothing, with only a gas mask for protection from noxious gas. He has photographed volcanoes on the Canary Islands, and in Ethiopia, Italy, Greece and Hawaii among others, and has a long list of other lava-spewing craters he intends to visit.

Patrick standing on the edge of a lava fountain on the most active volcano on Earth, Kilauea, Big Island, Hawaii. The molten lava here is over 2,012 °F (1,100 °C).

At this burning lava lake in the crater of active volcano Erta Ale, the surface is constantly moving and bubbling, spewing potentially lethal sulphur dioxide gas. The surrounding terrain is rough and crumbling, meaning Patrick has to watch his footing very carefully to avoid falling in to the lava lake.

Scissor Spider

Security guards at American airports confiscate hundreds of scissors and other potential weapons every day. Artist Christopher Locke collects these spiky tools and bends them into sculptures, including spiders made from twisted scissors and creepy crawlies made from knives and multi-tools.

BIRD LOVER

A male traveler arriving at Los Angeles International Airport, California, in 2009 was found to have 14 live birds strapped to his legs under his pants. Customs officials became suspicious after spotting bird feathers and droppings on his socks, and tail feathers protruding beneath his pants.

LATE DEMAND

A German mathematician, who had been dead for 450 years, received a letter in 2009 demanding that he pay long-overdue TV license fees. The bill was sent to the last home address of algebra expert Adam Ries, even though he had died in 1559—centuries before the invention of television.

CLONED MOUSE

Japanese scientists have created clones of a mouse that had been frozen for 16 years. The same method of extracting brain cells and injecting their nuclei into female egg cells could be used to bring back extinct animals such as the wooly mammoth or the sabre-toothed tiger.

ROTTEN STENCH

In May 2009, rotten food in a refrigerator released odors so vile that hundreds of people were evacuated from a building in San José, California, and seven others were sent to the hospital. One of the few people who didn't need treatment was the office worker who was cleaning out the fridge at the time—suffering from allergies, luckily she couldn't smell a thing.

ELDERLY MOM

In November 2008, Rajo Devi from the state of Haryana, India, gave birth to a healthy baby at 70 years of age.

MODERN CANNIBALS

The journalist Paul Raffaele reported in 2006 that he had discovered a modern headhunter tribe on the island of New Guinea that still removed the heads of their enemies and cannibalized their remains, and they have the skulls to prove it.

BOTTLE VOYAGE

A bottle with a note inside thrown into the ocean in 1969 off the coast of New Jersey was discovered 39 years later—just 400 mi (645 km) away in Corolla, North Carolina.

Silk Cocoon

A motorist returned to his car in Rotterdam, the Netherlands, in 2009 to find it buried beneath a giant silk cocoon created by an army of caterpillars. His Honda car had somehow been mistaken for food by spindle ermine larvae, which weave silk webs to protect themselves from birds and wasps, allowing them to gorge on leaves for six weeks before finally transforming into butterflies.

CUCUMBER THEFTS

In 2009, police in Adelaide, Australia, investigated a series of thefts involving cucumbers. More than $8,500 worth of cucumbers were stolen in 11 separate burglaries on market gardens over a period of three months.

CASH CATCH

Two Australian teenagers who went on a fishing trip to Tuntable Creek, near Nimbin, New South Wales, in September 2009 landed a surprise catch—a plastic package containing $87,000 in cash.

TASTY ORGANS

A restaurant in Tokyo, Japan, serves up sushi body parts hidden inside an edible human "corpse." The corpse, which has a dough "skin" and "blood" sauce, is wheeled into the restaurant on a hospital gurney and placed on a table. The hostess begins by cutting into the "body" with a scalpel, after which the patrons also dig in, opening up the flesh to reveal edible "organs" made of sushi.

Sumo Cyst

A Chinese woman thought she was pregnant with her first child, only to find that she was instead carrying an ovarian cyst weighing 7 lb 11 oz (3.5 kg). Surgeons at a hospital in Haikou successfully removed the cyst—the largest ovarian cyst found in over 20 years.

PIGEON SERVICE

A carrier pigeon in South Africa proved faster at delivering data than broadband Internet. The pigeon took 1 hour 8 minutes to fly the 50 mi (80 km) from Pietermaritzburg to Durban with a data card strapped to its leg—and including download, the transfer took just over two hours. In that time only four percent of the data had been transferred using the South Africa's leading Internet service provider.

STRETCHED LEGS

In an attempt to be taken more seriously at work, Hajnal Ban, a politician from Logan, Queensland, Australia, paid a Russian surgeon $30,000 to break her legs and stretch them so that she would be 5 ft 4 in (1.62 m) tall, three inches taller than her original height.

FLIGHTLESS LADYBUG

By disrupting the insect's gene for wing development, researchers at Nagoya University, Japan, have produced a wingless ladybug. Although ladybugs have been employed as eco-friendly pest killers for years, farmers had previously been unable to stop them from flying away.

Giant Grave

After 990-lb (450-kg) José Luis Garza died in Juarez, Mexico, in 2008, carpenters built him a special extra-large coffin, which had to be lowered into a massive grave by 20 people.

MARATHON MARRIAGE

Rachel Pitt and Garry Keates of Hertfordshire, England, got married while running the 2009 London marathon. They took a detour 24 mi (38.6 km) into the race to jog down the aisle of St. Bride's church, on Fleet Street. Still wearing running shoes, they later completed the remaining 2¼ mi (3.5 km) hand-in-hand before the groom carried his new bride over the finish line as she threw her bouquet into the crowd.

WINNING TICKET

Two months after her husband Donald's death, Charlotte Peters of Danbury, Connecticut, checked through his belongings and found a $10 million winning lottery ticket. He had bought the ticket just hours before suffering a fatal heart attack in November 2008.

BOXED CLEVER

A prisoner escaped from jail in Willich, Germany, in November 2008 by hiding in a box that was part of a courier's shipment.

HIDING PLACE

Two-year-old Natalie Jasmer from Greenville, Pennsylvania, did such a good job of hiding during a 2009 game of hide-and-seek that her family had to call police and firefighters to help find her. After an hour's search, she was finally found by the family dog, having fallen asleep in a drawer beneath the washing machine.

MOON CHECK

A $10.50 check signed by Neil Armstrong hours before he took off for the Moon was sold for $27,350 at an auction in Amherst, New Hampshire, in July 2009—40 years to the day after it was written. Armstrong had written the check—for money borrowed from a NASA manager—in case anything happened to him during the lunar mission.

GRATEFUL THIEF

An Italian thief thanked police for rescuing him from a group of irate Korean tourists whom he had just robbed. The thief had stolen a handbag from the family during their visit to Rome, but they gave chase and floored him with taekwondo moves, before subjecting him to a beating. They stopped only when an officer arrived to arrest the 48-year-old man.

DEATH EATERS

The ancient Greek historian Herodotus wrote of a nomadic tribe in Iran that killed and ate members of their community when they became old and weak, cooking them with their cattle. According to his writings, this was the way that they preferred to go.

SNAIL MAIL

In July 2009, Wendy Bosworth from Wolverhampton, West Midlands, England, received a postcard sent from a Greek island—22 years after it had been mailed. The card had been posted by her niece, Joanne Bosworth, who was holidaying on the island of Nisyros in 1987.

EMOTIONAL ROBOT

Scientists at Waseda University in Japan have developed a robot that can express seven different human emotions. The Emotional Humanoid Robot, named Kobian, uses motors to move its lips, eyelids and eyebrows into various positions and can also strike a range of poses to back up its expressions. To show delight, Kobian puts its hands over its head and opens its mouth and eyes wide; to express sadness, it hunches over, hangs its head and holds a hand up to its lowered face.

BROKEN LEG

After suffering decades of pain, Steve Webb from Essex, England, discovered he had been walking around with a broken leg for 29 years. He broke his left leg in a motorbike crash when he was 20 and in 2009 found that it had never actually healed.

SAME NAME

Kelly Hildebrandt, a student from Miami, Florida, announced her engagement in 2009 to... Kelly Hildebrandt. Bored one evening, she had entered her name on the social networking website Facebook to see what would appear and found one match—a Kelly Hildebrandt from Lubbock, Texas. She sent him a message, they became friends and after visiting her in Florida, he proposed.

EXPENSIVE TASTE

Gennaro Pelliccia, a London-based Italian coffee taster with more than 18 years of experience, has had his tongue insured for nearly $14 million. His job is to test every batch of raw beans before they leave the firm's roastery and he is banned from eating curry within two days of tasting sessions in case the spices dull his sensitivity.

A Game of Squash

Austrian artist Willi Dorner is causing a stir across Europe by squeezing bodies into nooks and crannies across the continent. Groups of dancers, climbers and performers, wearing brightly colored clothes, run through busy malls and high streets and suddenly cram themselves into doorways, trees and any gap they can find.

CLOSE RELATIVES

After not seeing each other for 60 years, long-lost siblings George Culwick and Lucy Heenan discovered in 2008 that they had been living just 4 mi (6.5 km) apart in Birmingham, West Midlands, England.

GARLIC BALLS

American First Lady Eleanor Roosevelt used to eat three chocolate-covered garlic balls every morning. They were prescribed by her doctor to improve her memory.

GRAVE DISCOVERY

In March 2009, while planting bushes, Sheila Woods of Devon, England, uncovered a grave, complete with headstone, coffin and corpse from 1833, in the middle of her garden.

BEETLE TERROR

In December 2008, police in Osaka, Japan, arrested a man for releasing thousands of beetle larvae onto an express train to scare female passengers.

ZERO GRAVITY

A couple from Brooklyn, New York, proved they were head over heels in love during their wedding by getting married in zero gravity. Science fiction fans Noah Fulmor and Erin Finnegan paid over $15,000 to have their wedding at Kennedy Space Center in a converted Boeing 727 jet airplane which, in the course of a special 90-minute flight, undertakes spectacular roller-coaster-style dives, which simulates the weightlessness experienced by astronauts on space walks. As they floated on air, the couple exchanged rings made from precious metal fragments of a meteorite that crashed to Earth in Namibia 30,000 years ago.

Family Whiskers

Dhanna Ram of Rajasthan, India, has been growing his mustache since 1988—and by 2009 it measured 4½ ft (1.4 m) long. He was inspired by the death of his father, Karna Ram Bheel, who himself had a mustache that measured a whopping 6½ ft (2 m) long!

Ram Raid

A ram in Helgoysund, Norway, was stranded 15 ft (4.5 m) up a telegraph pole for an hour after it tried to abseil down an electricity cable to reach a field of ewes. The lovelorn sheep slid down the cable from a higher field with his horn stuck on the wire, before stopping against the pole. Eventually a group of German tourists managed to loop a rope around the sheep and lower it to the ground.

CHILI GRENADES

To control rioters and fight insurgents, Indian security forces have been conducting trials using hand grenades that contain red-hot chili powder. The grenades use Bhut Jolokia chilis, which are 200 times hotter than the average jalapeño, to choke rioters' respiratory tracts and cause their eyes to water.

BILLION FROGS

Up to one billion frogs are eaten by people around the world each year.

CHILD'S PLAY

Three-year-old Pipi Quinlan from Auckland, New Zealand, visited an online auction site in 2009 and bought a mechanical shovel for $12,000 while her parents were asleep.

BOTTLE VOYAGE

A message in a bottle thrown from a cruise ship by a U.S. teenager in the Bahamas in 2004 was found five years later on a beach in Cornwall, England—4,000 mi (6,440 km) away. The message had been written by Daniel Knopp of Baltimore, Maryland.

Traveling Twins

Chang and Eng Bunker (1811–74) were the original Siamese twins, the rare condition being named after their birthplace of Siam (modern-day Thailand). They were joined at the stomach by a small piece of cartilage and were later exhibited as a curiosity. They went on to marry two sisters and had a total of 21 children. In 1874, Chang suffered a stroke in his sleep and when Eng awoke to find his brother dead, he refused to be separated from him and bled to death three hours later, because the blood was not being pumped back from his twin's body.

FAKE FISH

A shoal of 5-ft-long (1.5-m) robot fish have been built that are fitted with tiny chemical sensors so that they can detect pollutants in the water. Developed by the University of Essex in England and modeled on carp, the robot fish cost around $30,000 each to make and are designed to be lifelike in appearance and swimming behavior so as not to alarm real fish. They can swim at about 3 ft (1 m) per second and run on batteries that are recharged every eight hours.

STEEL VELCRO

German scientists have developed a steel version of Velcro that is strong enough to support buildings. Using the same hook-and-loop fastening system as Velcro, Metaklett can bear loads of around 3.6 tons per sq ft (35 tonnes per sq m) at temperatures as high as 1,472°F (800°C).

FALLING FISH

Leighann Niles was driving near Marblehead, Ohio, in August 2009 when her car windshield was smashed by a falling fish dropped from the talons of an eagle. She said the impact of the fish—a Lake Erie freshwater drum—felt like a brick hitting her car.

LAWN RANGER

Stan Hardwick of North Yorkshire, England, owns a lawn mower for every day of the year. Known as the Lawn Ranger, he has spent thousands of dollars on more than 365 mowers, some dating back to the mid-19th century. He keeps his favorites in the house for visitors to admire, and stores the rest in his garden shed.

BLUE DOTS

Headhunters of Borneo would mark one finger joint with a blue dot for each victim they had killed. Chief Temonggong Koh had completely blue hands by the time of his death in the late 20th century.

DOLPHIN GAMES

A woman who had been playing with a friendly bottlenose dolphin called Moko in the sea off Mahia Beach on New Zealand's North Island got into difficulty when the dolphin stopped her from returning to shore. Her cries for help eventually alerted rescuers who rowed out to find her exhausted and cold, clinging to a buoy. Locals say the dolphin gets lonely in the winter when there are fewer people around and just wanted to keep playing.

CASH FIND

While walking to his car in Syracuse, New York, in 2009, David Jenks noticed a number of bags apparently containing trash lying by the side of the street—but when he went to move them he discovered that they were filled with $250,000 in banknotes.

DELAYED DELIVERY

Dave Conn of Hudson, Ohio, received a postcard in his mailbox 47 years after it was sent. The card had been sent by a woman from Helena, Montana, in 1962, but the delay meant it never reached its intended recipient, who had died in 1988.

SWALLOWED PHONE

When Andrew Cheatle lost his cell phone on a beach at Worthing, West Sussex, England, he thought it had been swept out to sea and that he would never see it again, but a week later it turned up—in the belly of a huge cod. The 25-lb (11-kg) cod had been caught by fisherman Glen Kerley, who was gutting it for his fish stall when he found the phone—which still worked—inside the fish's stomach.

FROZEN FEAST

For the last 15 years of his life, eccentric U.S. movie producer Howard Hughes (1905—76) existed almost solely on a diet of ice cream. He usually ate the same flavor until all his local suppliers had run out.

SPRAY WATCH

To deter attackers, Serge Cotaina of France invented a wristwatch that can release a burst of pepper spray. A small cartridge hidden inside the watch's housing emits the spray from the side of the timepiece.

DOUBLE LIFE

Two women who worked at the same factory in Zhengzhou, China, were shocked to learn they were both married to the same man. Cui Bin divided his time between the two households, making excuses for his frequent absences.

Meanwhile, the two wives had become friends through a shared love of karaoke, never dreaming that they were also sharing a husband.

Claws Encounter

Inspired by *Edward Scissorhands*, Valentino LoSauro has developed fingertip scissors, which are made from elastic and razor-sharp steel. They cut hair twice as fast as hand-held scissors, claims LoSauro, a pianist, who wanted to apply the light-finger touch of piano playing to styling hair. "When I cut hair I use methods I call 'Flight of the Bumblebee,' " he says, referring to the quick-finger action he now uses at his Florida salon. "I can't believe how long a cut used to take."

STRAY BULLET

In July 2009, Janifer Bliss was accidentally shot while sitting on the toilet, when the person in the next-door cubicle dropped their gun and it went off. Bliss was sitting in the cubicle in a hotel bathroom in Tampa, Florida, when she was hit in the leg by the stray bullet, which was fired as the handgun fell to the ground.

DOUBLE MONEY

In August 2009, customers flocked to a faulty cash machine that was paying out double money at a supermarket in London, England. The store closed the machine as soon as it learned of the fault, but by then lucky customers had taken over $7,500 from it.

BODY BOMBS

Newly discovered species of marine worms use bioluminescent "bombs" to distract attackers. The worms, which live on the floor of the Pacific Ocean more than 1.8 mi (3 km) beneath the surface, cast off green glowing body parts when disturbed. Scientists from the University of California, San Diego, who made the find, say the worms are able to regenerate the body parts.

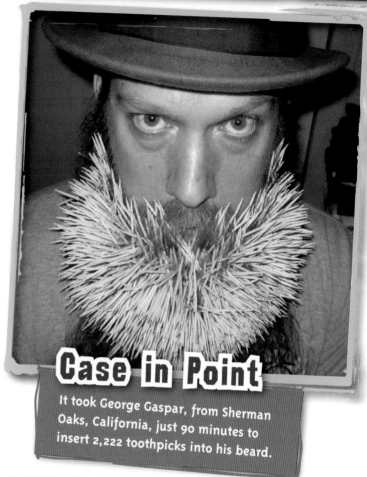

Case in Point

It took George Gaspar, from Sherman Oaks, California, just 90 minutes to insert 2,222 toothpicks into his beard.

UNBURIED HEADS

Headhunting rituals took place in Europe well into the 20th century. Tribes in Montenegro would remove the heads of people they had killed to prevent them receiving a proper burial.

HOARD UNCOVERED

An elderly Japanese businessman lost $4 million in cash when a thief found it buried in his garden.

SNAP DECISION

An anti-Mafia police unit in Naples, Italy, seized a crocodile that was used by an alleged mobster to intimidate local businessmen. Officers said the gangster would invite extortion victims to his home and threaten them with the crocodile, which weighed 88 lb (40 kg) and was 5 ft 7 in (1.7 m) long, unless they paid him protection money.

On the Ball

Ripley's loved the giant rubber-band ball made by Joel Waul so much that it bought it.

The problem was getting the giant ball, made from 780,000 rubber bands, to Ripley's Orlando warehouse for storage. At 9,400 lb (4,264 kg) and 7 ft (2.1 m) tall, the ball is not easy to maneuver and can be dangerous—Ripley's previously reported that, when the ball was just 400 lb (181 kg), it rolled over and sprained

Waul's hand. In October 2009, a Ripley's team arrived at Waul's Lauderhill, Florida, home with a transporter truck and crane. The ball was carefully hauled up from Waul's drive (it smells too bad to have been kept in his house) and loaded onto the truck, before making a slow journey to the Ripley's warehouse.

Archivist Ed Meyer meets Joel to collect the ball.

The ball is so heavy it took a crane to lift it...

...and a truck to move it!

The ball safe and sound at the Ripley Warehouse in Orlando, Florida.

337

Hair Sculpture

Chinese hairdresser Huang Xin spent seven days and nights creating this sculpture of Barack Obama from 9 lb (4 kg) of human hair collected in his shops. After washing and dying the hair—he used only women's hair because it is softer—he glued it on to paper before rolling it into different shapes. Huang Xin has also created a detailed model of Beijing's Tiananmen Gate Tower from hair.

ID PROBLEM

A judge presiding over a drug trafficking case in Kuala Lumpur, Malaysia, released the defendants—identical twins—because police officers couldn't prove which one had originally been arrested.

DENTAL DISCOVERY

A customer shopping at a Walmart store in Falmouth, Massachusetts, said he found ten human teeth hidden in a zipped compartment of a wallet he was about to buy. Police said the teeth belonged to an adult, but since there was no blood or gum tissue present, it would not be possible to perform DNA tests to identify whose teeth they were.

ILLUMINATED DRESS

British fashion student Georgie Davis has designed a dress that lights up when the wearer's cell phone rings. The right shoulder of the dress, which is connected to the phone by wireless technology, has translucent white scales that move and light up.

FROZEN MUMMY

In 1995, two climbers in the Andes discovered the mummified body of a young girl, frozen solid on the side of Mount Ampato. Although it is thought she died in the 15th century, her body was remarkably well preserved.

MISSILE CATCH

Commercial fisherman Rodney Salomon from St. Petersburg, Florida, landed the catch of his life in 2009—an 8-ft-long (2.4-m), American-made, air-to-air guided missile that could have exploded at any moment. Despite the danger, he reeled in the missile, strapped it to the roof of his boat and kept fishing in the Gulf of Mexico for another ten days—even during electrical storms—before returning to port.

LODGED IN BRAIN

A large metal pin broke off and lodged itself in the brain of 19-year-old Chris Clear from Penrose, Colorado, while he was helping a friend move a rototiller. Luckily, the pin narrowly missed several major arteries and, after a nine-hour operation to remove it, Clear was able to return to work as a volunteer firefighter. There is not even a scar to remind him of the accident, but he kept the pin as a souvenir.

PURPLE PEARL

A Florida couple stumbled across a potential fortune in their seafood dinner. George and Leslie Brock were eating steamed clams at a restaurant in Lake Worth when Mr. Brock bit on something hard—a rare, perfectly round purple pearl. Purple pearls are most commonly found in large New England quahogs—clams known for violet coloring on the insides of their shells—and the finest specimens can be worth as much as $25,000.

GUILTY CONSCIENCE

A man who robbed a Walnut Creek, California, bank in July 2009 apparently felt so guilty that three days later he walked into a church, confessed to the crime and handed over $1,200 to a priest before leaving.

Roadkill Calendar

Kevin Beresford traveled all over Britain taking photographs of roadkill for a 2010 calendar that became a best-seller. He sold hundreds of copies of his quirky Roadkill Calendar, which featured pictures of squashed squirrels, flattened foxes and mashed magpies.

Car Crazy

After spending 17 years building his own Lamborghini sports car in the cellar of his Wisconsin home, Ken Imhoff realized that he had no way of getting it out. Undeterred, he built a ramp and hired a mechanical digger to gouge out a slope in his garden, even removing a section of the house's foundations. At the end of a delicate 2½-hour operation, the new car finally emerged above ground.

WARNING SUIT

To make people aware of the threat of skin cancer, a Canadian company has designed a two-piece bathing suit that changes color to warn women when the sun's rays are too strong. The bikini is held together with pale decorative beads that turn dark purple if the UV rays reach harmful levels.

BEER LAKE

A beer lake was formed in the German city of Kassel in December 2008 after a truck carrying 12 tons of freshly brewed beer lost its load while taking a sharp turn. Some 1,600 bottles smashed as they hit the road, but their contents quickly froze in temperatures of around 25°F (-4°C).

PARROT TALK

A U.S. firefighter who lost his power of speech in a road accident in 1995 has been taught to speak again by parrots. Brian Wilson from Damascus, Maryland, suffered such a serious head injury that doctors told him he would probably never be able to speak coherently again. However, two of the pet parrots that he had kept since childhood continually talked to him, and eventually he began to respond. To show his gratitude, he now provides a home for abandoned or unwanted parrots.

Featureless Face

If visitors to the Chiesa della Santa Church in Bologna, Italy, gaze long enough into a grated opening in the church wall, a strange, dark, almost featureless face will stare back at them. The spooky apparition is the mummified relic of St. Catherine of Bologna. She died in 1475, but after a series of miracles, her body, inexplicably showing little sign of decay, was exhumed by nuns. A few years later, Catherine appeared to one of the nuns in a vision, asking to be placed in the small chapel, sitting upright. So they dressed her in nun's clothing, placed a golden cross in her hand and sat her in a golden chair, where she has remained for more than 500 years.

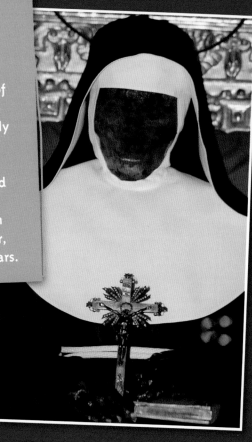

TEXT DOCTOR

Caroline Tagg, a postgraduate academic at Birmingham University, England, hasbeen awarded a doctorate in text messaging. She spent 3½ years writing an 80,000-word thesis on SMS texts and their language after studying more than 11,000 texts (that contained a total of around 190,000 words) sent by friends.

LOTTERY LUCK

In 2002, Mike McDermott from Hampshire, England, won the lottery twice with the same numbers, beating odds of 5.4 trillion to one.

ROWERS' RESCUE

The pilot of a light aircraft forced to bale out in the middle of the Irish Sea had a lucky escape when he was spotted by a team trying to row its way around Britain. The four-man crew was ten days into its time challenge when one of them saw the plane half-submerged in the freezing water. Pilot John O'Shaughnessy, who had been flying from Wales to Ireland, was standing on the wing.

INVISIBLE DOORWAYS

Using a technique called transformation optics, researchers in China have discovered a way of altering the pathway of light waves that could eventually enable them to create doorways or portals that are invisible to the human eye—like the one to platform 9¾ in the Harry Potter books.

CHOCOLATE LOVER

Peggy Griffiths from Devon, England, eats 30 bars of chocolate a week—and in 2009 she celebrated her 100th birthday. She has eaten an estimated 70,000 Cadbury's Dairy Milk bars in her lifetime, amounting to an incredible 4 tons of chocolate. Chocoholic Peggy used to run a candy store in the 1930s, but it closed down because she ate all the profits.

TINY LAMP

Scientists at the University of California in Los Angeles have created a tiny incandescent lamp that utilizes a carbon filament only 100 atoms wide—one one-hundred-trillionth of the size of the carbon filament used by Thomas Edison in his original lightbulbs. To the naked eye, the UCLA filament is invisible when the lamp is turned off, but it appears as a tiny point of light when the lamp is turned on.

ALL'S WELL

An 84-year-old man survived with only minor injuries after spending four days trapped in a well in June 2009. Bob Bennett had entered the 8-ft-deep (2.4-m) well shaft on his remote property at Benson Lake, British Columbia, Canada, while searching for a water source.

£21,000, THE BIGGEST WAGER ON RECORD!

This amount will be won if the above gentleman accomplishes the feat of WALKING ROUND THE WORLD adhering to certain conditions.

Masked Man

For a century it was believed that in 1908 adventurer Harry Bensley had set off from London on a six-year trek around the world, wearing an iron mask and pushing a pram to win a $100,000 bet with eccentric American millionaire J. Pierpont Morgan. However, far from reaching China and Japan as he had claimed, there is now doubt that Bensley ever left Britain. His family can find no evidence of him venturing abroad, and when he resurfaced he showed no signs of wealth, even though his supposed winnings were the equivalent of over $2 million today. So the mysterious case of Harry Bensley remains unsolved.

Eye Popper

Avelino Perez Matos, the Cuban Eyepopper, first appeared in the August 3, 1929 cartoon, then featured at the 1933 Chicago Odditorium. Believe it or not, Avelino Perez Matos of Baracoa, Cuba, could dislocate his eyes out of their sockets at will! The amazing stunt is still performed by brothers Antonio and Hugh Francis from Essex, England, who can both pop their eyes out of their sockets. Antonio demonstrated his talent on TV show *Britain's Got Talent*.

WALK-IN COCKTAIL

The Alcoholic Architecture bar in London, England, pumps out an intoxicating vapor of gin and tonic to leave visitors feeling slightly merry without even having a drink. Customers don protective suits to avoid smelling like a distillery, and to create the impression that they are actually inside the drink, the bar is decorated with giant limes and massive straws while a soundtrack carries the noise of liquid being poured over ice cubes.

TROPHY BODIES

The Sausa tribe from Peru would skin their enemies, before filling the skin with ash, sewing it back up and displaying it as a trophy and status symbol.

GREENBRIER GHOST

A ghost once helped convict a murderer. Zona Shue's death in Greenbrier County, West Virginia, in 1897 was presumed natural until her spirit appeared to her mother and described how she was killed by her husband Edward. Her mother persuaded the local prosecutor to reopen the case and an autopsy on the exhumed body verified that Zona had been murdered. Edward was subsequently convicted of the crime.

LIQUID VISION

Professor Josh Silver of England's Oxford University has invented inexpensive, fluid-filled eyeglasses that can be adjusted to anyone's vision needs. The lenses contain circular sacs filled with fluid that are connected to a small syringe attached to either arm of the eyeglasses. The wearer adjusts a dial on the syringe to increase or reduce the amount of fluid, thus altering the power of the lens.

MAKING HAY

A farmer's son, Markus Schmidt, spelt out his marriage proposal to girlfriend Corinna Pesl by rolling 150 bales of hay to form the words "Will you marry me?" Each bale of hay weighed 661 lb (300 kg) and each letter was 11½ ft (3.5 m) high. Corinna saw the 227-ft-long (70-m) message when she looked out of the bedroom window of her home in the Upper Bavaria region of Germany.

SCORPION HOME

Suang Puangsri gave up the bottom floor of his two-story home in Thailand to more than 4,600 pet scorpions. A practicing Buddhist, he spends an hour every day meditating inside their enclosure, often placing scorpions in his mouth. He says he has been stung so many times that he has become immune to their venom.

Snap!

Conjoined crocodile twins were born at the Samut Prakarn Crocodile Farm and Zoo near Bangkok, Thailand. The animals, named Chang and Eng after the world's most famous Siamese twins (see page 332), each had a head and four legs, but shared a common lower body with one tail.

HIDDEN PAIN

In April 2009, doctors treated Mrike Rrucaj of Albania for severe head pain and found a bullet that had been lodged in her cheek for 12 years without her knowing it.

UNDERWATER RESTAURANT

Seating 14 people and entered via a spiral staircase at the end of a jetty, the Ithaa restaurant in the Maldives is situated underwater, 16 ft (5 m) below sea level, offering customers a 180-degree panoramic view of the coral reef that surrounds it. Made mostly from acrylic, the 175-ton restaurant was lowered into the water and secured with concrete to four steel piles that had been hammered into the seabed.

ROBOT TEACHER

Children at a school in Tokyo, Japan, had a new teacher in 2009—a robot called Saya. Beneath a humanlike face, Saya has a system of 18 motors that work like muscles to give her facial expressions including surprise, fear, anger, happiness and sadness. She has a vocabulary of 700 words, has the ability to speak in any language and is programmed to respond to both words and questions.

POTATO DIET

Joanne Adams from Cleveland, England, used to live on 16 bags of potato chips a day. For some 20 years she ate hardly anything but potatoes, and as a result she kept breaking fingers and her hair grew so slowly she needed to wear extensions.

SKUNK STENCH

Israel has developed a new organic weapon called Skunk, which smells so horrible that, when sprayed from a water cannon, the stench cannot be removed for at least three days. The offensive weapon is a mix of yeast, baking powder and a few secret ingredients.

PARKING TICKET

A traffic warden in Darwin, Northern Territory, Australia, gave a dog a parking ticket after it was left outside a shopping market. An elderly lady left the dog tied to a fence outside the Rapid Creek market while she went shopping, but when she returned she found that an inspector had attached a ticket to the dog's lead.

Head Drill

Chinese kung fu master Hu Qiong can insert a fast-spinning electric drill into his temple and belly for a full minute and walk away unharmed. Known as "The Unbreakable Body," Hu can also catch a running electric saw with his bare hands.

Man of Steel

Builder Hu Zhuyin had a lucky escape after impaling himself on a crowbar 1 in (2.5 cm) thick when he slipped while climbing scaffolding in Qingdao, China. The solid steel crowbar sliced through his chest, missing his aorta by just ½ in (1 cm). Before medics could operate, firefighters had to cut through the bar so that Hu could lie flat on the operating table.

MISTAKEN IDENTITY

Assistants at a convenience store in Waterloo, Ohio, that had been robbed twice in two months mistook a drunken customer for a robber and threw a bag of cash at him. The man ignored the money and staggered out of the store.

GOOD LUCK HEADS

The feared Wa tribe from the jungles of Burma (Myanmar) would regularly cut off people's heads, and did so up until the 1970s. They believed that the severed heads prevented disease and brought good luck.

BODY HOAX

After receiving a tip-off about what appeared to be a body wrapped in a sleeping bag in a forest near Izu City, Japan, police officers took it back to the station for a post-mortem examination—but when the medical examiner opened the bag, he found it contained a life-size doll wearing a brown wig, a blouse and a skirt.

CRAZY CRAVINGS

Thirty-seven-year-old Rakesh "Cobra" Narayan, of Moala, Fiji, will eat just about anything—including floor tiles, pieces of concrete, clothes, shoes, furniture and even a lawn mower. His crazy cravings started when he was ten and chewed some chicken wire. Then, because he was still feeling peckish, he ate a raw chicken. Now he eats nuts and bolts, insects, lizards, grass, grease and his favorite, broken fluorescent-tube lights. At first the sharp objects used to cut the inside of his cheeks but since he learned to cope with the diverse materials in his mouth, he claims to have never suffered any ill effects.

EXPLODING FRIDGE

Kathy Cullingworth of West Yorkshire, England, was woken with a start one night when her fridge suddenly exploded. She found the fridge doors had been blown off, scattering food all over the kitchen.

ONION POWER

To save electricity, some people have started powering up their MP3 players with onions. They bore two holes in the onion, soak it in an energy drink and then stick a USB cable into it—and by doing that they can charge their iPod for an hour. Most vegetables can power iPods because they contain ions that react with the energy drink to create a charge.

SECOND BABY

Julia Grovenburg of Fort Smith, Arkansas, stunned doctors by conceiving for a second time while already pregnant. When Mrs. Grovenburg went for her first ultrasound scan, she thought she was about eight weeks pregnant—and she was, with a baby boy. However, she was also almost 11 weeks pregnant with a baby girl, who was developing next to her younger brother in their mother's womb. The non-twins are thought to represent an extremely rare case of superfetation.

Body Snatchers

Welcome to the world of the parasite, and what a world it is! These guys are frighteningly smart—they live on, or in, another organism and manipulate the behavior of their unsuspecting hosts to their advantage, often killing them in the process.

HUNTER HUNTED
Tarantula Hawk wasps hunt tarantulas and paralyze them with a powerful sting—one of the most painful ever recorded. The spider is dragged back to its own nest, where the wasp lays an egg on its body. When the wasp larva hatches, the paralyzed spider is eaten alive.

DEADLY MUSHROOM
These fungi infect caterpillars and other insects, killing them and mummifying the body as they spread. Some fungi make insects into zombies, whereby the insects crawl along and die in the best place for the fungi spores to spread into the air and infect other insects.

WOMB INVADER

A parasitic barnacle attaches itself to crabs, invades the egg pouch and forces the crab to look after parasite eggs. If the crab is male, the parasite sterilizes and enlarges its abdomen, essentially turning the male crab female.

TASTE BUDDY

This creature clamps onto the tongue of a fish, sucking blood from the tongue until it withers and dies. The parasite then remains firmly attached in the fish's mouth, working just like the original tongue, dining on blood, mucus and scraps of food.

STUCK FOR LIFE

Male anglerfish are much smaller than female anglerfish. They bite onto the body of females until their skin and eventually their blood vessels fuse together. The withered male then becomes part of the female body forever, useless except for his role in fertilizing the female's eggs.

UNWANTED CUSTOMERS

Shoppers at a food store in Puyallup, Washington State, were forced to flee in 2009 after cattle broke away from a fair parade and ran amok in the aisles. A year earlier, in 2008, a bull from the same fair charged into a bank.

TEQUILA DIAMONDS

Mexican scientists have turned the country's national drink, tequila, into diamonds. They discovered that, when deposited on a stainless steel base, the heated vapor from tequila blanco can form tiny diamond crystals.

PRECIOUS PARMESAN

At some banks in the Emilia-Romagna region of central Italy, a deposit of Parmesan cheese can be used to guarantee a loan. An 88-lb (40-kg) round of Parmesan is worth more than $400, and if the borrower defaults on repayments, the banks recover their losses by selling the cheeses. One bank holds over 400,000 rounds of Parmesan.

Up in Flames

In 2009, 17 people were each completely engulfed in fire without oxygen supplies at the same time in South Russell, Ohio. The group, led by local man Ted Batchelor, walked around Bell Road with their bodies in flames for an amazing 43.9 seconds. The team prepared for eight months for the event in their burn suits, and not one person sustained even a minor injury as the feat took place.

NEW SKULL

A man whose skull was partially removed after an accident over 50 years ago has stunned doctors by growing a new one—something that is thought to have happened only once before. Gordon Moore of Northumberland, England, had worn a metal plate for half a century after being involved in a car crash, but when surgeons removed the plate in 2009 to treat an infection, they were amazed to find he had grown a completely new skull underneath.

WAYWARD SHOT

History buff William Maser, whose hobby is re-creating 19th-century military firearms, accidentally fired a 2-lb (1-kg) cannonball through the wall of his neighbor's home in Georges Township, Pennsylvania, in September 2009. He fired the cannonball, about 2 in (5 cm) in diameter, outside his own home, but it ricocheted and hit a house 400 yd (365 m) away, smashing through a window and a wall before landing in a closet.

BAR BLAZE

In 2008, a fire crew from the town of Bournemouth in Dorset, England, was sent to extinguish a blaze at a bar called The Inferno—which was situated next to another bar called The Old Fire Station.

HOSPITAL FOOD

Hospitalis, a restaurant in Riga, Latvia, is hospital-themed with waitresses dressed as nurses, food served in flasks, cocktails served in test tubes and beakers, and medical implements for cutlery.

Light Show

Thousands of people saw a mysterious giant spiral of light appear in the sky over Norway on the morning of December 9, 2009. It began as a spinning circle of white light centered around a bright moonlike star and then spread out, sending a blue-green beam down to Earth. The eerie phenomenon, which was visible for hundreds of miles, was in the sky for several minutes. Theories included it being a misfired Russian missile, a meteor fireball or a previously unseen variation of *aurora borealis*, the northern lights.

BANK ERROR

After Josh Muszynski of Manchester, New Hampshire, swiped his debit card at a gas station to pay for a pack of cigarettes in July 2009, he checked his account online and saw that he had been charged over $23 quadrillion. The Bank of America corrected the error the following day.

EGG-STREME DIET

To build up their body weight for the 2010 Commonwealth Games, India's rugby players were ordered to eat seven meals and at least 15 eggs a day for over a year.

CRAZY HORSES

The Madagascar Institute, a New York-based arts group, has created a high-speed fairground carousel where the horses are powered by jet engines!

ICING ON THE CAKE

When Neil Berrett of San Francisco, California, decided to quit his job at a naval shipyard in 2009, he had his letter of resignation written in icing on top of a cake.

Legend of the Yeti

U.S. TV-show host Josh Gates displays a cast of what may be footprints of the elusive Yeti, an apelike creature whose existence has been shrouded in mystery for nearly 200 years. The tracks—measuring about 13 in (33 cm) long—were found in 2007 at an altitude of 9,350 ft (2,850 m) near Mount Everest in Nepal.

PENGUIN POOP

Scientists were able to locate the breeding colonies of Emperor penguins in Antarctica after spotting giant poop stains from space. Satellite images picked up huge, red-brown stains on the ice, which helped identify 38 breeding colonies, totaling up to 400,000 breeding pairs of penguins.

SNAKE BITE

Until health authorities stepped in to stop the practice, a prized delicacy on the menus of restaurants in the southern Chinese province of Guangdong was meat from a chicken that had been bitten to death by a poisonous snake.

LOW MAINTENANCE

The Beverly Clock, located at the University of Otago in Dunedin, New Zealand, is a working mechanical clock that has not been wound since 1864. It is powered solely by changes in pressure and temperature.

TEARS OF BLOOD

Teenager Calvino Inman of Rockwood, Tennessee, has a medical condition that leads to him crying tears of blood. The bleeding, which can last for up to an hour, occurs at least three times a day.

Maori Mummies

Maori tribes of New Zealand used to mummify heavily tattooed heads of warrior adversaries, skin, hair, teeth and all.

Maori warriors would collect as trophies the decapitated, tattooed heads of notable enemies they had killed in battle, and the heads of their own dead leaders and family members were also removed and treated with respect—sometimes to prevent other tribes escaping with them It has been reported that entire bodies were preserved, although none remain. Maori facial tattoos, known as *ta moko*, were a long and painful process, which made use of carved bone chisels to make cuts in the face. In the 18th century, European visitors began to buy the skulls as interesting artifacts, and soon the trade in mummified *ta moko* became so popular that appropriately tattooed enemies were killed solely in order to supply the market with fresh heads. This murderous practice was eventually outlawed in the 19th century.

A mummified head preserved by the Maori tribes.

HEAD SHRINKERS

Some of the most unbelievable discoveries that Robert Ripley made on his travels were the shrunken heads of South America. The Jivaro tribes of Ecuador and Peru would take the heads of fallen enemies, remove the skin whole, and shrink it to the size of a fist. Tsantas, as the shrunken heads were known locally, were used to banish the vengeful spirits of their previous owners, with their lips sewn shut to stop the spirits from escaping. When Western tourists began to visit the area in the 19th and 20th centuries, a demand for gruesome souvenirs fueled the practice, and it is said that people were killed just to keep up the supply. Robert Ripley reported in his journal that a German scientist who attempted to find Jivaro headhunters came out of the forest as nothing more than a shrunken head with a red beard. A TV documentary team recently unearthed a Polish videotape from the early 1960s that not only seemed to prove that tsantas were still being made by the Jivaro tribe at that time, but also provides remarkable video footage of the head-shrinking process.

Wooly Wedding

Shepherdess Louise Fairburn from Lincolnshire, England, got married in a wedding dress made of wool from one of her own flock. Husband Ian wore a woolen waistcoat made from the same sheep. The dress took 120 hours to make and cost around £3,000. Louise, who even carried a Bo Peep-style crook on her big day, loves her sheep so much that they featured in her wedding photos.

DOGGY ICES

A company from North Yorkshire, England, has devised a range of luxury ice creams—for dogs. The frozen yogurt treats come in three flavors and contain hidden dog biscuits as well as yucca extract to reduce the unpleasant odors from flatulence!

TRICKY PROBLEM

Capable of 200 trillion calculations per second, a computer network in Jülich, Germany, spent more than a year computing the answer to a single physics question.

INSEPARABLE TWINS

Identical twins Peter and Paul Kingston from West Sussex, England, have been almost inseparable for over 75 years. They worked for the same electronics firm and then as entertainers at the same holiday camp, and for the past 40 years they have shared the same house with their respective wives.

JELLYFISH ASSAULT

In September 2009, a 41-year-old man was arrested on Madeira Beach, Florida, accused of throwing jellyfish at teenagers.

MANY BEERS

Over 5,000 different types of beer are brewed in Germany. There are about 1,300 breweries in the country, and the Weihenstephan Abbey Brewery in Bavaria has been making beer for nearly a thousand years—since 1040.

WEDDING RUSH

Tens of thousands of Chinese people rushed to get married on September 9, 2009, believing that the 09/09/09 date was a good omen for a long marriage. The ninth day of the ninth month, "jiu, jiu" in Chinese, is a homonym for "jiujiu," which means "for a very long time."

CHIMP CANDIDATE

A bad-tempered chimpanzee that had a habit of throwing excrement at visitors to Brazil's Rio de Janeiro Zoo was nominated by a satirical magazine to run for the city's 1988 mayoral election. Tiao polled more than 400,000 votes, finishing third out of the 12 candidates.

FAMILY LINE

After six generations spanning 217 years, the last Dr. Maurice of the town of Marlborough in Wiltshire, England, finally hung up his stethoscope in 2009. Dr. David Maurice's retirement brought to an end an unbroken line of family members caring for the town's sick people dating back to 1792.

Musical Heights

In 2008, extreme cellists set themselves a 48-hour time limit to climb the four highest mountains in Britain and Ireland with cellos, perform a concert and cover the 1,000 mi (1,600 km) between the peaks. The challenge, completed successfully, followed performances in or on the roofs of 42 British cathedrals—a feat that they managed in just 12 days—and a concert at every street on the London Monopoly board in a day.

GIANT ORGANISMS

Researchers in The Bahamas recently discovered giant single-celled organisms the size of grapes living on the sea floor. If a person's cells were that size, the human body would be 3½ mi (5.6 km) tall!

GLOWING JELLO

By including food-safe quinine as an ingredient, gastronomes Sam Bompas and Harry Parr from London, England, have created a jello that glows blue in the dark.

CARDBOARD CUTOUTS

Flat daddies and flat mommies, life-size cardboard cutout photos of U.S. soldiers stationed abroad, are used to connect families with absent spouses and parents.

ROBOT ACTORS

Robots appeared on stage alongside human actors in a play that premiered in Osaka, Japan, in 2008. The machines were specially programmed to speak lines with humans and move around the stage.

Mountain Bike

Extreme yoga artist Khiv Raj Gurjar from Jodhpur in Rajasthan, India, balances in extraordinary positions on his bicycle just inches from the edge of rocky outcrops 300 ft (90 m) high. Khiv, who has been practicing and studying yoga since the age of 13, decided to combine both his loves—cycling and yoga—to create this striking discipline in 2006. Now in his sixties, Khiv practices daily for an hour and can perform up to 36 yoga moves balancing on his BMX bike.

Shark Attack

Craig Clasen from Mississippi fought a tiger shark for over two hours in a ferocious battle of life or death. Craig, an expert spear fisherman, was hunting bluefin tuna in the Gulf of Mexico with a small group when a 12-ft (4-m) shark began circling one of them. Craig instinctively grabbed his speargun and stabbed the shark when it made a move to attack. Once he had injured the creature, Craig said he felt a moral obligation to finish the job and kill the shark as humanely as possible. He shot it six times in the head with his spears, but sharks are extremely resilient and he was eventually forced to kill it with a blade knife through its skull. An experienced diver and fisherman, Craig has come into contact with thousands of sharks in his lifetime and said that this encounter was rare and the first incident in which he has had to take serious action to protect himself.

WILD CHILD

A Russian girl spent the first five years of her life being brought up by cats and dogs. The girl, from the Siberian city of Chita, adopted the behavior of the animals she lived with, even barking like a little dog and jumping at the door when people left the room.

CONCEALED WEAPON

Despite being searched several times, obese 540-lb (255-kg) George Vera was able to smuggle a gun into two different Texas jails by hiding it within his rolls of fat.

COLD COMFORT

Immigration officials in Llandudno, Wales, found a Chinese chef living in a freezer inside a restaurant where he was employed.

RICH FOOD

Fifteen gourmands paid $30,000 a head for a special meal prepared by the world's top chefs at a hotel in Bangkok, Thailand, in 2007. The banquet featured ingredients flown in from 35 cities around the world, including lobsters from Maine and oysters from France.

MAGNETIC IMPACT

After suffering massive head injuries in a car crash in 2005, Josh Villa of Rockford, Illinois, was eventually roused from the coma into which he had fallen by a magnetic field. An electromagnetic coil was held over the front of his head to stimulate the underlying brain tissue, and within a few weeks he had begun responding to simple commands.

BUCKET CEREMONY

In keeping with a tradition in Xi'an, China, that the bride's feet should not touch the ground during the journey from home to the ceremony, a couple got married in 2008 in midair in two large tractor digger buckets. The bride and two bridesmaids stood in one bucket, while the groom and two best men stood opposite them in a second bucket.

DOUBLE EGG

Farmer Jeff Taylor from Herefordshire, England, got the shock of his life when he found an egg inside another egg! Both eggs were intact and perfectly formed. Double eggs are thought to be the result of some malfunction in the hen's rhythmic muscular action, which moves a developing egg down the oviduct.

AIRPLANE DEBRIS

Wissam Beydoun of Dearborn, Michigan, was standing outside his home talking in 2009 when he was hit on the shoulder by a piece of metal that had fallen from an airplane. The aluminum scrap, which measured 8 x 6 in (20 x 15 cm) and weighed about a quarter of an ounce, left him with nothing worse than a bump.

FOLDING BATHROOM

Paul Hernon from West Yorkshire, England, has invented a fold-away bathroom that could prove ideal for small apartments. The space-saving unit, called the Vertebrae, stacks a sink, water cistern and showerhead into a single 8-ft (2.4-m) steel column.

MARS CROP

NASA scientists say that the soil on Mars would be good enough to grow asparagus and turnips, but unfortunately not fertile enough for strawberries.

RAW BLOOD

A restaurant in Hanoi, Vietnam, serves customers a bowl of raw pig or duck blood at 75 cents each. Equally popular is a frozen pudding made from the fresh blood of the same animals.

FREE SALAMI

Motorists in the Bulgarian capital Sofia were awarded free salami in 2009 for driving courteously. As part of a police road-safety initiative, a salami factory offered lunch to any driver who yielded to pedestrians at marked street crossings.

BABY SWITCH

Kay Rene Reed Qualls and DeeAnn Angell Shafer learned at the age of 56 that they had been accidentally switched at birth and had grown up with each other's parents. The girls were born at Pioneer Memorial Hospital in Heppner, Oregon, in 1953, but the mistake was only confirmed when they took DNA tests in 2009.

Top-heavy Turban

For a 2009 Sikh celebration in Amritsar, India, Baba Balwant Singh wore a 130-lb (60-kg) turban on his head that weighed more than he does! When unwound, the turban stretched for an incredible 2,300 ft (700 m)—that's equal to the length of seven football fields.

Index

Page numbers in *italic* refer to the illustrations

Abdulazizov, Abdurakhman 171
Abreu, Emerson de Oliveira 281
abseiler, elderly 167
accordions 237, 268
Acimovich, Nada 215
Acton, Patrick 242, *242*
actors 249, 360
Adamovich, Dr. David 127
Adams, Joanne 347
advertising, flies carry 97, *97*
aging, premature 193
Agrawal, Himanshu 273
airplanes
    airline solely for pets 295
    birds smuggled on 324
    Bleriot's flight repeated 317
    chimpanzee as passenger in 77
    crash lands on toilets 306
    creates cloud 149, *149*
    dog flies in business class 114
    dog hidden in luggage 120, *120*
    first flight for centenarian 319
    flying cars 153
    lands on road 283
    man hit by metal from 362
    men pull 282, 293, *293*
    mended by passenger 185
    paper airplane contest 183
    pilot dies in mid-flight 148
    pilot rescued from sea 342
    school lessons in 19
    spending a month in 159, *159*
    teaches cranes to migrate 93
    traveling round world without using 300
    very young pilot 170
    wing-walking 186, *280–281*, 281
airport runway, turtles shut 89
Aker, Stian 153
Al Mamari, Omar 158
albino animals 67, *67*, 74, *74–75*
Albu, Elena 127
Alder, Alec 106
Aldrin, Buzz 261
Allen, Lou 283
allergy, to own baby 205
alligators
    arm recovered from stomach 215
    shot with crossbow 167
    teeth 74
Allwood, John 300

alphabet, very short 47
Amaral, Dr. Terry 200
Amazon River, walking length of 146, *146–147*
Amge, Jyoti 198, *198–199*
amino acids, found in comet 53
amnesia 193, 222
Andersen, Hans Christian 43
Anderson, Jolene *118–119*, 119
anglerfish 351, *351*
animal parks, multiple visits to 120
animation, young teacher 117
Antarctica
    altitude 44
    hidden mountain range 48
    penguin poop stains 355
    skiing race in 153
ants, chemical production 99
Anze, Fabio 76
apartments
    abandoned apartment found 50
    block with only one tenant 29
    crystal cave in 52, *52–53*
aqueduct, long time to build 54
Arch, Derek 127
Aretz, Mark 50
armadillo, scrap metal 238
arms
    armless and legless woman 210, *210*
    enormous biceps 192, *192*
    one-armed pianist 254
    one-armed surfer 173
    one-armed table tennis player 299
    recovered from alligator's stomach 215
    very long hair on 214, *214*
Armstrong, Neil A. 127, 328
arrows 97, 127
asteroid, precious metals in 47
astronauts
    couches for 109, *109*
    sharing name with 127
    space station toilets 17
    space tourist 113
    test pilot in space 316, *316*
    valuable check 328
Athay, Harriet and Andrew 118
Auer, Dirk 298, *298–299*
Auger, James 47
Aukscionis, Kajus 153
Austen, Jane 264
Aykroyd, Dan 229
Azevedo, Nele 264

babies
    conceiving while pregnant 349
    crawling contest 153
    dog saves life 76
    enormous 215
    fetus left in body 216
    kept alive in dead mother's womb 197
    memorable birthdays 205
    mother performs cesarean on herself 203, *203*
    pink hospital for birth 29
    preserved in formaldehyde 208, *208*
    switched at birth 362
    three generations born at same time 205
    village with high birth rate 48
baboons, empty suitcases 77, *77*
Babu, S. Ramesh 167
bacon, used as bookmark 259
badger, drunken 70
Ball, John 304, *304*
balloons, mass ascent 281
balls
    bouncing multiple times 113
    crowd spins basketballs on fingers 310
    enormous ball of popcorn 169
    enormous sculpture of basketball 54
    giant ball of paper 283
    giant ball of rubber bands 336, *336–337*
    keeping in air 154, 169
    very fast juggling 173
    very large matzo ball 317
Ban, Hajnal 327
banknotes 326, 333
banks
    bull in 352
    cheese guarantees loan 352
    quadrillion dollar debit 354
    robber confesses to priest 339
Barbie dolls 241
Barley, Scott 22
barnacles 42, *42*, 351, *351*
bars
    alcoholic vapor in 345
    bartender's long career 310
    fire in bar called The Inferno 353
baseball
    mass potato chip crunch 283
    multiple swings 173
    success in two teams on same day 289
basketball
    bouncing multiple times 113
    crowd spins balls on fingers 310

basketball (*cont.*)
  elderly player 292
  enormous sculpture of 54
  first-time player's success 167
  long career in 281
  long winning streak 285
  playing on pogo stick 153
  playing with echolocation 222
Bassett, Dr. Stephen 67
Basso, Kevin *168*, 169
Bateman, Aiden 197
Bathory, Countess Elizabeth 33, *33*
bathroom, fold-away 362
bathtubs
  blown on to power cables 19
  look like shoes 241
  on roof 18
Bauman, Barry 259
beaches
  green sand 22
  large litter collection from 29
  refrigerated 53
  stolen sand 135
beads, flag made of 261
beaks, new beak for stork 66
beards
  free admission to zoo 313
  multiple toothpicks in 335, *335*
  styling champion 292
bears
  breaks into bakery 74
  eats chocolates 76
  given to U.S. President 68
  scalps man 229
Bedingfield, Daniel 265
bedroom, Hindu temple in 29
beds 110, 158
beer 341, 359
bees 68, 296, *296*
beetles, larvae on train 330
Belden, Judge Stephen 120
bench, very long 29
Bendikov, Alexander 187
Benedict XVI, Pope 16
Bennett, Bob 343
Bensley, Harry 343, *343*
Benz, Eleanor 197
Beresford, Kevin 340, *340*
Berg, Bryan 300
Bergbauer, Hildegard 67
Berrett, Neil 354
Bertoletti, Patrick 164, 292
Beydoun, Wissam 362
Bheel, Karna Ram 330

bicycles
  balancing on 360, *360*
  folds up very small 169
  intelligent bike 180
  large load on *132–133*, 133
  long-distance wheelie 171
  odd-shaped wheels 164
  symphony for bicycle bells 243
  very fast 173
  very long journeys on 174, 297
bigamy 334
bikini, skin cancer warning 341
billiards, playing nonstop 318
Binder, Alysa 295
bioluminescence 228, 335
bionic body parts *46*, 46, 51, *51*
birds
  budgerigar found at sea 84
  carrier pigeon saves lives 96
  eagle drops fish onto car 333
  huge bird made of rocks 47
  living life as a penguin 119
  never touch ground 94
  new beak for stork 66
  owl adopted by dog 93
  paintings on feathers *260*, 260
  parrots teach man to speak 341
  pelican swallows cell phone 97
  police capture emu 114
  poop stains seen from space 355
  smuggled on plane 324
  speaks on phone 94
  spider catches 83, *83*
  teaching to migrate 93
birthdays
  family born on leap day 197
  memorable dates 205
  party for fridge 110
  twins born in different years 310
Biswas, Ansuman 265
Björk 309
Blair, Daniel 139
Blank, Gerrit 194
Blazova, Jana 318
Bleriot, Louis 317
blindness
  boxer 285
  contact lenses for animals 84
  golf player hits hole-in-one 161
  guide dog for blind dog 80
  limbo skating under car 125
  in mountain race 153
  sight recovered after stroke 229
  uses echolocation 222

Bliss, Janifer 335
Bloch, Ingrid Goldbloom 254, *254*
Block, Ken 176, *176–177*
Blomberg, Ernst 34–35
blood
  crying tears of 355
  donations pay for concert tickets 264
  restaurant serves 362
  samples given away with book 265
  sculpture of head in 221, *221*
  vampires 30–39
blowtorch, in mouth 289, *289*
BLT, enormous 153
Boardman, Chris 180
boats and ships
  bomb used as anchor 125
  dolphins save from pirates 63
  elderly round-the-world sailor 279
  paralyzed sailor 174
  rowing solo across Indian Ocean 173
  sea lion takes over boat 139
  shipwrecks 137, 212
  standing on keel 307, *307*
  Titanic fans watch film in 166, *166*
  underwater 162, *162–163*
  very large collection of models 153
  young round-the-world sailors 105,
    278–279, *278–279*
body piercings, multiple 195, *195*
bog, barrel of butter found in 50
bogsnorkeling 114
bomb, used as boat anchor 125
Bonds, Briana 310
bones
  lengthening for small woman 225
  growing new skull 353
  huge whale skeleton 68
  isolated bone 212
  man becomes museum display 113
  skeleton found in tree 40
books
  bacon used as bookmark 259
  balancing on head 281
  blood and hair samples given away
    with 265
  enormous encyclopedia 264
  Moon rock in 261
  novel published on Twitter 254
  very overdue library book 272
Borsodi, Bela 249, *249*
Bosworth, Wendy and Joanne 328
bottles
  balancing matchsticks on 187
  buildings made of 44

bottles (*cont.*)
  contortionist in 191, *191*
  messages found in 325, 331
Boukamha, Larbi 237
box, prisoner escapes in 327
boxing 93, 285
bra, cash in stops bullet 298
Bradác, Zdenek 173
Bradford, Mark 238
Bradford, Robert 239, *239*
Bradt, Tyler 158
brain
  chopstick in 225
  knitted replica of 274
  magnetism rouses man from coma 362
  metal pin in 339
  missing half 205
  sight recovered after stroke 229
  surgeon suffers heart attack 214
Braun, Frederick and Gerrit 272
bread
  Mona Lisa in toast 256, *256*
  sculpture made from 255, *255*
Brewer, Tiger 280–281, 281
bricks, smashing with hand 173
bridge, butter to stop suicides 18
Brock, George and Leslie 339
Brooks, Paul and Caragh 135
brothers, long-lost 121
Brown, Harry 120
Brown, Ian 252, *252*
Brown, Mark 148, *148*
Brown family 39, *39*
Brumbach, Katie 313, *313*
Brunei, Sultan of 114
bubble, very large 127
bubblegum, buffalo sculpture 270, *270–271*
Bucci, Tom 283
Buck, Stanley and Christine 250
Buddha-shaped pears 172, *172–173*
buffalo 104, 270, *270–271*
Buford, Craig 309
bugs, eating 130, *130*
buildings
  crossword puzzle on 48
  elderly abseiler 167
  glass viewing platforms on 44
  height restrictions 46
  home on exterior wall of 17, *17*
  large number of windows 17
  made of bottles 44
  palace built of salt 53
  supported with Velcro 333

buildings (*cont.*)
  trompe l'oeil art on 238
  very narrow 18
bullets
  book of psalms save man 203
  cash in bra stops 298
  catching in hands 127
  collide in midair 143
  found in face 110, *110*, 346
  hits lemon 261, *261*
  man spits out 194
  stopped by hair weave 310
bulls
  in bank 352
  bull-leaping 308, *308*
  in hotel room 124
  wedged on roof rack 297
bungee jumping, over volcano 19
Bunker, Chang and Eng 332, *332*
Buntine, Patty 90
burglars 121, 141
Burnett, Charles III 297
buses 75, 174
butter 18, 50
buttocks
  ear stitched to 202
  needle removed from 284
Byron, Lord 245

Cabrera, Marino 137
cactus, very tall 53
cake frosting, artist licks off floor 272
cakes
  enormous 154
  realistic 236, *236*
  resignation letter on 354
calamari, speed-eating 292
Caldwell, Margaret 185
Caldwell, Ron 50
calendar, roadkill photos 340, *340*
Camejo, Luis Enrique *140*
camels 77, 94
camera, replaces eye 51, *51*
Cameron, Marc 148, *148*
Cammarata, Angelo 310
camouflage paintings 234, *234–235*
Campbell, Chad 141
Canada 28, 174
cancer, warning in bikini 341
candies, filled with insects 124
cannonball, fired through house wall 353
cans
  giant structure built from 310
  underwear made from 254, *254*

canyons 22, 24
Cao Fengying 84
Cardozo family 289
carousel, jet-powered horses 354
cars
  animals in trunk 125
  art from hubcaps 238
  boys drive 169, 306
  built in cellar 341, *341*
  car crash sculpture 167, *167*
  cat gets head stuck in wheel 99
  caterpillars cocoon in silk 325, *325*
  coyote survives crash 116, *116*
  dragging with eyelids 292, *292*
  driving to Australia 309
  eagle drops fish onto 333
  early snowmobile 165, *165*
  flying 153
  jet pack races 167
  jumping on snow 176, *176–177*
  limbo skating under 125
  lottery ticket replica of 112, *112–113*
  multiple traffic citations 319
  pulling with hair 180, *180*
  re-creating with light 148, *148*
  salami for courteous drivers 362
  snakes cause accident 106
  steam-powered 297
  stretch limousine racing car 158
  very small 165
Carson, Rob 215
Carter, Kevin 196, *196*
cartoonist, elderly 252
Case, Brent 229
cash machine, pays out double 335
cassette tapes, portraits made from 252, *252*
Castelar, Jose 149
castle, built in cliff 53
caterpillars
  cause emergency 141
  multiple head cases on 98, *98*
  parasites 350, *350*
  silk cocoon on car 325, *325*
Catherine of Bologna, St 342, *342*
Catlin, George 271
cats
  bald 67
  child brought up by 361
  clothes for 67
  dials emergency number 119
  facial disfigurement 96, *96*
  found in couch 139
  grows wings 75

cats (*cont.*)
head stuck in car wheel 99
junk removed from stomach 71
kitten survives in washing machine 93
rescued from collapsed building 93
survival kits for earthquakes 93
travels on bus 75
very obese 92, *92*
cave, castle built in 53
Cavey, Charlie 245
cell phones
dress lights up when it rings 339
found inside fish 333
multiple text messages 186
pelican swallows 97
cellar, car built in 341, *341*
cellos
extreme cellists 359, *359*
made from LEGO® 259
cells, giant 360
cemeteries
collection of paintings 271
vampire in 39
centenarians
eats a lot of chocolate 343
journalist 185
letter from prime minister 47
lives in house for long time 54
makes first flight 319
paraglider 310
quits smoking 117
cesarean section, mother performs on herself 203, *203*
Chacaliaza, Cesar 93
chain, very long 274
chameleon, fire brigade deal with emergency 134
chandeliers 17, 152, *152*
Chapman, Jenny 213
Cheatle, Andrew 333
check, valuable 328
cheese
addiction to 194
guarantees bank loan 352
infested with maggots 121, *121*
obstacle race for wheels of 54
cheesecake, giant 295
cheetahs, as pets 72–73, *72–73*
Chepkurgor, Godwin 124
chess, simultaneous games 300
Chestnut, Joey 297
chewing gum sculpture 238, 241

chickens
adopts puppies 84
giant plaster nugget 171
lays bowling-pin shaped egg 81
lays egg inside egg 362
lays enormous egg 96
restaurants serve chicken killed by poisonous snakes 355
chili peppers
riot control with 331
speed-eating 107, *107*, 181
chimpanzees 77, 359
chin-ups, multiple 215
chocolate
bear eats 76
centenarian eats a lot of 343
garlic balls covered in 330
giant eclair 283
giant slab of fudge 179
locusts covered in 131, *131*
choking, boy saved from 197
chopsticks
in brain 225
speed-eating M&Ms with 149
swallowing 225
Chou, Ya Ya 152, *152*
Christie, Agatha 249
churches
in base of cliff 40
built in canyon 24
echoing ceiling 141
large church stolen 44
turned into gym 54
cigars, enormous 149
cinemas
marriage proposal in 265
in shed 29
Titanic fans watch film in boats 166, *166*
very small 54
Cioanca, Ioana 254
circuses, flea 58–59, *58–59*
cities
abandoned city found 22
art works left in 261
covered by dust storm 22
paper model of 250, *250*
shaped like Evita 19, *19*
toothpick model 264
clam, purple pearl in 339
Clarke, Simon 184
Clarke, Stephen 174
Clasen, Craig 361, *361*
Clear, Chris 339

cliffs
castle built in 53
church built in 40
dog survives fall over 143
graves on 28, *28*
monkey pushes woman off 110
riding unicycle on trails 170
sleeping on 311, *311*
climbing
climbers find mummy 339
free climbing 290–291, *290–291*
sleeping on cliffs 311, *311*
very young climber 317
Clinton, DeWitt 271
Clinton, Hillary and Chelsea 124
clocks
"decimal time" 17
no need to wind 355
"Sandringham Time" 50
clones 84, 324
clothes
designer outfits for dogs 142
dress lights up when cell phone rings 339
dress made of raw meat 105, *105*
enormous pants 237, 273
faces made from 249, *249*
Jane Austen fans wear period costume 264
made from hair 254
man smuggles 130
paper wedding dress 271
for pets 67
very cheap wedding dress 119
wedding dress with very long train 242
woolen wedding dress 358, *358*
clouds
airplane creates 149, *149*
new type of 20–21, 21
volcano blows hole in 41, *41*
Clough, Lucy 289
clover, four-leaved 117
clowns 113, 129
Coca-Cola, addiction to 164
cockatoo, python kills 82, 83
cockroaches, eating 104, *104*
cocktails, pouring multiple 183
coconuts, piercing with finger 181
coffee 257, *257*, 328
coffins 169, 179
coins 114, 237
Coleman, Rory 113
Coles, Lesley 97
Coles, Melanie 29

Colet, Lluis 153
Colin, Cammie 167
Collins, Jim 158
coma, magnetism rouses man 362
comet, amino acids found in 53
computers
  computer-related tattoos 213
  cremation ashes stored in 135
  lengthy calculation 358
  paralyzed man communicates via 194
concrete blocks, smashed on chest 314, *314*
Condori, Mauricio Zanes 203
Coney Island 206–211, *206–211*
conjoined twins 332, *332*, 346, *346*
Conn, Dave 333
Connery, Sir Sean 197
contact lenses 84, 196, *196*
contortionists 190–191, *190–191*
Cooksey, Damian 293
coral, roads made of 41
corkscrews, swallowing 304, *304*
corpses
  edible human "corpse" 326
  feared to be vampire 33
  motorcycle like 182, *182–183*
  stuffed skins as trophies 345
Cortez, Revoli 268
cosmetic surgery, to look like Nefertiti 216
cosmonauts, toilets segregated 17
Cotaina, Serge 334
couch, cat found in 139
countries
  "doubly landlocked" 47
  founded as practical joke 17
  shifting border 50
  without transport 24
courts
  defendant's mouth taped shut 120
  man chops finger off 222
  parrot ordered to appear 139
Courtney, Lisa *174–175*, 175
cows
  accordion music calms 237
  bullock traps head in ladder 84, *84–85*
  offered for Chelsea Clinton 124
  run amok in food store 352
  six-legged 70, *70*
  steer with very long horns 62
  two-headed calf 137
coyote, survives car crash 116, *116*
crabs 93, 351, *351*
cranes, microlight teaches to migrate 93

crawling, contest for babies 153
cream tea, enormous 184
cremation ashes
  buried in pub 127
  head-shaped urn 117, *117*
  in paintings 273
  stored in computer 135
crickets, paintings on 265, *265*
crocodiles
  conjoined twins 346, *346*
  hippo kills 78, *78–79*
  hotel in shape of 18, *18*
  Mafia use to intimidate 335
  playing with 94, *94*
  put in prison 134
crop circle, Oprah Winfrey's head as 50
crosses, vampire protection 35
crossword puzzle, on apartment block 48
Croucher, Brian 252
crowbar, man impaled on *348*, 349
crutches, marathon on 186
crystals, apartment covered in 52, *52–53*
cucumbers, theft of 326
Cui Bin 334
Cullingworth, Kathy 349
Culp, Connie 307
Culwick, George 330
Cunningham, Rikki 318
curry, very expensive 180
custard pies, mass fight 299
cyanide, millipede produces 62
cyst, enormous 326, *326*

Da Silva, Luan 154
Dalek, matchstick model of 252
Dali, Salvador 153
Dalla Costa, Milko 161
dancing
  dog's ability 99
  mass commemoration of Michael Jackson 274
  mass dancesport class 260
  robot display 130
  simultaneous tango dancers 237
  very fast tap dancer 260
Darby, Malcolm 229
Darshandas, Guru Bharatdas 28
darts, climbing wall with *284–285*, 285
Darwin, Charles 313
"Dave" 223, *223*
David, Alfred 119
Davidhazy, Andrew 261, *261*
Davie, Ian 260, *260*

Davis, Georgie 339
de Marco, Alfonso 54
deafness
  kissing pops eardrum 225
  puppy learns sign language 88
death
  coming back from 127
  death and rebirth ceremonies 142
  delusions about 289
  feigning to avoid arrest 127
  long time to die after being shot 309
  multiple escapes from 106
  sculpture using dead animals 138, *138–139*
  tribe eats elderly members 328
Deck, Jeff 106
deer, swimming at sea 141
Deighton, Len 259
Deininger, Tom 244, *244–245*
Della Monaca, Massimiliano 241
Delvoye, Wim 230, *231*
dental treatment, under hypnosis 215
Derouen, Janelle 95
deserts, rain evaporates in 50
diamonds, tequila turned into 352
diaper, saves baby in fall 200
DiDonato, Tiffanie 225
Dieudonne, Anastasie 33
digger buckets, wedding in 362
Dillinger, John 110
diving
  extreme ironing 183
  into shallow water *286–287*, 287
  living underwater 306, *306*
  whale saves diver 122, *122–123*
  whales' ability 64
divorce, house sawed in half after 104
DJ, nonstop broadcast 238
Dobrin, Corneliu 174
doctors, six generations in family 359
dogs
  adopts owl 93
  adopts red pandas 93
  airline solely for pets 295
  banned from resort 106
  best man at wedding 118
  blown away by wind 97
  child brought up by 361
  child married to 130
  cloned 84
  clothes for 67, 142
  dancing 99
  deaf puppy learns sign language 88
  five-legged puppy 99

dogs (*cont.*)
  flies in business class 114
  given parking ticket 347
  guide dog for blind dog 80
  hair and chewing gum sculpture of 241
  hen adopts puppies 84
  hidden in luggage 120, *120*
  ice cream for 358
  learns to box 93
  long-lost 64
  paintings by 81
  phones for help 106
  puppy survives in lavatory 139
  puppy swallows arrow 97
  reading ability 66
  saves baby's life 76
  shopping 94
  strays travel on subway 139
  surfing 83
  survival kits for earthquakes 93
  survives fall over cliff 143
  survives on remote island 68
  swallowed by snake 90
  trapped in rabbit warren 127
  trodden on by horse 65
  very expensive 104
  very old 95
  walks on back legs 139
  wins lotteries 91
dollhouse, used to sell house 50
dolls
  Barbie 241
  on graves 28, *28*
  on island 24, *24–25*
  life-size doll found in sleeping bag 349
dolphins
  pink 67, *67*
  save ships from pirates 63
  stops woman from returning to shore 333
  swim through flooded forests 70
donkeys 50, 132, *132*
Donovan, Richard 171
doorways
  invisible 342
  squashing bodies into 329, *329*
Dorner, Willi 329, *329*
Dracula 31, 32
drains
  covers stolen 106
  elephant falls down 125, *125*
  living in 44
  man stuck in 124, *124*
drawing pin, in lung 217

drawings
  continuous line portrait 238
  Etch A Sketch® drawing of Barack Obama 310
  with sand 249
drill in head 347, *347*
Drummond, Jake 171
drumming, mass 237
dryer lint pictures 251, *251*
Duan Qiongxiu 90
ducks
  eating embryos 134, *134*
  plastic duck race on river 148
  teaches boy to walk 201
dumbbells, live mortars as 116
dune, face of Jesus in 44
dung, frogs live in elephants' 68
Durrant, Dean 283
Düsseldorf Vampire 38
dust storm, covers Sydney 22
Dutta, Anandita 181

ears
  kissing pops eardrum 225
  lifting weights with 171, *171*
  stitched to buttocks 202
earthquakes 43, 93
Easter egg, giant 273
eBay, cheap wedding dress 119
echolocation, blind boy uses 222
Eckman, Allen and Patty 266–267, *266–267*
Eckstrom, Adam 112, *112*
eclair, giant 283
Edison, Thomas 343
Edward VII, King 50
Edwards, David 94
egg cartons, paintings on 246, *246–247*
Egger, Nalthasar 307
eggs
  bowling-pin shaped 81
  eating multiple boiled eggs 183
  egg inside egg 362
  enormous 96
  giant Easter egg 273
  smashing in elbow 192, *192*
Ekin, Namik 306
elections
  chimpanzee runs in 359
  donkeys deliver ballot papers 50
  playing cards settle 136
  polling station with one voter 28
electricity
  boy survives shock 225

electricity (*cont.*)
  onion-powered MP3 players 349
  solar panels on mausoleums 54
elephants
  duel fought on 44
  falls down manhole 125, *125*
  false foot for 91
  frogs live in dung 68
  hanged for killing handler 127
  moisturizer for 75
  painted like pandas 141
  plays harmonica 80
  prosthetic leg 95, *95*
  recognize people 65
  slippers for 68
  topiary hedge 238
Elliott, Rob 29
embroidery, Sistine Chapel ceiling 271
emotions, robot expresses 328
emu, police capture 114
encyclopedia, enormous 264
England, Christine 120
Entwistle, Thomas 300
Etch A Sketch®, drawing of Barack Obama 310
Ettlin, Beat 76
Evans, John 281
Evason, Maureen 225
Everest, Mount 114
Everett, Vince 284
eX de Merci 224, *224*
exorcism, of vampire's tomb 39
eyebrows, very long 216
eyelids, dragging car with 292, *292*
eyes
  adjustable glasses 345
  camera replaces 51, *51*
  contact lenses for animals 84
  corneal tattoo 204, *204*
  half brain missing 205
  hand-painted contact lenses 196, *196*
  painting with 240–241, 241
  popping from socket 344, 345
  sight recovered after stroke 229
  sight restored with tooth 222
  three-eyed piglet 77
  twig impaled in 230

Fabelo, Roberto 140, *140*
fabrics, portrait of Rembrandt 268, *268–269*
face
  bullet found in 110, *110*, 346
  cat's disfigurement 96, *96*

face (*cont.*)
  covered in hair 227, *227*
  forest in shape of 43
  glass found embedded in 300
  made from clothes 249, *249*
  robot expresses emotions 328
  transplant 307
  very large tumor removed 197
Fahradyan, Davit 154
Fairburn, Louise and Ian 358, *358*
family
  all live in same street 18
  family tree in model houses 259
  long-lost siblings 330
  six generations of doctors 359
farming, noises used in music 251
feathers, birds painted on 260, *260*
Federer, Roger 161
Feeney, Simone and Ryan 137
feet
  extra toes 202, *202*, 222, 229
  false foot for elephant 91
  snake grows foot 90, *90*
  twisted backward 200, *200–201*
  webbed toes 229, *229*
  writing with 318
Fehr, Jeff 160, *160–161*
Fernandez, Ramon 174
Fewins, Tom 300
Filchock, Martin 252
Filippone, Mike 173
fingernails, very long 212, *212*
fingers
  bionic 46, *46*
  cracking knuckles 124, 230
  crowd spins basketballs on 310
  enormous 136, *136*
  extra 202, *202*, 229
  giant finger painting 274
  man chops off 222
  piercing coconuts with 181
  single-finger push-ups 170, *170*
Fink, Richard IV 300
Finnegan, Erin 330
fire
  in bar called The Inferno 353
  fire-eating 288, *288*
  giant wall of 161
  human torches 301, *301*, 352, *352–353*
  tornado of wildfire 25
fish
  bouncing 65
  cell phone found inside 333
  eagle drops onto car 333

fish (*cont.*)
  goldfish survives in toilet 61
  goldfish survives out of tank 83
  parasites 351, *351*
  sculpture made from everyday items 244, *244–245*
  shoal of robot fish 333
  sleepy cuttlefish 84
  stolen using Internet photos 54
  stop eating 68
fishermen
  catch money 326
  catches missile 339
  child catches monster 64, *64*
  fishing through hole in floor 134
  large catch in 24 hours 319
flags
  coin mosaic of 237
  deterring wolves with 67
  made of beads 261
  tattooed on body 102, *102–103*
  wearing flag tie for long time 143
flea circuses 58–59, *58–59*
flies 97, *97*, 272, *272–273*
Flournoy, Bob 143
flowers 158, 245
Floyer, Ceal 237
flu shots, multiple 205
fog, water collected from 44
food
  crocodile tears syndrome 230
  eating anything 349
  eating insects 130–131, *130–131*
  giant structure built from cans 310
  rotten food in fridge 325
  speed-eating 107, *107*, 149, 164, 168, 169, 181, 292, 297
  unusual canned food 104, *104*
  very expensive banquet 362
footprints, Yeti 355, *355*
forests
  dolphins swim through flooded 70
  face-shaped 43
Forster, Marcelus 238
Foster, Billy 292
fox, steals shoes 64
Francenella, Giancarlo 268
Francis, Antonio and Hugh 345
Fraser, Al 317, *317*
freezer, chef lives in 361
French fry sculpting contest 243
fridges
  birthday party for 110
  exploding 349

fridges (*cont.*)
  rotten food in 325
  as works of art 140, *140*
frogs
  eating 331
  eight-legged 135, *135*
  enormous and aggressive 63
  false leg for 90
  live in elephant dung 68
  rare frogs rediscovered 93
  wedding for 61
Frost, Sophie 220
Fryer, Paul 274
Fryers, Tom 317
fudge, giant slab of 179
Fulmor, Noah 330
Funck, Devin 215
funerals 125, 169
fungi, parasitic 350, *350*
Furman, Ashrita 113, 149
Furze, Colin 169

Gao Xianzhang 172, *172–173*
garage doors, murals on 55, *55*
garbage bin, busker plays guitar in 245
garden, plasticine 245
Gardiner, Lillian 319
garland, very long 158
garlic 35, 330
Garrett, David 309
gas pipeline, letter sent through 309
gas station, covered with patchwork 26–27, *27*
Gaspar, George 335, *335*
Gates, Bill 297
Gates, Josh 355, *355*
Georgiev, Kiril 300
Gernsback, Hugo 164, *164*
Gheorghe, Andrei 251
Ghost of a Dream 112, *112*
ghosts 39, 345
giraffes 74, 273
glaciers 16, 50
glasses 164, *164*, 345
glove, very valuable 273
gnomes, large collection of 141
goats
  arrested by vigilantes 112
  friendship with giraffe 74
  lack of sleep kills 139
Goddard, Al 154
gold
  in asteroids 47
  metal detector finds treasure 141

gold (*cont.*)
  in sewage refinery 29
golf
  blind player hits hole-in-one 161
  caddie walks to tournament 292
  giant tee 161
  lightning strikes player 216
  tournament in snow 154
  very long game 283
  very long putt 170
Gonzalez, Mario Miguel 140, *140*
Gooch, Mick 170, *170*
gorillas 113, 268
Gormley, Antony 249
graduate, elderly 197
Graham, Kim 220
Granados, Ricardo 283
Granato, Leandro 240–241, *241*
Grand Canyon 310
grasshoppers
  candies filled with 124
  eating 187, *187*
graves
  dolls on 28, *28*
  exorcism of vampire's 39
  found in garden 330
  solar panels on 54
gravity, wedding in zero 330
Great Lakes, swimming across 316
Great Wall of China 53
Green, Keith 120
Grendol, Joseph 305, *305*
Grewal, Liz 88
Griffin, Tarrance and Tariq 310
Griffith, Jan and Dave 68
Griffiths, Peggy 343
grocery receipt, as artwork 237
Grovenburg, Julia 349
Guan Baihua 164
guitar, busker plays in garbage bin 245
gummi bears 152, *152*, 184, *184–185*
Gumpertz, Samuel W. 206
guns
  obese man smuggles into jail 361
  very valuable 110
  woman shot while sitting on toilet 335
Gurjar, Khiv Raj 360, *360*
Guzy, Rachel 174
gym, church turned into 54
gymnast, multiple turns on horizontal
  bar 154

Habu 181, *181*
Hadgu, Kiros 191, *191*

Haini, Salim 183
hair
  bullet stopped by hair weave 310
  clothes made from 254
  cutting with fingertip scissors 334, *334*
  deterring wild boar with 201
  on entire body 111, *111*
  face covered in 227, *227*
  fans request 245
  hair and chewing gum sculpture 241
  pays for road repairs 312
  in plaster on house 48
  pulling cars with 180, *180*
  samples given away with book 265
  sculpture of Barack Obama 338, *338*
  selling 201
  stomach filled with 137, *137*
  uncut for years 194
  very expensive haircut 114
  very long eyebrow hair 216
  very long hair on arm 214, *214*
Hale, Gordon 169
Hall, David 272
Hallett, Dave 91
Hallowes, Harry 48
Hamilton, Bethany 173
hands
  bionic fingers 46, *46*
  breaking ice blocks with 314, *315*
  catching knives and bullets in 127
  cracking knuckles 124, 230
  crowd spins basketballs on fingers 310
  enormous fingers 136, *136*
  extra fingers 202, *202*, 229
  man chops finger off 222
  piercing coconuts with finger 181
  pulled off in tug-of-war competition
   200
  rare disease diagnosed 216
  single-finger push-ups 170, *170*
  smashing bricks with 173
Harabis, Tomás 17
Hardacre, Sarah 238
Hardesty, Reina 186
Hardwick, Stan 333
Hardy, Alex 197
Hargreaves, Dominic 169
harmonica, elephant plays 80
Harris, Duncan 170
Hasaj, Lindsay 213
Hasan, Samat 179
Haseman, Nancy 68
Hawking, Stephen 297
hay bales, marriage proposal in 345

Hayes, Adrian 114
Hayes, Caroline 141
Haynes, Marques 281
Hayward, Tom 113
hazelnuts, hurled in festival 16
Hazelton, Dan 114, *114–115*
He Haoyang 225
head
  balancing books on 281
  blood sculpture 221, *221*
  chopstick in 225
  drilling 347, *347*
  growing new skull 353
  headhunters 325, 333, 335
  headless woman 211, *211*
  heads severed for luck 349
  man shoots himself with speargun 281
  metal pin in brain 339
  shrunken 357, *357*
  smashing watermelons with 300
  two-headed animals 65, 87, 137
  urn for cremation ashes 117, *117*
  vampire's 38, *38*
  wax heads in Ripley museums
   226–227, *226–227*
headdress, made of dead mice and
  rats 251
Heard, Michaela 283
heart
  bus driver has heart attack 174
  disco music helps resuscitation 230
  lightning cures heart condition 215
  moves around in body 309
  skydiver has heart attack 225
  surgeon has heart attack 214
Heath, Sam 127
Heather, Martin and Sharon 71
Heckler, Roy 59
Heckler, William 58–59
hedges, topiary 238, 245
Heenan, Lucy 330
Heine, Bill 23, *23*
helicopters
  bungee jumping over volcano 19
  home-made 179
  very young pilot 170
Hendrickx, Nicholas 272, *272–273*
Hendrix, Jimi 252
Herbert, Terry 141
Hernon, Paul 362
Herodotus 328
Herson, Benjamin 106
hide-and-seek, lost child 328
Hildebrandt, Kelly 328

Hill, Nate 138, *138–139*
Hiorns, Roger 52, *52–53*
hippos
    kill crocodile 78, *78–79*
    stuck in water tower 99
    unable to swim 91
Ho Eng Hui 181
Hoehle, Bernd 173
Hoekstra, Liam 203
Hof, Wim 283
Hogg, Gavin 238
Hogwarts, matchstick model of 242, *242*
Holbrook, Molly 171
Holmes, Bob 318
Hooper, Heidi 251, *251*
horns, steer with very long 62
horror story, on toilet paper 238
horses
    clothes for 67
    dog survives being trodden on by
        65
    pony with very short legs 80, *80*
Horseshoe Falls 156–157, *156–157*
Horvath, Al 54
hospitals
    children abandoned in 113
    hospital-themed restaurant 353
    pink décor 29
hot dogs 154, 297
hot-water bottles, inflating with nose
    282, *282*
hotels
    built with salt 139
    cheap weekend at 118
    customers on display 274
    pigeons stay in 139
    runaway bull in 124
    in shape of crocodile 18, *18*
Hou Guoying 110, *110*
houses
    built of LEGO® 251
    built of rocks 16, *16*
    cannonball fired through wall 353
    car built in cellar 341, *341*
    centenarian lives in for long time 54
    dollhouse used to sell 50
    estate sold in raffle 43
    family tree in model houses 259
    full of rubbish 116
    human hair in plaster 48
    pig refuses to leave 141
    sawed in half after divorce 104
    scorpions live in 345
    shark in roof 23, *23*

houses (*cont.*)
    temple built in bedroom 29
    very narrow 19
    walking 22
Howard, John 194
Howkins, Paul and Val 110
Hu Qiong 347, *347*
Hu Zhuyin *348*, 349
Huang Xin 338, *338*
Huang Yijun 216
Hubbard, Kamani 229
hubcaps, art from 238
Huggins, Colin 273
Hughes, Howard 334
Hultgren, Chayne 302–303, *302–303*
husband-carrying contest 46
hypnosis, dental treatment under 215

ice
    breaking blocks with hand 314, *315*
    driving on *154–155*, 155
    frozen man 220, *220*
    mountain range under 48
    sculpture made from 264
ice cream 334, 358
ice hockey 149, 293
icing, resignation letter written in
    354
illusions
    camouflage paintings 234, *234–235*
    trompe l'oeil art 238
Imhoff, Ken 341, *341*
Indian Ocean, rowing solo across 173
Ingham, David 238
inline skater, towed by motorcycle 298,
    298–299
Inman, Calvino 355
insects
    chocolate-covered locusts 131, *131*
    eating 130, *130*, 187, *187*, 309
    parasites 350, *350*
    sculpture made from 255, *255*
intelligence
    child with very high IQ 297
    dogs' 64
International Space Station 17, 113
Internet
    child shops online 331
    fish stolen using photos from 54
    giant jigsaw puzzle 158
    pigeons faster than broadband 327
iPods 220, 349
iron, ancient pillar of 40
ironing, by scuba divers 183

islands
    dog survives on remote 68
    dolls on 24, *24–25*
    lake on island in lake 46
    rat-free 16
    very low-lying 54
Itou, Wataru 250, *250*
Iwasaki, Keiichi 297
Izzard, Eddie 295

jack-o'-lanterns, speed-carving 174
Jackson, Michael 99, 265, *265*, 273, 274
Jacquet, Junior Fritz *274–275*, 275
jambalaya, giant 179
Jamison, Richard 194
Jasmer, Natalie 328
javelin, spears leg *128–129*, 129
jeans, enormous pair of 273
Jefferson, Thomas 68
Jeftichew, Fedor 227, *227*
jello, glows in dark 360
jellyfish, man arrested for throwing 358
Jem, Jia 105, *105*
Jenks, David 333
Jesus Christ
    image of in sand dune 44
    life-size LEGO® statue of 237
jewelry, human teeth in 264, *264*
Jian Liao *128–129*, 129
jigsaw puzzle, giant online 158
Jin Jeong-gun 237
Jivaro tribes, shrunken heads 357, *357*
Jo-Jo the Dog-faced Man 227, *227*
Jones, Martin 222
Jones, Merv 116
Joubert, Randy 121
journalist, centenarian 185
juggling, very fast 173
junk mail, art exhibit 254

Kagel, Mauricio 243
kangaroo, breaks into house 76
Kapral family 180
Karabay, Kim 306, *306*
karaoke, nonstop 310
Karia, Dhirajlal and Sushila 29
Kathan, Bill 310
kayaking, over waterfall 158
Keates, Gary 327
kebabs, mice 126, *126*
Keiichiro, Sako 17
Kenny, Victoria 213
Keogh family 197
Kerley, Glen 333

Kevan, Tim 83
Khan, Shantanu and Azeem 174
kibbeh, giant 292
kidney stone, enormous 212
Kiesewetter, Maiko 284–285, 285
Kim Sun-Ok 310
King, Natalie 319
Kingston, Peter and Paul 358
Kirkpatrick, Kerry 84
kissing
  mass Valentine's Day kiss 284
  multiple kisses 149
  pops eardrum 225
kite-surfing 310
kites 154
Kittinger, Joe 316, 316
knitting
  cozies for trees 238
  replica of brain 274
  replica of village 241
  shed covered in 238
knives, catching in hands 127
Knopp, Daniel 331
Knowles, Tim 259
knuckles, cracking 124, 230
Kobozevsa, Lilia and Liana 139
Kodritsch, Ronald 237
Koeberl, Franz 237
Kokane, Rohan Ajit 125
Kolodzinski, Jeff 319
Kolos, Farkas 300
Koster, Patrick 322–323, 322–323
Kourounis, George 14, 14–15
Krantz, Gordon 113
Kroon, Enno de 246, 246–247
Kürten, Peter 38
Kutcher, Ashton 229

Lackey, Tom 186
ladder, bullock traps head in 84, 84–85
ladybugs, wingless 327
Lai Thi Dao 197
Lake, Etta 213, 213
lakes
  acid 14, 14–15
  in Canada 28
  drains in two directions 50
  driving on ice 154–155, 155
  lake on island in lake 46
Laliberté, Guy 113
Lamberti, Nicolo 161
Lampard family 64
landownership
  in Britain 44

landownership (cont.)
  free land for families 29
  squatter wins rights 48
Lane, Cindy 83
Langdon, Professor 111, 111
Langley, Winnie 117
languages
  national anthem in five 255
  short alphabet 47
  whistling 44
Lao Du 284
Larratt, Shannon 204, 204
laughter therapy 222
lava 322–323, 322–323
lawn mowers 333
Lawrence, Annette 254
Lawson, Derek 184, 184–185
Le Mindu, Charlie 251
Leach, Bobby 157, 157
leap days, family born on 197
lecture, very long 153
Lee, Bruce 170
Lee, Hoon 272
Leggett, Nicki 245
LEGO®
  cello made from 259
  house built of 251
  life-size statue of Jesus Christ 237
legs
  amputated leg on display 228
  armless and legless woman 210, 210
  bone-lengthening 225
  broken for long time 328
  dog walks on back legs 139
  eight-legged frog 135, 135
  false leg for frog 90
  five-legged puppy 99
  horse leg extensions 220
  huge tumor removed from 307
  javelin spears 128–129, 129
  pony with very short 80, 80
  prosthesis for elephant 95, 95
  six-legged cow 70, 70
  stretched surgically 327
  twitching after detachment 94
lemon, bullet hits 261, 261
Leonardo da Vinci, Mona Lisa 256–257,
  256–257
Lester, Mark 193
Lewis, Greg 248, 248
Lewis, Katherine 274
Li Huiyan 134
Li Jingchao 225
Li Wenhua 296, 296

Lieshout, Joep van 237
life, amino acids found in comet's tail 53
light
  buffalo turns on 104
  emitted by body 228
  invisible doorways 342
  mysterious light in sky 354, 354
  re-creating cars with 148, 148
  tiny lamp 343
lightbulbs, eating 183
lightning
  cures heart condition 215
  iPod saves girl 220
  strikes golfer 216
  very long storm 22
limbo skating, under vehicles 125,
  148
Lin Rong 242
Lin Tinzhuan 218, 218–219
Linley, Claire and Stuart 116
Linton, Alex 305, 305
Lipnicka, Anita 264
lips
  canyon in shape of 22
  wooden plates in 226, 226
Lister, Hilary 174
litter 22, 29
Liu, Mr. 153
Liu Bolin 234, 234–235
Liu Ge 193, 193
Liu Hua 136, 136
lizards, two-headed 65, 87
llamas, at funeral 125
lobster roll, giant 281
Locke, Christopher 324, 324
Lockwood, Lara 300
Loco, Chiti 94, 94
locusts, chocolate-covered 131, 131
Lola, Princess 209, 209
Lomax, Finlay 201
Loos, Arthur 228, 228
Lopianowski-Roberts, Joanna 271
LoSauro, Valentino 334, 334
lotteries
  dog predicts winning numbers 91
  man dies after buying winning ticket
  327
  replica of Hummer made from tickets
  112, 112–113
  winning numbers repeated 106, 342
Lovering family 184
Lugosi, Bela 31
Luis, Jingle 200, 200–201
Lund, Anette and Kenneth 135

lungs
  foreign bodies in 197, 217
  tree growing in 213
Lussier, Jean 157, *157*
Lynch, John 195, *195*

McAlpine, Peggy 310
Macapagal-Arroyo, Gloria 268
McClure, Royce B. 158
McCrone, Terry 125
McDermott, Mike 342
McDonagh, Hannah 265
McGinlay, Sean 319
McGuinness, Eileen 205
McGuire, Thomas 136
Mach, David 268
Mackie, Joanne 205
Mackler, Scott 194
McLennan, Karl 215
McMahon, Aisling 75
McPherson, Stewart 69
Maddison, Robbie 297
Madigan, Roisin 110
Mafia, use crocodile to intimidate 335
Magar, Khagendra Thapa 217, *217*
maggots 121, *121*, 197
Magness, Dan 154
mail, long-delayed postcards 328, 333
mailbox, child trapped in 215
Mailer, Norman 261
Malcolm, Duncan 274
Malcolm, Keith 301, *301*
Malkoff, Mark 159, *159*
Malterud, Rune 153
mammal, venomous 68
Mamoyac, Derek 309
Manchester, Sean 39
mangroves 309
manhole covers, stolen 106
Manley, John 197
Mann, Alf 194
Mann, Gerry and Cindy 50
Maori, mummies 356, *356*
Maradona, Diego 265
marathons
  elderly runner 300
  family run in 180
  on seven continents 171
  walking on crutches 186
  wedding in 327
mariachi music 241
Marquis, Ken 238
marriage proposals 265, 345
Mars, soil fertility 362

Marsh, Jennifer *26–27*, 27
martial arts 314, *314–315*
Martin, Jim 149
Martz, Judge James 139
Mary, Virgin, art collector buys tattoo of 230, *231*
Maser, William 353
masked man, mystery of 343, *343*
Mason, Leslie 215
Massaneiro, Caua Felipe 200
matchsticks
  balancing on bottleneck 187
  gorilla sculpture 268
  model Dalek 252
  model of Hogwarts 242, *242*
  model of North Sea oil rig 243, *243*
math, dogs' ability 64
Matos, Avelino Perez *344*, 345
matzo ball, very large 317
Maurice, Dr. David 359
mausoleums, solar panels on 54
May, James 245, 251
Mayfield, Dr. 289, *289*
mayoral election, chimpanzee runs in 359
meat
  dress made of raw 105, *105*
  giant kibbeh 292
memory
  amnesia 222
  chocolate-covered garlic balls to improve 330
  elephants recognize people 65
  robber suffers from blackouts 193
  total recall 222
Mendenhall, Vickie 139
mermaid, made of toothpicks 248, *248*
Mertens, Silvia 18
metal detector, finds treasure 141
meteorites
  man survives being hit by 194
  Moon rock in book 261
  very large collection of 29
Meyer, Ed 337, *337*
mice
  clones of frozen mouse 324
  eating 126, *126*
  headdress made of dead 251
  nest made from $20 bills 70
Michelangelo 271
Mighall, Hannah 205
milkmen, long careers 127, 167
Miller, Alison 205
millipedes, very poisonous 62

miners, survive underground 229
Mink, Ken 292
Miramontes, Enrique 283
Misiura, Steve 245
missile, fisherman catches 339
Mo Zhaoguang 104
Modestou, Ken 114
Molnar, Donna 222
Mona Lisa 256–257, *256–257*
Monacelli, Elizabeth 81
money
  bag of found in street 333
  bullet stopped by cash in bra 298
  cash machine pays double 335
  fishermen catch 326
  mouse makes nest with $20 bills 70
  quadrillion dollar debit 354
  robber confesses to priest 339
  thief finds cash hidden in garden 335
monkeys 77, 110
Monks, Alyssa 272
Montroll, John 273
Moon, Anne 89
Moon rocks, in book 261
Moore, Gordon 353
Moose 268
moose, large collection of memorabilia 154
Morgan, J. Pierpont 343
Morgan, Jason 164
Morrison, Jim 252
Morrison-Jack, Ben 310
mosaics 237, 268
motorcycles
  backflip while jumping between bridge spans 297
  inline skater towed by 298, *298–299*
  like corpse 182, *182–183*
  massive jumps on 160, *160–161*, 165
  ridden by small child 174
  riding in high temperatures 158
  standing on 153
  very long 169
mountains
  blind woman in race 153
  climbers find mummy 339
  extreme cellists play on 359, *359*
  high-altitude golf tournament 154
  hiker survives fall by eating insects 309
  range hidden beneath ice 48
  school halfway up 22
  sleeping on cliffs 311, *311*
  tree saves woman from fall 225
  very young climber 317

mouth
blowtorch in 289, *289*
piglet with two 77
movies
marriage proposal in 265
shown in shed 29
Titanic fans watch in boats 166, *166*
vampires in 31, *31*
when to go to the toilet during 260
Moyen, Branden 169
Moyse, George 297
Mozart, Wolfgang Amadeus 22
MP3 players, onion-powered 349
Mueller, Edgar 262, *262–263*
Muller, Friedrich 312, *312*
mummies 38, *38*, 339, 342, *342*,
356–357, *356–357*
Munda, Sagula 130
Munday, Syb 205
Muñoz, Abraham 169
Munoz, Annie 124
Munro, Stan 264
murals, on garage doors 55, *55*
murderer, ghost convicts 345
Murray, Lucas 222
muscles, child with very big 215
museum, living in 265
music
accordion calms cows 237
album of musical screams 309
blood donations pay for concert
tickets 264
cello made from LEGO® 259
disco music helps resuscitation 230
elephant plays harmonica 80
extreme cellists 359, *359*
giant accordion 268
mass mariachi musicians 241
massed choir 243
nonstop karaoke 310
note held for long time 300
one-armed pianist 254
piano on subway 273
played on bicycle bells 243
popular recording 252
uses farm noises 251
violin played very fast 309
mustaches 129, 330, *330*
Muszynski, Josh 354

nails
hammering into nose 303, *303*
lying on bed of 314, *314*
single-finger push-ups on 170, *170*

Naismith, Graham and Eirene 309
Namita, Nileen 216
Narayan, Rakesh 349
Naresuan, King of Siam 44
NASA 109, *109*, 158
Nash, John 230
national anthem, in five languages 255
Native American, face in rocks 18
Natoli, Bobby and Robert 215
Navale, Abbishek 148
Neate, Adam 261
necks, stretching 227, *227*
needle, removed from butt cheek 284
Nefertiti, Queen 216
neon tubes, swallowing 304, *304*
Netherland, Chad 314, *314–315*
Newman, Peggy and Peter 259
Niagara Falls 156–157, *156–157*
Nieuwenhuizen, Riana van 72–73, *72–73*
Niles, Leighann 333
Nisbet, Gary 121
Noble, Kim 274
Norberg, Dr. Karen 274
Norman, Vic 281
North Pole 114
nose
hammering nail into 303, *303*
inflating hot-water bottles with 282,
282
like elephant's trunk 210, *210*
maggots removed from 197
pigs with misplaced nostrils 61, *61*
two-nosed rabbit 143
very large 193, *193*
novel, published on Twitter 254
nuclear test site, camels live in 94
Nyaumbe, Ben 88

Oakley, Karina 297
Obama, Barack
Etch A Sketch® drawing of 310
hair sculpture of 338, *338*
portrait on multiple bodies 223, *223*
octopuses, tentacles 65
O'Dell, Keith Jr. 187
Ogawa, Tadahiko 256, *256*
oil rig, matchstick model of 243, *243*
Olson, David 143
onion, powering MP3 players with 349
orangutan, whistling ability 81
organs, back-to-front 225
origami giraffe 273
O'Shaugnessy, John 342
Ostling, Geoff 224, *224*

Otto, Nina 84
Outen, Sarah 173
ovarian cyst, enormous 326, *326*

Packer, Phil 186
paintings
by dog 81
by trees 259, *259*
camouflage 234, *234–235*
collection in cemetery 271
cremation ashes in 273
giant finger painting 274
on crickets 265, *265*
on egg cartons 246, *246–247*
on feathers 260, 260
hidden image of pig in 259
large collection acquired cheaply 300
like photographs 272
Mona Lisa 256–257, *256–257*
multiple painting styles 274
painting with eyes 240–241, *241*
pigeons evaluate 89
portrait on multiple bodies 223, *223*
trompe l'oeil 238, 262, *262–263*
very young artist 310
Palychevsky, Gennady 220, *220*
pancakes 299, 319
pandas 93, 141
pangolins 99
pants, enormous pair of 237
paper
giant ball of 283
junk mail art exhibit 254
model city made of 250, *250*
origami giraffe 273
paper airplane contest 183
sculpture 266–267, *266–267*
wedding dress made of 271
papier-mâché, giant statues 54
paragliding 154, 289, 310
paralyzed people
communication via computer 194
sailor 174
sneezing breaks back 213
parasites 350–351, *350–351*
parking ticket, dog given 347
Parr, Don 29
Partyka, Natalia 299
pasta, restaurant serves giant bowl of
167
pastries, speed-eating *168*, 169
patchwork, gas station covered with
26–27, 27
Pe Fu 194

peaches, sculpture made of *118–119*, 119
pearl, in restaurant clam 339
pears, Buddha-shaped 172, *172–173*
peashooting championships 158
Peel, Mike 84
Peerlings, Pieter 18
Pelliccia, Gennaro 328
penguins 119, 355
Pereira, Ivonete 298
Perez, Inés Ramirez 203, *203*
perfume, overcomes bank workers 194
Perham, Mike 278–279, *278–279*
Peron, Juan and Eva 19, *19*
Perrin, Alan 161
Perruorria, Jorge *140*
Pesl, Corinna 345
Peterkin-Vertanesian, Brian 216
Peters, Charlotte and Donald 327
Peterson, Brooke 106
Petrella, Bob 222
Pettipas, Michael 158
Pharr, Daniel 225
phonebooks, portraits carved in 253, *253*
photographs
    cutout photos of soldiers 360
    of flies 272, *272–273*
    giant album 268
    giant mosaic 268
    paintings like 272
    of roadkill 340, *340*
    of volcanoes 322–323, *322–323*
pianos 254, 273
pies
    giant moon pie 158
    mass pie fights 171, 299
pigeons
    evaluate paintings 89
    faster than broadband 327
    prisoners use for smuggling 97
    saves lives 96
    stay in hotel 139
pigs
    hidden image in painting 259
    misplaced nostrils 61, *61*
    piglet swallows ring 89
    races for 76, *76*
    shakes hands 81
    terrorizes woman 141
    three-eyed piglet 77
Pinkard, April 309
pipeline, letter sent through 309
pirates, dolphins save ship from 63
pistol, very valuable 110
Pitt, Lorraine 153

Pitt, Rachel 327
The Pixies 309
pizzas 158, 289, 306
planets 22, 50
plant, traps rats 69, *69*
plasticine, garden made of 245
playing cards 136, 300
plinth, human artworks on 249
Plomdeur, Nicolas 34
Poel, Egbert van der 259
poetry, from posts on Twitter 251
pogo stick, playing basketball on 153
Pohjonen, Kimmo 251
poisons
    eating wasps 119
    living with venomous snakes 88
    millipedes produce cyanide 62
    snake wine 186, *186*
    venomous mammal 68
Pokémon, large collection of
    memorabilia *174–175*, 175
police
    prizes for mustaches 129
    sea lion takes over boat 139
    twins confuse 338
pollution, robot fish detect 333
ponds, colored 43, *43*
pool, very young player 187
popcorn, enormous ball of 169
popping eyes from sockets *344*, 345
population, in vast territory 41
Porter, John 264
portraits
    carved phonebooks 253, *253*
    drawing in continuous line 238
    Etch A Sketch® drawing of Barack
        Obama 310
    fabric portrait of Rembrandt 268,
        268–269
    of headmaster who expelled artist 238
    made from cassette tapes 252, *252*
    painted on bodies 223, *223*
postcards, long-delayed 328, 333
potato chips 283, 347
Potter, Dean 181
Potter, Harry 242, *242*
Powell, Don 237
Powell, Robert 288
power cables, typhoon blows bathtub
    on to 19
prayers, to stop glacier shrinking 16
pregnancy, conceiving during 349
Presley, Elvis 284
Price, Edna 304

Price, Joe *178–179*, 179
priest, bank robber confesses to 339
Primo, Tiago and Gabriel 17, *17*
Prior, Ken 20–21, *21*
prisoners
    caught coming back into prison 134
    drunk from hand gel 118
    escapes by hiding in box 327
    recaptured after long time 106
    use homing pigeons 97
prisons
    crocodile put in 134
    obese man smuggles gun into 361
psalms, stop bullet 203
pubs 68, 127
Pugh, John 238
Pugh, Les 167
pumpkins, speed-carving 174
Purcariu, Marius 197
push-ups 170, *170*, 215
pythons
    boy's friendship with 71, *71*
    found in shopping bag 97
    found in toilet 61
    kills cockatoo *82*, 83
    man escapes from 88
    recovered with tracking device 66

Qaboos Ibn Sa'id, Sultan of Oman 238
Qualls, Kay Rene Reed 362
Queral 253, *253*
Quinlan, Pipi 331
Quinn, Marc 221, *221*

rabbits
    addiction to soap operas 141
    dog trapped in warren 127
    enormous 71
    large number of pets 68
    two-nosed 143
    woman gives birth to 194
radio 238, 252
Raffaele, Paul 325
raffle, estate sold in 43
rain
    frog wedding for 61
    insurance against 120
    rapid evaporation 50
Raj, Jyothi 290–291, *290–291*
Ram, Dhanna 330, *330*
Ramathan, Bashir 285
Ramke, Hermann 173
Ramos, Enrique 265, *265*
Rantzau, Erik 61

Raph, Chris 183
rats
 display in shop window 60, *60*
 Hamelin overrun with 18
 headdress made of dead 251
 island cleared of 16
 new species discovered 83
 in temple *48–49*, 49
 trapped by plant 69, *69*
Ravel, Maurice 254
Raven, David 249
Ravi, Jeyaraman 261
Ray, Todd 86, *86–87*
reading, dog's ability 66
Ready, John 193
receipt, as artwork 237
refrigerated beach 53
Rehman, Aman 117
Reinfelder, Sarah 229
relationships, Museum of Broken
 264
Rembrandt, fabric portrait of 268,
 268–269
Renner, Ronnie 165
restaurants
 chef lives in freezer 361
 edible human "corpse" 326
 hospital-themed 353
 purple pearl found in clam 339
 serve chicken killed by poisonous
  snakes 355
 serves blood 362
 serves giant bowl of pasta 167
 underwater 346
 very expensive curry 180
 wedding in fast-food restaurant
  135
Reynolds, Bob 81
Reynolds, David 243, *243*
"Rham Sam" 111, *111*
ribs, speed-eating 164
Rich, Lucky Diamond 217
Ricketts, William 258, *258*
Ridlington, John 215
Ries, Adam 324
The Righteous Brothers 252
Riksfjord, Bernard 309
Rimsky-Korsakov, Nikolai 309
ring, piglet swallows 89
Ringling Bros. and Barnum & Bailey
 Circus 313
riots, chili powder controls 331
Ripley, Robert 6–9, *6–7*, 304, 357
Rishi, Guinness 102, *102–103*

rivers
 boy floats down on toy jeep 215
 of different colors 19
 plastic duck race on 148
 walking length of Amazon 146, *146–147*
roadkill calendar 340, *340*
roads
 airplane makes emergency landing
  on 283
 bachelors build to encourage brides 50
 hair pays for repairs 312
 made of coral 41
robberies
 bank robber confesses to priest 339
 bullet stopped by cash in bra 298
 burglar bites through steel bars 121
 burglar makes second visit 141
 drunken customer mistaken for thief
  349
 fish stolen using Internet photos 54
 monkey mugs woman 110
 pepper spray in wristwatch 334
 robber suffers from memory blackouts
  193
 theft of cucumbers 326
 thief eats to change appearance 132
 thief finds cash hidden in garden 335
 victims fight back 328
Robbins, Billy 283
Robert, Alain 290
RoboSteel 142, *142–143*
robots
 actors 360
 dancing display 130
 expresses emotions 328
 shoal of robot fish 333
 teacher 346
Rogers, Andrew 47
roller coaster, giant model of 169
roofs
 bathtub on 18
 giant Waldo painted on 29
 shark in 23, *23*
 tree growing on 47
Roosevelt, Eleanor 330
Rosenberg, Ally 238
Rosenberg, Lyssa 66
Ross, David 77
Rossi, Nicholas 215
rowing 173, 342
Rrucaj, Mrike 346
rubber bands, giant ball of 336, *336–337*
Rubik's cube, *Mona Lisa* made from
 257, *257*

rugby, diet to increase weight 354
running
 around Britain 295
 elderly marathon runner 300
 family run in marathon 180
 keeping soccer balls airborne while 169
 marathons on seven continents 171
 race in high heels 297
 wedding in marathon 327

sailing
 elderly round-the-world sailor 279
 paralyzed sailor 174
 standing on keel 307, *307*
 young round-the-world sailors 105,
  278–279, 278–279
Saint, Heather 119
saint, mummified body of 342, *342*
Saito, Minoru 279
salami, for courteous drivers 362
Salis, Edmond 317
Salomon, Rodney 339
salt
 colored ponds of 43, *43*
 hotels built with 139
 palace built of 53
Sambath, Uorn 71, *71*
sand
 drawing with 249
 face of Jesus in dune 44
 green 22
 stolen 135
Sandow, Eugene 312, *312*, 313
sandwiches
 boy saved from choking on
  197
 enormous 153, 184
Sandwina 313, *313*
Santana, Julián 24
Sarkadi, Sandor 212
sasquatch, protection for 19
Sassenbach, Thomas 55, *55*
Saturn, lightning storm on 22
sauna, in skull 237
sausage, enormous 297
Savelyev, Sergey 136
Savini, Maurizio 270, *270–271*
Sawaya, Nathan 259
Scanlan, Jo 260
Scarpino family 71
Schmeissing, Anna 153
Schmidt, Markus 345
Schnepp, Jeanne 216
Schollmayer, Dominik 238

schools
  classrooms in shipping containers 46
  halfway up mountain 22
  lessons in airplane 19
  robot teacher 346
Schreck, Max 31, *31*
Schröder, Andrea 93
Schwarz, Julia 202
scissors
  cutting hair with fingertip scissors
   334, *334*
  spider sculpture 324, *324*
scorpions, live in house 345
Scott, Eric 167
screaming 136, 309
scuba divers, extreme ironing 183
Scudamore, Wendy 81
sculpture
  armadillo made from scrap metal 238
  blood head 221, *221*
  bread and insects 255, *255*
  bubblegum buffalo 270, *270–271*
  car crash 167, *167*
  chewing gum 238
  dead animals 138, *138–139*
  enormous basketball 54
  fish made from everyday items 244,
   244–245
  French fry sculpting contest 243
  giant papier-mâché statues 54
  gummi bear chandelier 152, *152*
  hair and chewing gum 241
  hair sculpture of Barack Obama 338,
   338
  ice 264
  life-size LEGO® statue of Jesus Christ
   237
  made from peaches *118–119*, 119
  made from toys 239, *239*
  matchstick gorilla 268
  paper 266–267, *266–267*
  recycled materials 251
  scissor spiders 324, *324*
  scrap metal 142, *142–143*
  toilet paper tubes 274–275, *275*
  toothpick mermaid 248, *248*
  in trees 258, *258*
  used teabags 238
sea lion, takes over boat 139
Selvey, John 274
Semyonova, Alexei and Dmitry 139
sewage, gold in 29
Sexton, Brian 54
Sha Sha 271

Shackleton, Edwin 316
Shafer, DeeAnn Angell 362
sharks
  attacks surfer 173
  babies born through wound *88–89*, 89
  battle with man 361, *361*
  jumps out of aquarium 93
  in roof 23, *23*
  skin 71
  surfer saved from 205
Sharma, Rakesh 171, *171*
Shaw, Justin 214, *214*
sheds 29, 238
sheep
  at wedding 358, *358*
  shrinking 96
  trapped on electricity cable 331, *331*
  very expensive 70
Sheng Wang 212, *212*
Shi, Mr. 200
Shine, Benjamin 268, *268–269*
ships *see* boats
Shivnani, Ashok 225
shoes
  bathtubs look like 241
  fox steals 64
  race in high heels 297
  slippers for elephant 68
shops
  cattle run amok in food store 352
  dogs do shopping 94
  rat display in window 60, *60*
  swarm of bees traps people in 68
shower, mass 309
shrapnel 193, 194
Shue, Zona and Edward 345
Siamese twins 332, *332*
sick leave, very long 215
Sidorkin, Artyom 213
sign language, deaf puppy learns 88
signs, typographical errors 106
Silk, Kate 194
Silva, Orico 222
Silver, Josh 345
silver, protection from vampires 35
Simmons, Erika 252, *252*
Simonova, Kseniya 249
Simson, Pete 265
Singh, Bara Balwant 363, *363*
Singh, Kailash 205
Singh, Mika 198
Singh, Ravi 119
singing
  massed choir 243

singing (*cont.*)
  nonstop karaoke 310
  note held for long time 300
sinkhole, woman trapped in 216
Sistine Chapel ceiling, in cross-stitch 271
sitcom, marathon viewing 245
skiing
  long distance traveled on 307
  South Pole race 153
  on watermelons 54
skin
  growths on 218, *218–219*
  huge folds of 228, *228*
  moisturizer for elephants 75
  premature aging 193
  sharks 71
  very stretchy 213, *213*
skulls
  growing new 353
  sauna in 237
  surgery with power drill 215
  tower made from 45, *45*
  vampire's 38, *38*
skydiving
  elderly skydiver 297
  female formation 319
  mass head-first dive 318, *318–319*
  skydiver has heart attack 225
Skylab space station 22
slacklining 181, 293, *294–295*, 295
Slayer 309
sleep
  on cliffs 311, *311*
  lack of sleep kills goats 139
  sleepwalker falls out of window 197
  survey of beds 110
sleeping bag, life-size doll found in 349
slippers, for elephant 68
small people 198, *198–199*, 217, *217*, 225
smells
  alcoholic vapor in bars 345
  rotten food in fridge 325
  vile-smelling weapon 347
Smith, Errick 170
Smith, Melissa 96
Smith, Sophie 281
smoking, centenarian quits 117
snails, giant *98–99*, 99
snakes
  boy's friendship with python 71, *71*
  cause car accident 106
  grows foot 90, *90*
  living with venomous 88
  man escapes from python 88

snakes (*cont.*)
  python found in shopping bag 97
  python found in toilet 61
  python kills cockatoo 82, 83
  recovered with tracking device 66
  restaurants serve chicken killed by 355
  snake wine 186, *186*
  swallows dog 90
  toads eat 84
  tries to eat own tail 81, *81*
  two-headed 87
sneezing, breaks back 213
snoring, very loud 213
snow
  early snowmobile 165, *165*
  golf tournament in 154
  naked low-temperature walk 283
  woman survives in drift 222
snowboarding, long jumps 176, *176–177*
soap operas, rabbit's addiction to 141
soccer
  keeping balls airborne 154, 169
  player's blood and hair samples given
    away 265
soil, fertility on Mars 362
solar panels, on mausoleums 54
Solar System 18
soldiers, cutout photos of 360
Soliman, Jayne 197
Song Weiguo 228
South, Mabel 117
South Pole 114, 153
space, test pilot in 316, *316*
space stations
  company fined for littering 22
  segregated toilets 17
  space tourist 113
speargun, man shoots himself with 281
speech, parrots teach man 341
speed-eating
  calamari 292
  chili peppers 107, *107*, 181
  hot dogs 297
  M&Ms with chopsticks 149
  pastries *168*, 169
  ribs 164
Spence, Rob 51, *51*
spiders
  catches bird 83, *83*
  happy face on 91, *91*
  liquefy prey 90
  live underwater 71
  made of scissors 324, *324*
  parasites 350, *350*

spine, sneezing breaks 213
Spooner, Alison 283
squatter, wins valuable land 48
Squibb, Casey 114
squid, piglet 66, *66*
Stafford, Ed 146, *146–147*
Stalin, Joseph 229
Stalnaker, Joe 106
starfish, enormous 93
steam-powered car 297
Steele, George 225
Steiner, Tim 230, *231*
Stephanson, Paula 316
Stevens, LeRoy 309
Stewart, Matt 254
stilettos, race in 297
Stoker, Bram 31
stomach
  arm recovered from alligator's 215
  chopstick in 225
  filled with hairball 137, *137*
  junk removed from cat's 71
stork, new beak for 66
storm drains, living in 44
storms, on Saturn 22
story, printed on toilet paper 238
Strauss, Jakob 215
Stroe, Giuliano 215
strongmen/women 312–313, *312–313*
  bending metal bars with teeth *178–179*,
    179
  breaking ice blocks with hand 314, *315*
  dragging a car with eyelids 292, *292*
  elderly strongman 216
  enormous biceps 192, *192*
  lifting people 135
  lifting tables with teeth 171, 317, *317*
  multiple chin-ups 215
  pulling airplanes 282, 293, *293*
  pulling cars with hair 180, *180*
  pulling railway carriages 171
  single-finger push-ups *170*, 170
  very strong children 203, 215, 230
  weight lifting with ears *171*, 171
  weight lifting with teeth 171
  weight lifting with tongue 181, *181*
Suang Puangsri 345
Subramaniyan, K.V. 202, *202*
Subramaniyan, Sethu 238
subways 139, 273
suicides 18, 40, 156
suitcase, baboons empty 77, *77*
Sun, size of 18
Sun Chien 94

Sunderland, Zac 105
Sunshine, Paula 48
superheroes 114, *114–115*, 126
surfing
  dog's ability 83
  kite-surfing across Bass Strait 310
  one-armed surfer 173
  surfer saved from shark 205
surgery
  legs stretched 327
  power drill used on skull 215
  surgeon suffers heart attack 214
sushi, body parts made of 326
Suzuki, Koji 238
Swart, Johannes 88
swimming, across Great Lakes 316
sword swallowing 302–305, *302–305*

table tennis, one-armed player 299
tables, lifting with teeth 317, *317*
tadpoles, fall from sky 47
Tagg, Caroline 342
tall people 316
Tamm, Peter 153
tango, simultaneous dancers 237
tap dancer, very fast 260
tarantulas 350, *350*
Tattersall, Anne 184
tattoos
  art collector buys 230, *231*
  computer-related 213
  on eyeball 204, *204*
  flags 102, *102–103*
  Maori mummies 356, *356*
  multiple 195
  over whole body 217, 224, *224*
  "tear outs" 114, *114–115*
Taviano, Marla 120
Taylor, Annie Edison 156, *156*
Taylor, Darren 286–287, 287
Taylor, Jeff 362
Taylor, Moulton 153
teabag sculpture 238
teacher, robot 346
tears
  of blood 355
  crocodile tears syndrome 230
teeth
  alligators 74
  bending metal bars with *178–179*, 179
  communication via implant 47, *47*
  dental treatment under hypnosis 215
  found in wallet 339
  human teeth in jewelry 264, *264*

teeth (*cont.*)
lifting weights with 171, 317, *317*
monkeys floss 77
sight restored with 222
telephones
cat dials emergency number 119
cell phone found inside fish 333
dog phones for help 106
dress lights up when cell phone rings 339
inability to identify voices on 197
missing bird speaks on 94
pelican swallows cell phone 97
television
marathon sitcom viewing 245
rabbit addicted to soap operas 141
television glasses 164, *164*
Temonggong Koh, Chief 333
temples
built in bedroom 29
made of bottles 44
rats revered in 48–49, 49
tennis, very successful player 161
tentacles 42, *42*, 65
tequila, turned into diamonds 352
text messages 186, 342
theater
multiple performances by actor 249
robot actors 360
thermal baths 40, *40*
Thomas, Richard 127
Thompson, Val 273
Thomson, Alex 307, *307*
thumb, enormous 136, *136*
ties, wearing same for long time 143
tightrope walking 179, 181, 293, 294–295, 295
time
"decimal time" 17
"Sandringham Time" 50
time zones in China 43
Tiny Iron 192, *192*
Titanic, fans watch film in boats 166, *166*
Tkeshelashvili, Jemal 282, *282*
toads 53, 84
toast, *Mona Lisa* made from 256, *256*
Toda, Takuo 183
toes
extra 202, *202*, 222, 229
webbed 229, *229*
Toft, Mary 194
toilet paper, horror story printed on 238
toilet paper tubes, sculpture 274–275, 275

toilets
airplane crash lands on 306
crowd visits 293
goldfish survives in 61
leisurely users locked in 16
puppy survives in 139
python found in 61
segregated on space station 17
when to go to during films 260
woman shot while sitting on 335
tomato fight 150, *150–151*
tongue
coffee taster insures 328
lifting weights with 181, *181*
parasites 351, *351*
very long 99
whale's swollen 62, *62–63*
toothpicks
mermaid made of 248, *248*
model city 264
multiple in beard 335, *335*
topiary hedges 238, 245
tornado, of wildfire 25
tortoise, very old 312
tower, made from skulls 45, *45*
Towers, John 182, *182–183*
town, model of 250
toys, statue made from 239, *239*
tractor, tows coffin 169
traffic citations, multiple 319
trains
beetle larvae released on 330
enormous train set 272
man clings to outside of 106
overcrowding 108, *108–109*
pulling carriages 171
track stolen 300
Tran, Dennis 158
transplant, face 307
transport, using many different types of 316
trees
growing in lung 213
growing on roof 47
knitted cozies for 238
large number of mangroves planted 309
paintings by 259, *259*
saves woman from fall 225
sculpture in 258, *258*
secret location for rare 25
skeleton found in 40
Trenk, Adam 136
trompe l'oeil art 238, 262, *262–263*

trucks, driving on ice *154–155*, 155
tug-of-war, hand pulled off 200
tumors, enormous 197, 307
tuning forks, giant 274
tunnels 24, 44
turban, giant 363, *363*
turkey, stuffed with smaller birds 300
Turner, Bill 68
turtles
albino 74, *74–75*
conjoined twins 86, *86–87*
shut airport runway 89
swims to hospital 81
TV license, dead man asked to pay for 324
twins
born in different years 310
conceiving at different times 349
confuse police 338
conjoined twins 332, *332*, 346, *346*
of different colors 283
inseparable 358
marry twins 139
multiple sets of 220
with different fathers 230
woman with two wombs 229
Twitter 251, 254
typhoon, blows bathtub on to power cables 19
Tyson, John 158
Tyson, Mike 139

underwater
boat 162, *162–163*
living in tank 306, *306*
restaurant 346
spiders live 71
underwear, made from trash 254, *254*
Unger, Donald L. 124
unicycle, riding on cliff trails 170
urination, Mozart's commemorated 22
Utley, Michael 216

vacations, insurance against rain 120
vampires 30–39, *30–39*
Van der Glas, Polly 264, *264*
Van Duzer, Scott 306
Vance, Chad 106
Vangelakos, Victor 29
vans
bull wedged on roof rack 297
very speedy bread van 161
vase, enormous 254
Velcro, buildings supported with 333

Vera, George 361
Versailles, smiley face found in grounds 41
Vidiz, Claive 184
Villa, Josh 362
village, knitted replica of 241
violin, played very fast 309
Vistica, Olinka 264
Vitale, Claudio 214
Vlad Draculea III, Prince 32, 32
Vlosich, George III 310
Vogel, Herb and Dorothy 300
voices, inability to identify 197
volcanoes
  acid lake 14, 14–15
  blows hole in clouds 41, 41
  bungee jumping over 19
  photographing 322–323, 322–323
  thermal baths 40, 40
  volcano boarding 161
volleyball, one-man team 318

wages, paid in coins 114
Wagner, Aloisia 210, 210
Waldo, painted on rooftop 29
walking, backward in Grand Canyon 310
Wallachia 17, 32, 33
wallet, teeth found in 339
Wang, Mrs. 104
Wang Guoqiang 139
Wang Houju 307
Wanstell, Jessica 64, 64
Warren, Bo 141
Was, Lauren 112, 112
washing, forgoing for male child 205
washing machine, kitten survives in 93
Washington, Mia 230
wasps 119, 350, 350
water, collected from fog 44
water skiing, very long jump 153
waterfalls 156–157, 156–157, 158
watermelons, skiing on 54
watermelons, smashing with head 300
Watkins, Perry 165
Waul, Joel 336, 336–337
weapons
  bomb used as anchor 125
  cannonball fired through house wall 353
  chandeliers made from 17
  live mortars used as dumbbells 116
  shrapnel from 193, 194
  vile-smelling 347
Webb, Steve 328

Weber, Herbert 179
Webster, Patricia 230
wedding dresses
  made of paper 271
  very cheap 119
  very long train 242
  woolen 358, 358
weddings
  bachelors build road to encourage brides 50
  balancing on poles 129
  bee suits for bride and groom 296, 296
  bigamy 334
  bride and groom with same name 328
  child married to dog 130
  in digger buckets 362
  dog as best man 118
  in fast-food restaurant 135
  for frogs 61
  lucky date for Chinese 359
  in marathon 327
  mass parade of brides 174
  multiple 135, 137
  multiple toasters given 116
  in Shrek costumes 120
  twins marry twins 139
  in zero gravity 330
Weight, James 310
weight lifting see strongmen/women
Weisser, Elmar 292
well, man trapped in 343
Werle, Petra 255, 255
whales
  diving ability 64
  huge skeleton displayed 68
  saves diver 122, 122–123
  swollen tongue 62, 62–63
  topiary 245
Wharton, Charlotte 153
wheelbarrows, human 289
wheels, bicycle with odd-shaped 164
whisky 184
whistling 44, 81
White, Doug 148
Whitlark, "Dad" 190
Whittingham, Sam 173
The Who 309
Wickens, Jacqueline 230
Wiesel, Dan 295
wig, bullet stopped by 310
wild boar, deterring with hair 201
Williams, Gareth 241
Williams, Sidney 216
Williamson, Kieron 310

Wilshaw, Brian 43
Wilson, Brian 341
Wiltshire, Natalie 81
wind farm, lack of sleep kills goats 139
windows, office block with large number of 17
winds
  blows bathtub on to power cables 19
  dog blown away by 97
  tornado of wildfire 25
Winehouse, Amy 252
Winfrey, Oprah 50
Wing Ma 225
Winstanley, Paul 149
Witte, Frank and Barbara 65
Wittgenstein, Paul 254
Wogan, Terry 170
wolves, deterring with flags 67
wombs
  fetus left in body 216
  women with two 213, 229
Woods, Sheila 330
Woodward, Jack 127
worms
  bioluminescent defenses 335
  enormous 76
  lollipops filled with 124
  worm charming championships 281
Wray, Andy 222
wristwatch, pepper spray in 334
writing, with feet 318
Wu Zhongyuan 179

Xiao Ming 217
Xie Long 116

Yamada, Keizo 300
Yan Hongxia 296, 296
Yang Guanghe 292, 292
Yang Yun 122, 122–123
Yeti, footprints 355, 355
Youngblood, Joel 289

Zak, Heinz 294–295, 295
Zamoratte, Hugo 191, 191
zebra, riding to pub 68
Zhang Tingting 180, 180
Zhao Liang 316
Zhao Peng 242
Zhou Juchang 110
Zhu Zhu 271
Zigun, Dick 206
zombies 126, 185
zoo, free admission for beards 313

381

Acknowledgments

COVER (sp) © Evgeny Kuklev—iStock.com, (b) Alex Smith - www.as-images.com, (t) Andrew J.K. Tan; 12 (c) John R. Chu, (b/r) www.style-your-garage.com; 13 (l) Elizabeth Mackenzie-Barrett, (c) Feliciano Guimarães, (r) NASA/JSC; 14–15 Furious Earth; 16 Feliciano Guimarães; 17 Reuters/Bruno Domingos; 18 Geoeye Satellite Image; 19 (t/r) Geoeye Satellite Image, (t/l) Keystone/Getty Images; 20–21 Over Schiehallion, Perthshire, Scotland. © Ken Prior; 23 Tim Graham/Getty Images; 24 (b/l) Elizabeth Mackenzie-Barrett, (c/r) Sharon O'Dea/Bizarre Magazine; 25 Photo by Deb Hall; 26–27 International Fiber Collaborative; 28 © Jeremy Horner/Corbis; 29 SNAP/Rex Features; 30 (b) © PixAchi—Fotolia.com, (r) SNAP/Rex Features; 35–36 Fortean Picture Library; 37 (t) Paul Huber, (b) Reuters; 38 (b/r) Pamela Bohnenstiehl, (t/l, t/r) Bishop Sean Manchester; 40 Courtesy Alexander Turnbull Library, Wellington, New Zealand; 41 NASA/JSC; 42 Wenn.com; 43 Jerry Ting; 45 John R. Chu; 46 David Cheskin/PA Wire/Press Association Images; 47 SSPL via Getty Images; 51 Kosta Grammatis, lead engineer for team eyeborg; 52–53 Aisling Magill/Barcroft Media Ltd; 55 www.style-your-garage.com; 56 Picture by Ian McLelland on behalf of PDSA; 57 (l) Todd Mecklem, (c) Reuters/Cathal McNaughton, (r) Zak-n-Wheezie hatched on 6/14/07 to Frank and Barbara Witte of www.fresnodragons.com; 58 (b) © Bettmann/Corbis, (r) © Hulton-Deutsch Collection/Corbis; 59 © Nicole Duplaix/Corbis; 60 Todd Mecklem; 61 Wenn.com; 62–63 Wenn.com; 64 Bournemouth News/Rex Features; 65 Zak-n-Wheezie hatched on 6/14/07 to Frank and Barbara Witte of www.fresnodragons.com; 66 Gary Florin/Rex Features; 67 Caters News Agency Ltd/Rex Features; 69 www.redfernnaturalhistory.com; 70 ChinaFotoPress/Photocome/Press Association Images; 71 Heng Sinith/AP/Press Association Images; 72–73 Caters News Agency Ltd/Rex Features; 74–75 © UPPA/Photoshot; 76 Reuters/Cathal McNaughton; 77 Martin Birchall/Rex Features; 78–79 Vaclav Silha/ Barcroft USA Ltd; 80 Chris Ison/PA Archive/Press Association Images; 81 Rex Features; 82–83 Cindy Lane/Newspix/Rex Features; 83 (b) Newspix/Rex Features; 85 Wenn/SSPCA; 86–87 (c, t) Dana Fineman Courtesy of The Venice Beach Freakshow; 87 Asia Ray Courtesy of the Venice Beach Freakshow; 88–89 Kelly Tarltons Underwater World; 90 © EuroPics[CEN]; 91 Caters News; 92 Picture by Ian McLelland on behalf of PDSA; 94 Barry Bland/Barcroft Media Ltd; 95 Apichart Weerawong/AP/Press Association Images; 96 Melissa Smith; 97 Jung von Matt/Neckar; 98 (b) Drew Fitzgibbon/Newspix/Rex Features, (t) © NHPA/Photoshot; 100 Sculptures from recycled steel by RoboSteel www.Robosteel.com; 101 (l) Courtesy of NASA-JSC, (c) Irish Revenue Commissioners, (r) Jeff Barnett-Winsby; 102–103 Guinness Rishi; 104–105 Wenn.com; 107 Wenn.com; 108–109 Khalid Tanveer/AP/Press Association Images; 109 (t) Courtesy of NASA-JSC; 110 Wenn.com; 112 Jeff Barnett-Winsby; 114–115 Tattoo by Dan Hazelton; 116 David Lovere/Rex Features; 117 Rex Features; 118–119 Wenn.com; 120 Irish Revenue Commissioners; 121 David McLain /Getty Images; 122–124 © EuroPics[CEN]; 125 AP/Press Association Images; 126 Reuters/Thomas Mukoya; 128–129 © EuroPics[CEN]; 130 Tony McNicol/Rex Features; 131 Olycom SPA/Rex Features; 132 Reuters/Nozim Kalandarov; 133 Reuters/Nir Elias; 134 www.tropix.co.uk/V. and M. Birley; 135 AP/Press Association Images; 136 © UPPA/Photoshot; 137 Wenn.com; 138 Kevin Walsh; 140 East News/Rex Features; 142–143 Sculptures from recycled steel by RoboSteel www.Robosteel.com; 144 Concept, design, sculpture by John Towers of Blue Flame Alley Studios, Florida / Photos courtesy of Horst Rösler, Germany / Special thanks for Kate Towers for her endless support; 145 (r) Johnny McCormack; 146–147 Photo's by Keith Ducatel www.keithducatel. com; 148 Marc Cameron/Mark Brown/Rex Features; 149 Rex Features; 150–151 Getty Images; 152 YaYa Chou; 155 National Geographic/Getty Images; 157 (t) Niagara Falls (Ontario) Public Library; 159 Mark Malkoff; 160 Getty Images; 162–163 Scubacraft 2010; 164 Time & Life Pictures/Getty Images; 165 AP/Press Association Images; 166 Chris Jackson/Getty Images; 167 John MacDougall/AFP/Getty Images; 168 Getty Images; 170 Chatham News; 171 Simon De Trey-White/Barcroft Media Ltd; 172 Wenn.com; 175 Paul Michael Hughes/Guinness World Records/Rex Features; 176–177 Johnny McCormack; 178 Hulton Archive/Getty Images; 180 AFP/Getty Images; 182–183 Concept, design, sculpture by John Towers of Blue Flame Alley Studios, Florida/Photos courtesy of Horst Rösler, Germany/Special thanks for Kate Towers for her endless support; 184–185 Vat19.com; 187 Reuters/Natalie Behring; 189 (c) Photographer: Sridar Sri; 190 Archive Holdings Inc./Hulton Archive/Getty Images; 191 (c) Geoffrey Swaine/Rex Features, (b/r) Rex Features; 192 Beretta/Sims/Rex Features; 193 © EuroPics[CEN]; 195 Rex Features; 196 Kevin Smith/Solent News/Rex Features; 198–199 Simon De Trey-White/ Barcroft Media Ltd; 200–201 Richard Drew/AP/Press Association Images; 202 Photographer: Sridar Sri; 203 Jaime Puebla/AP/Press Association Images; 204 Lane Jensen/ BizarreArchive.com; 206–207 (l, r) Christophe Boisson—Shutterstock.com, (dps) Hamidisc—Shutterstock.com; 207 (b/r) Elena Moiseeva—Shutterstock.com, (sp) Courtesy Everett Collection/Rex Features; 208–209 (l, r) Christophe Boisson—Shutterstock.com, (dps) Hamidisc—Shutterstock.com; 208 (t/l, b/l) Elena Moiseeva—Shutterstock.com, (t) Time & Life Pictures/Getty Images, (b) Getty Images; 209 (sp) Time & Life Pictures/Getty Images, (t/l) Elena Moiseeva—Shutterstock.com, 210 (t/l, b/l) Elena Moiseeva—Shutterstock.com, (t) D. B. Denholtz Collection, (b) Eileen Darby/Time Life Pictures/Getty Images; 211 (c/r) Elena Moiseeva—Shutterstock.com, (c) Time & Life Pictures/Getty Images; 212 © EuroPics[CEN]; 214 Miami New Times/Colby Katz; 217 Getty Images; 218–219 © EuroPics[CEN]; 220 © EuroPics[CEN]; 221 Dazed & Confused/Rex Features; 223 Reuters/Yiorgos Karahalis; 224 James Elsby/Newspix/Rex Features; 229 © NHPA/Photoshot; 231 Picture courtesy de Pury & Luxembourg, Switzerland & Studio Wim Delvoye, Belgium; 232 (sp) Terence Bogue, (r) Leandro Granato; 233 (l) Heidi Hooper, (c) Professor Andrew Davidhazy; 234–235 Caters News; 236 Zubova Zhanna; 239 © Robert Bradford 2012. All Rights Reserved, DACS; 240–241 Leandro Granato; 242 Rex Features; 243 Solent News/Rex Features; 246–247 Enno de Kroon; 249 NTI Media Ltd/Rex Features; 250 SWNS.com; 251 Heidi Hooper; 253 Alex Querel; 254 Dean Powell; 255 Unimedia Images/Rex Features; 257 (b) ©Invader/Solent News/Rex Features; 258 (sp) Thomas Becker, Arnstadt, Germany, (b/r) Copyright Parks Victoria; 259 Solent News/Rex Features; 260 Ian Davie; 261 Professor Andrew Davidhazy; 262–263 Edgar Mueller/Manfred Stader/Rex Features; 264 Terence Bogue; 266–267 eckmanfineart.com; 268–269 Benjamine Shine; 270–271 Caters News; 272–273 Nicholas Hendrickx; 274–275 Matthieu Gauchet; 277 (l) Bill Tremblay/The Independent, (c) www.lloydimages.com; 278–279 PPL Media; 280 Shaun Curry/AFP/Getty Images; 282 AFP/Getty Images; 284–285 Marcus Brandt/DPA/Press Association Images; 286–287 Michael Martin/Barcroft Media Ltd; 288 Andrew J.K. Tan; 290–291 Niklas Halle'n/Barcroft Media Ltd; 292 ChinaFotoPress/Photocome/Press Association Images; 293 Bill Tremblay/The Independent; 294 Barcroft Media; 296 © EuroPics[CEN]; 298–299 www.JW-SPORTFOTO.de; 301 M & Y Agency Ltd/Rex Features; 302–303 (dps) Niall Carson/PA Archive/Press Association Images; 303 (t/r, t/c) The Space Cowboy; 307 www.lloydimages.com; 308 Mery Nunez/Barcroft Media Ltd; 311 (sp) Topher Donahue/Getty Images, (b) Photolibrary.com; 312 Time & Life Pictures/Getty Images; 313 Getty Images; 314–315 Chad Netherland; 316 National Museum of the United States Air Force; 318–319 Norman Kent/Barcroft Media Ltd; 320 (r) Dr Robert A. Patzner; 321 (c) Ian & Louise Fairburn; 322–323 Patrick Koster/Barcroft Media Ltd; 324 heartlessmachine.com; 325 © UPPA/Photoshot; 326 Wenn.com; 327 Monica Rueda/AP/Press Association Images; 329 Lisa Rastl/Barcroft Media Ltd; 330 Reuters/Pawan Kumar; 331 Caters News; 332 Blank Archives/Getty Images; 334 Barry Bland/Barcroft Media Ltd; 335 Wenn.com; 338 Imagine China; 340 Kevin Beresford; 341 Wenn.com; 342 Michelle Enemark of CuriousExpeditions.com; 343 Bournemouth News/Rex Features; 346 Reuters/Sukree Sukplang; 347–348 © EuroPics[CEN]; 350 (t) © NHPA/Photoshot, (b) Mark Moffett/Minden Pictures/FLPA; 351 (t) Dr Robert A. Patzner, (c/r) Norbert Wu/ Minden Pictures/FLPA, (b/l) Professor Nico Smit; 352–353 Amy Sancetta/AP/Press Association Images; 354 Jan Petter Jorgensen/Rex Features; 355 Reuters/Gopal Chitrakar; 356 Werner Forman Archive/Formerly Hooper Collection/Sold at Christies; 358 Ian & Louise Fairburn; 359 © Extreme Cello; 360 Simon De Trey-White/Barcroft India/Barcroft Media Ltd; 361 D.J. Struntz/Barcroft Media Ltd; 363 Narinder Nanu/AFP/Getty Images

Key: t = top, b = bottom, c = center, l = left, r = right, sp = single page, dp = double page
All other photos are from Ripley Entertainment Inc.
Every attempt has been made to acknowledge correctly and contact copyright holders and we apologize in advance for any unintentional errors or omissions, which will be corrected in future editions.